THE WO...
DANIEL O'...

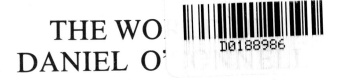

Christmas

To:- Rozelle with love.
Patricia.

Daniel O'Connell. A portrait by Bernard Mulrenin R.H.A.

THE WORLD OF DANIEL O'CONNELL

Edited by

Donal McCartney

Published for
The Cultural Relations Committee of Ireland
by
THE MERCIER PRESS
Dublin and Cork

ISBN 0 85342 589 2

The aim of this series is to give a broad, informed survey of Irish life and culture, past and present. Each writer is left free to deal with his subject in his own way, and the views expressed are not necessarily those of the Committee. The general editor of the series is Caoimhin Ó Danachair.

The editor of this collection is Donal McCartney, Professor of Modern Irish History and Dean of the Faculty of Arts in University College, Dublin.

941. 508092

RS3641X

Contents

List of Illustrations

Preface

As befitted a man born in and formed by the eighteenth century, Daniel O'Connell was concerned with the rights of man: not merely with the rights of Irishmen. The brand of nationalism to which he subscribed was not exclusive. He made an impact outside of Ireland; and Europe and the English-speaking world responded by taking an interest in O'Connell's Ireland. The Irish party, which was O'Connell's creation, often concerned itself in the British Parliament in matters which were not specifically Irish. As nationalism developed, however, in Ireland as elsewhere, it became more self-centred. By the end of the nineteenth century the Irish party under Parnell in the House of Commons was paying less attention to matters non-Irish. By the early twentieth century, in the days of Griffith and Pearse, Irish nationalism was even more intensively self-occupied. The men of the Easter Rising proclaimed a separatist republic. The movement known as Sinn Féin (Ourselves) broke the parliamentary link with Westminster completely. So long as Irishmen were concerned to give their country its own political identity, understandably they remained preoccupied with their own nationalistic affairs.

Preoccupation with one's own nation and the self-indulgence which was part of it represent a kind of nationalism that now belongs to the past. Today independent Ireland is enthusiastically involved not only in the European Economic Community but also in many other spheres of internationalism. The following essays grew out of an idea that the bicentenary of O'Connell's birth should be noted in a manner fitting to a patriot who was never narrowly nationalistic. At a time when Ireland is playing an international role greater than ever before, it is considered appropriate that these essays should deal primarily with O'Connell's impact outside of Ireland and with his image abroad. A limited nationalistic approach to O'Connell can only mislead. These essays are offered in the conviction that the external dimension can assist in placing O'Connell's contribution to politics in proper focus and enrich our understanding of one of Ireland's greatest historical figures. They are especially offered to readers who are not Irish but who wish to know us better by probing a little more deeply into our history and into the personality and various images of a man who was one of the great formative influences in the development of the political mind of modern Ireland.

Chapter 1
The World of Daniel O'Connell

Donal McCartney

Daniel O'Connell's political career began with a speech in 1800 against the proposed union of Ireland with Great Britain. When that career closed with his death forty-seven years later, the union, despite all the colossal striving of half a century of effort, was still intact. Although O'Connell had failed even in the limited objective of establishing a parliament in Dublin subject in certain important respects to the imperial parliament in London, nevertheless he was called, paradoxically, the Liberator by millions of his countrymen. And it was under that name that his fame reverberated throughout Ireland and the United Kingdom, through the English speaking world of America and the Empire, and throughout continental Europe. It is a paradox that is worth trying to unravel, and it is no doubt the same paradox which the contemporary French traveller, Gustave de Beaumont, had in mind when he observed:

> "O'Connell did not make Ireland free but without him she would never have become free."[1]

An old-fashioned if rather simplistic way of regarding O'Connell's career was to see it divided into three well-defined phases. The first, or Catholic Emancipation phase from 1800 to 1829; the second, or parliamentary phase from 1830 to approximately 1840; and the third or Repeal phase from 1840 to 1847.

Phase 1800–1829

A political and social system had operated in Ireland throughout most of the eighteenth century under which the religion of the vast majority of the Irish people had been persecuted, their property rights restricted, their education interfered with and their social advancement halted. Most of these Penal Laws had been removed from the statute book by the time O'Connell began his public career. The family to which he belonged, Catholic, middle-class, land-owning in the remote southwest of the country, not only managed to survive but might be said to have flourished during this period of the Penal Laws. The comparative proximity of France and Spain to the coasts of County Kerry and the smuggling trade which this facilitated accounted for the comfortable

---

1. Quoted in John Hennig, 'Continental Opinion', in M. Tierney (ed.), *Daniel O'Connell: Nine Centenary Essays*, p. 260.

circumstances of the O'Connells. They were a family who, in a very real sense were outward-looking and European, in advance of most others in the island. And of this circumstance the Penal Laws were unintentionally the cause. O'Connell himself received his education on the continent, in St Omer and in Douai, before completing his legal studies in London. His uncle Maurice (Hunting Cap) financed the education of his nephews, partly at least out of the money he made from trading with French and Spanish ships. Another celebrated uncle, General Count Daniel O'Connell, also illustrated the family's continental links by serving in the Irish Brigade of the Wild Geese under King Louis XVI. And when the monarchy fell in France, Count O'Connell organised the Loyalist refugees into Pitt's Irish Brigade in the British army. A brother of O'Connell became an officer in this Brigade and died in action in San Domingo. A son of O'Connell served in the Irish Legion which fought with Bolivar in South America before becoming an officer in the Imperial Austrian army.

The O'Connells were not only wide-ranging in their travels, they were also prolific in the era which saw the Irish population explode to over eight millions at home and over-spill into the English speaking world. The Liberator was one of ten children. He married one of a family of eleven of a local physician and he and his wife had eleven children, of whom seven survived. It was a family that cushioned him financially and socially, accounting, no doubt, for that optimistic sense of psychological and political security which this chieftain of his clan exuded. In financial terms the member of the family to whom O'Connell owed most was the uncle 'Hunting Cap', who had cultivated the lucrative (but sometimes illicit) trade with French merchantmen. This uncle had also been careful, however, to show that he was on the Government's side when the revolutionary French threatened an invasion of Ireland in the 1790s. It was a situation which provided him with something of the best of both worlds. To survive in a world that was neither English nor Irish and which had, at the same time, strong continental links, Hunting Cap had to be ambidextrous. His nephew, who inherited his wealth and possessions, inherited also these ambidextrous skills and applied them to the world of politics.

During the first two decades of the nineteenth century, O'Connell established himself as one of the foremost advocates in the history of the Irish Bar. It was because of his reputation as a defence lawyer that he first passed into Irish folklore as 'The Counsellor'. In popular poetry and story the image of O'Connell grew to Mosaic proportions. The *aisling* or vision poetry of Irish literature which, in the eighteenth century, had promised that the Pope and France and Spain would come to the aid of an oppressed Ireland personified as Cathleen Ni Houlihan, soon replaced these with O'Connell as the sole deliverer; and the folktales mirrored the self-confidence of the new democracy which O'Connell had created.

The right to sit in parliament had not yet been restored to the Catholics and it was to promote this objective that they organised themselves into a Catholic Committee, afterwards called the Catholic Board. The reputation which

O'Connell was acquiring for himself in the courts and the talents which were earning him that reputation also brought him to the forefront in the councils of the Catholic Committee. By 1808 he was playing a prominent role in its affairs. In the controversies over the question of whether to concede a veto to the Crown in the appointment of Catholic bishops and over the issue of the payment of the Irish clergy by the state, O'Connell inspired the independent and popular cause. One significant effect of his successful anti-veto campaign was that it made Rome realise that Irish Catholicism was something separate from British Catholicism, and that ecclesiastical affairs in Ireland were primarily the concern of the Irish clergy and laity, and not of the British Government, as Rome had hitherto tended to regard them. The Catholic Committee's custom of (gently) petitioning parliament to concede Emancipation was soon backed by a more vigorous agitation and by the demanding of Catholic rights at public meetings which provided O'Connell with the opportunity to exercise his great oratorical talents to the full.

The Catholic Association, founded by O'Connell in 1823, introduced novel methods of organisation which produced revolutionary results. The subscription of one penny a month opened up associate membership to the mass of the people, and priests were included as ex officio members. This Catholic Rent provided a big fighting fund, some of which was set aside for the legal protection of the peasants. A most significant psychological effect of the rent was that it gave contributors a strong sense of proprietary interest in the politics of Emancipation, thereby enrolling the Irish people, suddenly aware that they were an awakening giant of enormous strength in what was arguably the first mass movement of organised democracy in Europe. The clergy became O'Connell's lieutenants, his local organisers and his supervisors of the rent collection. Parish branches were encouraged to forward information about local grievances to headquarters in Dublin where a central committee took on all the appearances of a popular native Parliament. The network of nation-wide branches made possible a series of meetings by which O'Connell's propaganda could filter down to the remotest parts of the country. The Association, at first, supported the candidacy of liberal protestants seeking election, and then, in 1828, decided on the radical policy of supporting a Catholic candidate, O'Connell himself, in the County Clare by-election. The campaign of civil disobedience and passive resistance was thus successfully introduced into Irish politics by O'Connell and led directly to the Emancipation Act of 1829.

Phase 1830–1840

In Irish historiography it was at one time customary to regard the Emancipation struggle of the 1820s and the Repeal movement of the 1840s as the two great peaks of O'Connell's career. In both phases the emphasis was on the extra-parliamentary organisation and agitation at home in Ireland, and there is no doubt about O'Connell's massive impact in these areas. The decade of the 1830s, on the other hand, when O'Connell's energies were concentrated on parliamentary activity in London, was looked upon as the valley years in between the peaks of Emancipation and Repeal. "Ten years . . . of barren labour", was how Sean O'Faolain described the parliamentary career of O'Connell during this decade. P. S. O'Hegarty was another historical writer who stressed the barreness of the policy of trying to get justice for Ireland in the English Parliament. 'Ploughing the Sands' is the title of the chapter covering the 1830s in Denis Gwynn's biography of O'Connell, and not one of the *Nine Centenary Essays,* edited by Michael Tierney, dealt specifically with the decade of O'Connell's parliamentary career.

Yet, it is in this decade that the real O'Connell is revealed—the utilitarian pragmatist, the political opportunist; and anyone who has understood the O'Connell of these years could never have expected him—as Young Ireland did—to act in a doctrinaire fashion on the Repeal issue. As a radical reformer O'Connell gave his attention to all the great questions of the day and was one of the most widely reported and controversial figures in the British Parliament where, in his first year, 1831, he spoke three to four times a day on average during the session. He played an important role in the 1832 Reform Bill and he advocated triennial parliaments, male suffrage, the secret ballot and an elective House of Lords. He championed religious toleration and the abolition of slavery and he condemned discrimination against the Jews. He advocated the abolition of capital punishment and flogging in the army, and he pressed for various reforms of the legal system.

A political deal with the Whigs, known as the Lichfield House Compact, amounted to a power-sharing alliance by which O'Connell and his Party kept the Whigs in office in return for good Government measures and an impartial administration of Ireland. Municipal reform, a Poor Law extended to Ireland, settlement of the Tithe War, and the appointment of Catholics to posts of responsibility were among the reforms obtained during this period of O'Connell's alliance with the Whigs. He had succeeded in creating the first influential independent Irish Party in the British Parliament and thereby established a force in British parliamentary politics and set a pattern of Irish nationalist behaviour which lasted until the Act of Union was finally dissolved in 1922. He had also played a significant role in the van of democracy and of liberalism at a critical stage in their development.

Not that the British then, anymore than the Irish since, always appreciated the extent of O'Connell's contribution to the parliamentary sphere. The attitude of the British Tories to O'Connell was sometimes one of loathing and fear, and always one of distrust and opposition. For them, he posed a dangerously formidable challenge which threatened to destroy their establishments, their status and their world. Whigs and Liberals, on the other hand, in their reforming endeavours often found themselves on the same side as O'Connell sometimes desperately needing his support. They were always greatly relieved, however, not to be dependent on him. British radicals wooed him since his objectives and theirs usually overlapped, but in the end

O'Connell was too big an oak of the Irish forest ever to be restricted within the tradition of British radicalism.

Phase 1840–1847

The Repeal of the Union agitation which O'Connell launched in the early 1840s, brought him to the peak of his fame. He would make a revolution, he said, not as the French had done with blood, but with the moral force of public opinion. And to that end he organised the nation behind the Repeal agitation, which bore many of the same organisational features as the earlier Emancipation movement. The most notable characteristic of the Repeal Movement, however, was the massive outdoor meeting. Through these monster meetings, held on various historic sites all over Ireland, O'Connell introduced the mass of the Irish people to practical democracy and liberalism and nationalism at a time when these were no more than ideological concepts in the minds of intellectuals in other parts of Europe. The greatest political artist which Ireland had ever known worked on the peasantry who were his unlikely material and moulded them into the political consciousness of being the Irish people. It was O'Connell, therefore, who, in the political sense, created the Irish people and stamped them for good and ill in his own image.

His gigantic campaign, his imprisonment, the failure of the policy to achieve Repeal despite O'Connell's boundless optimism, and his death in 1847 in the midst of a famine which swept away nearly one million of his countrymen by hunger and disease and another million by emigration, captured worldwide attention. Amongst the millions of Irish, scattered over the world, to America, to Britain, to Australia, Canada and to elsewhere in the British colonies, O'Connell exerted a powerful influence. For Irish emigrants, wherever they settled abroad, it was a source of deep pride and of self-esteem that their nation had produced a man of O'Connell's political calibre. O'Connell, for his part, contributed powerfully to the development of the idea of an Irish spiritual empire. The fact that he was never a republican separatist enabled him to think of the British Empire as, in a large part, Irish. He exaggerated the number of Irishmen in the British forces and he was proud of the victories they had won. He recommended his Irish friends to the government for appointment in the colonies. He insisted that full civil liberty was not only for the Irish at home, but also for the Irish abroad. He realised that his influence with the British government on behalf of Catholics in the colonies was more powerful than it could ever be in the American republic on behalf of the Irish emigrants there. He subscribed to the idea that the Irish nation was one, however far-flung its children might be. He viewed the Empire not only in practical terms as a home for the Irish emigrant, but as something they had helped to create, and in which they could make the progress too often denied them at home. Above all, he saw the Empire as a global mission field where the Irish could fulfil their destiny, which, according to O'Connell in writing to an ecclesiastical friend, was catholicising other nations. Ireland's Empire, as conceived by O'Connell, was partly mundane since Ireland was constitutionally an integral portion of the United Kingdom, and partly spiritual because of the religious or missionary aspect. It was also, however, psychological in so far as it was a form of compensation for the political frustration at home, and it was in addition a substitute for the profane imperialism of the ancient enemy. For decades following O'Connell's death the concept of Ireland's spiritual empire could be used to make a virtue out of the grim necessity of emigration.

O'Connell's Impact outside of Ireland

O'Connell's impact on the Irish living outside of Ireland was conditioned, of course, by local circumstances and produced varying reactions in different places. The acquisition of political power and influence by the Irish in the United States of America was doubtlessly related to their massive exposure to political experience and to their training in technique and organisation under O'Connell. For, in pre-Famine Ireland, politics had become a very large part of the social life of the masses and seemed to have become second nature to the Irishman. Because of the language they spoke, as well as the experience they had gained within the British system, no other emigrant group was as well equipped as the Irish to win political power from the descendants of the earlier American colonists, while at the same time not threatening in any way radically the American political inheritance. On the contrary, they slotted into the American political scene almost naturally. Part of their contribution to the American cultural melting-pot lay in the fact that they acted as a solvent between the dominant Anglo-American Protestant ethos and the Roman Catholic immigrants from central Europe and for that reason, if for no other, Irish-American nationalism could never be simply an extension of native Irish politics. Love of their homeland, hatred of what they regarded as the English oppression from which they had fled, and the pride that enabled them to claim that they had come from a freedom-loving people, ensured their support for O'Connell's Irish causes. Not living in Ireland, they could afford to be more militant and separatist than O'Connell, and, living in America, they could not afford to be as liberal as he was on the question of slavery. Slavery in O'Connell's eyes was not merely an institution in need of overhaul in an age of reform in Britain, and it was not merely a stain upon the American character; it was universally wrong. Anti-slavery was a moral as well as a humanitarian cause. After his role in the successful struggle for the abolition of slavery in the British Empire, O'Connell was largely responsible for directing the force of the British anti-slavery movement into the camp of the American abolitionists. He was indeed one of the most significant European accessions to the cause of anti-slavery in America, and American abolitionists appreciated that O'Connell, unlike other notable European nationalists, was prepared to take political risks for the principle of anti-slavery. Ireland and Irishmen wherever they were, he pleaded, should be foremost in seeking to effect the emancipation of mankind. By their memories of Ireland, Irish Americans should love liberty, hate slavery , and treat the blacks as their brethern. There were times when he had to balance his advocacy of anti-slavery against the consequential loss of support, both financial and political, for his repeal movement. On these occasions he showed himself unwilling to barter his abolitionist principle in return for aid for his domestic Irish causes. When one remembers just how expedient a politician he could be on most matters, his principled behaviour on the slavery issue does him all the greater credit. He returned money to Irish-American allies when it was accompanied with arguments in favour of slavery, as he did when it was accompanied with arguments in favour of physical force to solve the Irish question. He did not want blood-stained or slavery-tainted money. If, because of his advocacy of anti-slavery he immediately lost many Irish-American friends for his repeal cause, he gained friends for Ireland from among the American abolitionists, men of the calibre of Wendell Phillips, who long after the death of O'Connell continued to befriend the cause of Irish independence.

The image of O'Connell in Australia differed considerably from that in America. In Australia O'Connell was generally seen to be an important ally working for reform and harmony within the Empire. His loyalty to the Crown and to the Empire was something his contemporaries in Australia could enthusiastically share with him. They could also applaud his achievement of civil liberty for the Catholics and his condemnation of bloodshed as a political weapon. As a leading member of the Imperial Parliament O'Connell, for his part, maintained a close interest in the affairs of the colony. He used what political patronage he had to get his friends appointed to important posts in Australia and he was kept informed of developments there by his Australian correspondents. Acts of maladministration were noted publicly by him. Just as he had championed the cause of the blacks in the West Indies and in America, he likewise held that no distinction should be made between free settlers and emancipated convicts in Australia, but that all should be treated as equal citizens. Australians, however, could also be cautious in their attitudes to O'Connell. His political technique and the flamboyancy of his tactics did not always appeal to the respectable Irish Australians. His radicalism and his democratic principles were not always regarded as quite relevant to their circumstances. Some Catholics of New South Wales showed less than enthusiasm for O'Connell's repeal objective because a significant Irish Party in the Imperial Parliament might be of greater benefit to them in Australia than the establishment of an Irish Parliament in Dublin. By the time of the celebrations in connection with the centenary of O'Connell's birth (1875) Irish Australians were anxious to stress that their hero was neither narrowly Irish nor narrowly Catholic, but rather a defender of human rights and a benefactor of mankind.

Canada too had its own peculiar reaction to O'Connell. Among the Irish who settled in Newfoundland were fishing colonists who had hailed from the south east of Ireland, more particularly Waterford and its immediate hinterland, and these seasonal migrants had kept up a regular traffic with the homeland. Sweetmans, a Waterford merchant family, annually transported hundreds of Irishmen for the fishing trade.[2] The attachment of these migrants to O'Connell had been formed in the days of the Waterford election (1826). Not surprisingly, therefore, their views of his politics were little different from the views held by those who had never emigrated from home. Catholic French Canadians, under British administration, could also identify with O'Connell and look to him as their own champion. 'Friends of Ireland' societies among French Canadians in Montreal, Quebec and Three Rivers in 1828 and 1829 had passed resolutions praising O'Connell and his fight for Catholic Emancipation.[3] The programme of reform advocated by the Canadian radicals won the support of O'Connell and his English radical allies. When the constitution granted to Newfoundland in 1832 was abolished in the early 1840s, O'Connell protested vigorously in parliament. He asserted that the real reason behind the abolition was that the majority of the people of Newfoundland were Roman Catholic and that the alterations made by Westminster were an attempt to deprive recent immigrants, many of whom were from Ireland, of the right of voting. The Bishop of Newfoundland had kept O'Connell well briefed on this matter.[4] As a memento of their appreciation of O'Connell, 'the man of the people', framed engravings of the Irishman in juxtaposition with the Virgin and the Crucifix were to be found in the remote homes of the French Canadians.[5]

If, in their sore social and economic needs during the era of O'Connell, the Irish discovered a refuge in the English speaking world of America, Australia, Canada and elsewhere in the British Empire, it might be said that it was in that same era that continental Europeans discovered an Ireland which O'Connell had put on the map. This was true even in the case of the Papacy, which obviously had to be concerned with a compaign for civil rights for Irish Catholics, especially since the clergy and laity in Ireland were united in an organisation of novel and massive proportions and of wide implications. There was also for the Pope the delicate matter of maintaining that friendly relationship with Britain which had been established during the Napoleonic conquest. The diplomatic protection occasionally accorded by Britain was appreciated by the Papacy and had to be fostered. The question of a British royal Veto on the appointment of Irish bishops was of deep interest in Rome, and it was an issue which had implications for the Papacy's relations with the heads of other states, Prussia, Russia, France and Spain. The question of a Protestant state's involvement in the education of Irish Catholics was also a matter of grave concern in Rome. In all of these areas the Papacy had to tread warily between the warring camps, Irish Catholics whose loyalty to Rome was proverbial and a friendly British government. O'Connell therefore was liable to become a pawn in a diplomatic game of which he was often himself innocent.

2. See J. J. Mannion, *Irish Settlements in Eastern Canada* (Toronto, 1974) p. 18.
3. Helen Taft Manning, *The Revolt of French Canada 1800-1835* (1962) p. xiv.
4. M.F. Cusack (ed.) *Speeches and Public Letters of the Liberator,* ii, pp 92-101 (speech of 30 July 1842).
5. Manning, op.cit., p. 206.

O'Connell's campaigns gradually won Rome's appreciation of the fact that the minority Catholic population in the United Kingdom included a major grouping which was distinctly Irish and would have to be treated as such. The change in the papal treatment of Ireland was a reflection of the growing awareness in Europe generally of this separate Irish identity.

Before O'Connell's time the secular European powers had been interested in Ireland largely as a source of embarrassment to England. Ireland was the Achilles heel of the British monarchy. The interest in Ireland exhibited, for example, by Spain in the sixteenth century, or by France in the seventeenth and eighteenth, was in direct ratio to the degree of hostility existing between these states and England. Apart from this, what happened in Ireland was of little interest to, and of less consequence for, the states of Europe. In O'Connell's time, however, what happened in Ireland began to have an influence on developments on the continent. Ireland had become more significant for Europe than at any time since the Middle Ages; it had become a source of interest in itself and not merely because of its relations with England. It still remained true, however, that any signs of disunion in the United Kingdom which had played so powerful a part in the defeat of Napoleonic France were bound to attract attention. And the more it was realised that the Irish were trying to free themselves from English political domination, the more curious did Europeans become about Ireland. But it is also true that the romanticism of the time accounted in a large part for the interest shown by continentals in a people about whose origins, literature and customs little enough was known.

Europeans had been stirred in a great variety of ways by the overthrow of the ancien régime and by the ideals and achievements of the French Revolution and the Napoleonic era. In 1820 there had been attempts in Spain, Portugal, Piedmont and Naples to re-assert liberal democratic constitutions against the restored legitimate monarchs. The revolt of the Christian Greeks against the tyranny of the Turks in the 1820s appealed to all the well springs of political and literary romanticism in Europe. And the establishment of Greek independence in 1830 became a symbol of resurgence for all nationalists elsewhere in Europe, who were opposed to the domination of their countries by foreign governments. The suppression of the widespread revolts of 1830 and the exile of numerous rebels produced an international fraternity of liberals and nationalists enthusiastic for the progress of each other's causes. The July Revolution in France overthrew the illiberal Bourbons. Its repercussion in the southern provinces of the Netherlands resulted in Belgian independence under an elected constitutional monarch. O'Connell heartily welcomed the progress of liberalism in France and Belgium in 1830, as he had applauded the revolt in Spain in 1820. The French revolt was "consolatory and deserving of the highest praise. The people were in everything right, the government in everything wrong .... patriotism was in this instance victorious and tyranny completely overthrown." One feature in this "great and satisfactory change" which was especially hailed by O'Connell was "the complete severance of the church from the state". In his view the first French Revolution had unfortunately convinced the French clergy that the safety of their religion was inseparable from the security of the throne. Under the restored Bourbons had emerged an unhallowed mixture of zeal for religion and servile attachment to the crown. Religion was thus placed in a false position; Catholicism in France, like Protestantism in Ireland was considered to be the enemy of the people and of liberty. The revolt of 1830, however, had altered all of that and religion had been left to fructify in its freedom, uncontaminated by association with the state.[6]

In his characteristically superlative way O'Connell asserted that there never yet had been a "more atrocious act of tyranny" than the imposing of a "gross Dutchman" as king on the people of Belgium by England and the Holy Alliance. In this "undisguised piece of despotism" the Belgians had not been consulted nor had any regard been paid to their feelings or their interests. The Protestant king had used his authority to oppress the Catholic people with regard to clerical appointments, education and private property.[7] When the Dutch king was overthrown and the time came to elect the new constitutional monarch, O'Connell himself was named in the public press as a possibility for the honour but, given the concern of all the great powers with the principle of royal legitimacy, his candidature could scarcely have received very serious consideration or support. In the event Prince Leopold of Saxe-Coburg-Gotha of a German dynastic family became King of the Belgians as Leopold I.

This climate of liberal and nationalist enthusiasms sustained European interest in Ireland. Thanks to O'Connell more books on Ireland by continental writers were published during the 1830s and 1840s than during any other period of similar length in the eighteenth or nineteenth centuries. And this interest was also extended to the periodicals and the continental daily press. For the oppressed and liberal and romantic, Ireland had something of the same appeal as Greece or Poland. In 1829 a French author, Dufau, in his introduction to Croker's *Fairy Legends of the South of Ireland,* wrote: "It would be indeed inconsistent to emancipate Greece but to leave the system in Ireland unchanged. A lively sentiment of pity in favour of the distressed peasantry of Ireland has been moving the whole continent." And, addressing a repeal meeting in Paris in July 1843, a French politician, Ledru Rollin said: "We drink to Ireland at whose name the secret sympathies of all nations are excited." After one has allowed for oratorical exaggeration and literary licence, the fact of Europe's absorbing interest in Ireland remains. Ireland was no longer a remote island. Rather was it a mirror in which many struggling Europeans saw the reflection of their own problems. They could therefore readily identify with the issues raised in Ireland by O'Connell, and in supporting him they were, in fact, pursuing their own objectives. Many would have agreed with Gustave de Beaumont's verdict that "Ireland is a small

6. Fitzpatrick (ed.) *Correspondence of Daniel O'Connell,* ii, 222-4 O'Connell to Fitzsimon, 11 September, 1830.
7. O'Connell to Walsh, 11 September 1830 (*Ibid,* ii 219–221).

country on whose soil a battle is in progress on the greatest problems of politics, morals and humanity." This interest by Europeans in Ireland was something which O'Connell, with his supreme faith in the force of public opinion, consciously encouraged. He told his County Clare electorate: "The discussion which the attempt to exclude your representative from the House of Commons must excite will create a sensation all over Europe and produce such a burst of contemptuous indignation against British bigotry in every enlightened country in the world that . . . . the universal shout of the nations of the earth will overpower every opposition."[8]

O'Connell, of course, was not to win universal approbation in Europe. Prince Metternich, Chancellor of the Austrian Empire, presiding over that system which was threatened by agitations such as those led by O'Connell described O'Connell's triumph in 1829 as a revolutionary performance covering itself with a religious mask. Naturally ruling circles elsewhere in Europe shared Metternich's conservative attitude towards O'Connell. Goethe in Weimar, Cavour in Piedmont, Gregory XVI in Rome (however much the Pope might approve of his personal piety), had their reservations about him, and some German Catholics disliked O'Connell's association of Catholicism with revolutionary movements. But it was from those who were laying siege to the Metternich system that O'Connell received support. The attempts of the pre-Metternich era to enshrine liberalism in constitutions and nationalism in declarations of independence were everywhere being remembered and revived. O'Connell, with his important platform in the United Kingdom and a voice that was heard throughout the entire English speaking world, was well placed to spearhead the general movement even on the European continent. As a member of the Imperial Parliament in London, he occupied the centre of the stage of what the Italian, Ventura, called: "the greatest theatre in the world". The King of Bavaria had referred to O'Connell as "that energetical character inseparable for ever from the history of our age".[9] It was Metternich, however, who lent his name to the repressive and conservative aspects of the era. It would scarcely be an exaggeration to label liberal democratic and nationalist aspirations of the same era as 'O'Connellite'. Before O'Connell's time Ireland's relations with the continent had been passive and receptive in the sense that Ireland was influenced by European movements and never vice-versa. In O'Connell's time winds from Ireland began to make a stir in the world of politics outside of Ireland.

O'Connell's impact on the continent exhibited itself in a variety of ways. In 1836, for example, he was invited to act for the defence of a group of French prisoners known as the Lyons Conspirators, who were charged with treason when, in this second city of France, the centre of the silk industry, a ten day strike failed, leaders were arrested and the workers revolted and held the city for five days in what was the most important social uprising in France since

---

8. Quoted in M. MacDonagh *Daniel O'Connell* (1929), p. 157.
9. O'Connell (ed.), *Correspondence of Daniel O'Connell*, vii, no. 2914 fn 3, Ludwig of Bavaria to O'Meara, 12 October 1841.

the French Revolution. Unrest spread to other parts of France and resulted in the mass arrest and trial of republicans and workers' leaders, and in the severe restriction of liberty. The affair received widespread publicity, and in England O'Connell had presided over a meeting which was held in support of Beaumont, a British subject, on trial for treason in France with the other conspirators. Although he regarded it as a great honour to be asked to lead their defence, O'Connell's lack of fluency in French obliged him to decline the invitation.

European interest in O'Connell reached its peak in 1843, the so-called repeal year. That year O'Connell appealed to the sympathies of the people of Germany for support against English oppression. One response came from Dr. Charles Weil of Stuttgart in the Kingdom of Wurtemberg, who was editor of the liberal *Konstitutionellen Jahrbücher*. This paper was the organ of the German constitutional party and it had a circulation all over the Germanic Confederation. Amongst its foreign correspondents was the distinguished Lamartine. Its editor now offered O'Connell space for publicising Ireland's cause.[10] From various other quarters of the Germanic Confederation came evidence of support for O'Connell. Charles Zander, editor of the *Neue Würzburger Zeitung*, writing from Würzburg in Bavaria, expressed his feelings about: "The outrages upon public justice"occasioned by the arrest and trial of O'Connell. Priests in the Kingdom of Würtemberg collected a subscription for the repeal cause. Dr. Walter, a Professor of Law at the University of Bonn, collected signatures in Prussia in support of O'Connell. From Berlin came other supporting addresses with signatures. These addresses had difficulties with the respective governments in Bavaria, Wurtemberg and Prussia. Many of the sympathisers hoped indeed for reciprocal moral support from O'Connell, and as Zander said: "We doubt not we shall receive it."[11] Occasionally, as in the case of the wardens and congregation of the Roman Catholic church in Celle, in the Kingdom of Hanover, they were not beyond requesting financial aid.[12] Others requested no more than O'Connell's autograph. It greatly pleased O'Connell that King Ludwig I of Bavaria should have requested his autograph, not only because of the reverence in which O'Connell said he held a sceptred monarch, but also because that monarch respected popular institutions and manifested a zeal for the spiritual authority of the Holy See.[13] A similar request from the Czar of Russia was refused by O'Connell on the grounds of the Czar's cruelties perpetrated against the Poles.

The truth of the matter was that O'Connell was very useful on the continent for whatever one's cause happened to be. Democrats saw him as the most successful practical exponent of those ideals of the American and French Revolutions which stressed the right of resistance to oppression and popular sovereignty. It was the democrat in O'Connell which Balzac saw when he

10. *Ibid.*, no. 3009, Weil to O'Connell, 30 March 1843.
11. *Ibid.*, no. 3069, Zander to O'Connell, 8 April 1844.
12. *Ibid.*, no. 3176, Catholics of Celle to O'Connell, 14 November 1845.
13. *Ibid.*, vii, no. 2914, O'Connell to O'Meara, 9 September 1841.

described O'Connell as greater than Napoleon because he incarnated a whole nation. Roman Catholics on the continent regarded him as their special champion. Catholic Rhinelanders, opposed to the rule of Protestant Prussians, regarded O'Connell as their defender, and individuals like Dom Saulnier de Beauregard, superior general of the Trappists, successfully solicited O'Connell's aid when about seventy of his confrères, French, English and Irish, were banished from their Abbey at Mellery near Nantes in 1831.[14] Another individual Roman Catholic, Comte Louis Francois de Robiano-Borsbeck, who represented Ypres in the Belgian Chamber of Deputies and who became Director of the Catholic Library of Belgium, once described himself as one of those men for whom O'Connell had devoted his life.

O'Connell's liberal Catholicism was what made greatest appeal to the continental intellectuals struggling to free their church once and for all from the conservative shackles of the ancient régime, and trying to forge acceptable links between Catholicism and the new liberalism. That is why the visit of the young French nobleman, Montalembert, to O'Connell was something in the nature of a pilgrimage to the shrine of liberty. For Montalembert O'Connell was: "the great liberator, the man of the people". And the liberal Catholic paper, L'Avenir, of Lamennais, Lacordaire and Montalembert was only one of the many continental journals which aroused interest in O'Connell, shared his doctrines of the total separation of church and state, of liberty of conscience, freedom of education, and of the press, and the sovereignty of the people, found encouragement in his achievement and a model in his methods. Liberal Catholics on the continent, many of whom were his intellectual superiors but none of whom could match his organising genius, saw O'Connell as one of their most effective spokesmen. For Lacordaire, O'Connell had merited not only the title of liberator of his country, but also the 'ecumenical' title of liberator of the Church. Because of the crimes that had been committed in its name, especially during the revolutionary and Napoleonic era, liberalism was looked upon by the church as a highly dangerous ideology. As late as 1864 it was still being condemned by Pius IX in his Syllabus of Errors. Catholic intellectuals who had tried to reconcile liberalism with their religion found in O'Connell their best argument and their most successful model. For them his career was living proof of the natural union of liberalism and religion. The funeral orations by Father Orioli in Genoa, by Lacordaire in Paris and by Ventura in Rome eloquently testified to the contribution which O'Connell had made to the cause of Catholic liberalism. Ventura, one of the great preachers of the age, depicted O'Connell as the one who had baptised liberalism and made it christian. Louis Veuillot who, with Montalembert had once met O'Connell in Paris, wrote in his paper L'Univers on the occasion of the centenary of O'Connell's birth that O'Connell in the modern world "sprinkled the first drops of baptismal water upon that savage power . . . which we call democracy". A free church unhampered by government interference and an

14. *Ibid.*, iv, no. 1857, De Beauregard to O'Connell, 13 December 1831.

independent clergy uninhibited by secular and financial links with the state were seen to be possible as a result of O'Connell's career.

Accounts of O'Connell's life and translations of his speeches were made available in most European languages. Nationalists struggling to free their countries from the grip of the big empires took especial note of his activities. Italian nationalists aiming at the liberation of their country from the Austrian Empire and seeking to unite the separate states of Italy into one nation carefully chartered O'Connell's progress. Cavour, an anglophile, was not very pleased with the damage which O'Connell's agitation did to the good name, unity and strength of the United Kingdom which sympathised broadly with the Italian cause. But even Cavour, however variable he thought O'Connell's policies to be, could admire the constancy of his objective: the elevation of the political status of his countrymen and co-religionists. "In consideration of the constancy of his moving principle", wrote Cavour, "history will pardon his continual variations, his so various judgments of the same measure and the same men".[15] Mazzini, too, enjoying political asylum in England, preferred to regard O'Connell's movement as reformist, not nationalist. But while the big names of the Risorgimento distinguished between the reformer and the nationalist in O'Connell, other Italians drew inspiration from him. Brofferio, leader of the radicals in the Piedmont Chamber of Deputies, urged on his audience the example of O'Connell: "The great apostle of Irish liberty". Cesare Balbo also held out before the Piedmontese the example of a people united behind O'Connell and displaying strength and wisdom which seemed to Balbo truly classical and truly christian. In Venice, Tommaseo, referring to O'Connell, spoke of the spectacle of an "Advocate more powerful than warrior or sovereign who incites and restrains millions by his voice alone".[16] And in Rome Ventura saw him as something far greater than any mere nationalist could ever be, a man not of one nation alone, but one whose great pacific revolution spread out from Ireland and penetrated into all parts of Europe. He was speaking of O'Connell when he said "God does not create a great man for the use of a single age or a single people". It was what Montalembert also had in mind when he addressed O'Connell: "But you are not only a man of one nation, you are a man of all christendom".

In central and eastern Europe too, spokesmen of the suppressed nationalities like the Magyars, the Czechs and the Poles, showed a keen interest in the Irish struggle. They saw in O'Connell's agitation an inspiring instance of a great nationalist liberation movement. In articles in his *Journal de Prague* Havlitcheck informed his readers about the repeal struggle and pointed to it as an inspiration for his compatriots. European nationalists were correct in looking upon O'Connell's movement as nationalist, but, unlike so many of the continental nationalists, O'Connell was not a separatist nor republican nor doctrinaire. His form of nationalism did not stress the romantic cultural

15. Quoted in K.B. Nowlan, 'The Risorgimento and Ireland 1820-1848' in Edwards (ed.), *Ireland and the Italian Risorgimento* (Italian Institute, Dublin 1960), p. 23.
16. Quoted in N. Mansergh, *The Irish Question 1840-1921* (3rd ed. 1975) pp. 86-7.

ideologies which others associated with distinct national languages and national frontiers. Nor did he hold any romantic notions about the necessity of achieving national liberation through bloodshed and the sword. These views were the prerogative of O'Connell's younger contemporaries, the Young Irelanders, who formed the intellectual wing of the repeal movement in its later phase. That freedom was not worth a single drop of human blood was O'Connell's constant message. Human life was far more sacred to him than any political doctrine. That is why "the sovereignty of the people" was for him no mere political catch-cry much less a licence for regicide or fratricide. On the contrary, he understood the phrase in a particularly humane sense and O'Connell's continental admirers for the most part thoroughly grasped his meaning, even when they were choosing those parts of it which suited best their own particular circumstances. Lamartine, head of the provisional government in France in 1848 after the overthrow of the king, declared to an Irish delegation that waited on him, and who might have expected French encouragement for an intended republican revolt, that O'Connell had taught the world the most energetic although wisest means for the people to regain their rights—peaceful agitation.

Conclusion

Although Irish to the core, yet as a man formed by the eighteenth century, O'Connell was also intensely European and cosmopolitan. His cosmopolitanism saved him from being narrowly Irish and from becoming a rigid doctrinaire nationalist. And what was best in his Irishness gave him a universal appeal without ever losing his characteristic Irishness. In strictly Irish terms he was, in the first place, the representative of the will of the native Irish Catholic majority to survive the centuries of oppression. His life incarnated that spirit of optimistic self-confidence born of the conviction that, like a chosen people, his ancestors had survived all of the persecutions. That conviction sustained him at the most critical points of his career, and his numerous allusions to Ireland's history were clear and constant revelations of his attitude of mind and heart as for example, during his nomination for the Clare election when he declaimed: "Should I not deplore the cruel fate which places the Gores and other Protestants above me in my native land . . . yet this man in my native land—the land of my ancestors where my forefathers were for centuries the chieftains of the land and the friends of her people—make it a species of kindness that he honours me with his patronage. I treat with disdain and contempt the condescension of such patronage".[17] On the other hand, he was in more tangible, political lineage the heir of the liberal national tradition of the eighteenth century Protestant ascendancy. He donned the mantle of Grattan and he spread it open to embrace all of his country's people and their different political traditions. There were those who claimed that O'Connell's Catholic Emancipation agitation fostered sectarianism, but this was certainly

17. Quoted in MacDonagh, op,cit., p. 162.

never intended by O'Connell himself, although there were many forces at work in the circumstances which thwarted his best intentions. In his speech against the Union in 1800, as indeed on other occasions afterwards, he held out to his fellow Catholics an ideal of patriotism above that of sectarianism. In answer to the charge that the Catholics were willing to barter the Protestant parliament of Ireland in return for Catholic toleration by a United Kingdom government, he said: "I know that the Catholics of Ireland still remember that they have a country and that they would never accept any advantages as a sect that would destroy them as a people". And he tried to instil into his fellow Catholics a faith in their Protestant neighbours. "Let every Catholic who feels with me proclaim that . . . he would rather confide in the justice of his brethren, the Protestants of Ireland, who have already liberated him by giving him the franchise, than lay his country at the feet of foreigners." Although he roused the native Catholic people to the pitch of agitation, his statesmanship ever insisted on the acceptance of the Ango-Irish as Irish and an essential part of the country's tradition. Thoroughly versed in the political and constitutional traditions of the Anglo-Irish, he readily appreciated the ideals and achievements of the American colonists and he had owed much to their example.

If ever there was a case for describing a man as an Atlantic Revolutionary the description must surely fit O'Connell. For not only were his formative influences as well as his subsequent impact Irish and British and American, but they were also French. It is true that aspects of the French Revolution only horrified and disgusted him, but it is equally true that some of its ideals inspired him. He was never a republican or a socialist, and he despised the violence and the death that went with the French Revolution. Its Liberty, Equality and Fraternity he set himself to adapt to the circumstances of the United Kingdom of Great Britain and Ireland and his own political and religious principles. If he may be justly described as European in his political outlook, he was European above all in his loyalty to the concept of christendom, and at the heart of O'Connell's christendom was the Papacy. The decision to make a pilgrimage to Rome as the end of his life drew near and the dramatic gesture of the final legacy of his heart to Rome were symbolical of his loyalty. The Catholicism which O'Connell desired should be presided over by that Papacy was not, however, of the narrow political kind of the ancien régime which associated altar and throne all too closely for the good of religion. It was not a matter of pure coincidence that a favourite phrase of O'Connell's was: "The cause of the Catholics and of universal liberty". For him, civil rights for Irish Catholics was an essential part of the universal liberty of man. In the repressive era of Metternich he was one of the first political figures to organise a mass civil liberties movement, and his achievement and success set an example of strength and preached a message of hope to all oppressed Europeans. His liberal principles embraced the downtrodden wherever they were to be found, whatever the colour of their skins, or the religion they professed. By his Irish agitations and his role in the United

Kingdom Parliament, O'Connell made a significant contribution to democracy. His onslaught laid siege to oligarchy and aristocratic establishment. Discrimination on religious and racialist grounds was highlighted by his campaigns and if these were not altogether abolished from the world, at least ameliorative measures were introduced to parts of that world as a result of O'Connell's living and caring. Liberals, democrats, nationalists, reformers, philanthropists everywhere could appeal to O'Connell's example and adapt his methods for their own purposes. He is rightly seen as one of the eighteenth century founding fathers of the doctrine of the rights of man, and he is rightly seen as one of the prophets of the European christian democratic movement of our own time.

As significant as the object lesson which he gave in democratic and liberal principles were the methods which he employed. Physical force for the attainment of political objectives was deliberately rejected by him at all the great moments of his career. In his address to the electors of the county of Clare, dated 25 May 1829, he claimed: "We achieved emancipation in the most peaceful, loyal and constitutional manner. We committed no offence, we were guilty of no crime, we destroyed no property, we injured no man's person, we affected no man's life. The glorious revolution which gave us Catholic Emancipation was effected without the shedding of one drop of human blood." A few years later, in 1833, in the thick of the radical reform stage of his parliamentary career he announced: ". . . my political creed being, that the best possible political revolution is not worth one single drop of human blood."[18] During the celebrated debate on Repeal at the Dublin Corporation in February 1843 he proclaimed: "Not for all the universe contains would I, in the struggle for what I conceive my country's cause, consent to the effusion of a single drop of human blood, except my own." His controversial peace resolutions of July 1846 postulated that: "The greatest political revolution that ever was achieved is not worth one single drop of human blood."

An opportunist in so much else, O'Connell nevertheless insisted on the principle of non-violence as the method to be employed in pursuit of political objectives. His grounds, of course, were as much practical as they were theoretical. What he thought of the blood-sacrifice mystique so beloved by later Irish patriots as the most efficacious means of achieving independence is perhaps best summed up in his pragmatic remark that one live Repealer was worth a whole graveyard of dead ones. O'Connell, however, was not a pacifist. In his argument against the young militants in 1846 he defended the use of arms for self-defence. He had approved of the liberal and national revolts of 1830 in France, Belgium and elsewhere, and he gave his blessing to his son serving with Bolivar in South America. Far from condemning his fellow countrymen who had joined the British forces (as later nationalists would condemn them) he boasted of their military achievements, and complained about the lack of public recognition for their valour and their sacrifice. In this

18. M.F. Cusack op.cit., ii, 441.

mood he could toss off a statement like: "I trust in God the time is not distant when Irish blood will be shed in the name of Ireland."[19] He was innocently unaware that his 'Mallow defiance' speech of 1843 and other such militant pronouncements encouraged the more ardent Young Irelanders to think romantically about physical force. And it suited him that British newspapers and politicians regarded his language and his agitations as likely to lead to civil disturbances and war. He capitalised on the endemic violence in Irish society, and he indulged in a brinkmanship calculated to win concessions for his people while at the same time denouncing that very violence the existence of which he utilised so well to his own advantage. When his young supporters followed his example and talked war he became apprehensive lest their unguarded enthusiasm provide the authorities with legal weapons with which to destroy his constitutional organisation. In any event his calculatedly defiant language as well as his pseudo-pacifist pronouncements have always to be seen as the tactical rhetoric of the political opportunist. Besides, he said so much over so long a career that there were bound to be contradictions, both apparent and real, in his attitude to physical force as to other questions of the day. When all of this is admitted, however, there can be no doubt that the lessons which he constantly reiterated, and which were closest to his heart were those of non-violence and of the unconquerable power of organised moral force.

The universal renunciation of physical force was not acceptable to the Young Irelanders of his day, nor indeed to many contemporary nationalists elsewhere. Nor did his peace resolutions win much approval from either unionists or nationalists in the subsequent story of Irish politics. Irishmen today, however, as well as Europeans and others who have experienced all the horror and terrorism of twentieth century warfare, can no longer be as certain that O'Connell's peace resolutions are so demonstrably false as Pearse and a nationalist age once made them out to be. O'Connell's unshakable faith in the moral force of organised public opinion was to be one of his greatest political legacies to mankind.

The Liberator's contribution to politics had been not merely Irish but international in scope. Only the international perspective in history can take the full measure of O'Connell's contribution to the world of politics, and, more especially to the cause of freedom.

19. *Pilot*, 8 July 1846.

Chapter 2
O'Connell and His Family

Maurice R. O'Connell

The Barony of Iveragh forms the western end of the peninsula that runs out from Killarney into the Atlantic. It is mountainous and weather-beaten tourist country, of bays and coves and beautiful views, separated from the rest of Kerry by a solid range of mountains. In O'Connell's day it was a thickly populated area of small holdings where farmers cut their turf and supplemented their incomes by sea fishing and by grazing cattle and sheep on the mountains. It was also a region in which the Gaelic language survived among all classes into the nineteenth century. Surviving also were a number of Gaelic and Catholic landowning families—McCarthys, O'Connells, O'Mahonys and Sugrues—though their significance owed more to lineage and 'following' than to material wealth.

The O'Connells were the principal family in the barony for some centuries before Daniel O'Connell was born in 1775. The head of the family was his uncle, Muiris a' Chaipín, known to posterity as Hunting-Cap. This uncle enormously expanded his inherited land by farming, smuggling, lending money, hard bargaining and, above all, by thrift. By 1800 he was rich in both land and securities. Hunting-Cap's brother Morgan did likewise, though on a more modest scale and more humanely. In addition, he ran a general store, reared ten children, of whom Daniel was the eldest son, and died prosperous.

Being born into a family that had both lineage and financial success was important to the development of O'Connell's personality. Impoverished lineage can be a millstone, encouraging a man to substitute fancies of ancient grandeur for hard work and honest ambition. He feels deprived, and consequently comes easily to hate and envy success. O'Connell's family background, combining lineage with economic expansion, placed him above the reach of these temptations: he could look the British Government and the Irish Protestant Ascendancy straight in the face without feeling impelled to hate the former and to envy and feel inferior to the latter.

His mother was a daughter of John O'Mullane, a small Catholic landlord near Mallow, Co. Cork, described as 'Chief of his Name'.[1] His mother's sister had married Nicholas Nagle of Castletherry, Mitchelstown, Co. Cork, a first cousin of Edmund Burke. The connection is interesting in that O'Connell seems to have had no regard whatever for that great statesman. He probably could not forgive Burke for his absolute condemnation of the French

---

1. Basil O'Connell, "Catherine O'Mullane," *The Irish Genealogist*, ii, no. 10, (July 1953), p.311.

Revolution and his defence of the English landed aristocracy.

In 1802 O'Connell risked his prospects as the adopted son and heir of his rich but childless uncle, Hunting-Cap, by making an impecunious marriage. His bride was his distant cousin, Mary O'Connell, one of the eleven children of a Tralee physician who had died comparatively young. Mary was the daughter of a 'mixed' marriage, her mother a Catholic, her father a member of the Church of Ireland. In accordance with the custom of the time she and her sisters were reared as Catholics, her brothers as Protestants. When the ambitious Hunting-Cap learned that his promising young barrister nephew had married a girl without a dowry he 'wept with rage' and disinherited him. Some years later, however, he became reconciled to the erring young man and eventually bequeathed him a third of his wealth including Derrynane, the ancestral family home.

In those days the possession of a dowry, even though she had to hand it over to her husband, gave a woman self-respect. Mary was deeply sensitive on the point because, as late as 1825, after twenty-three years of marriage and the birth of eleven children, she could still say to her husband, when recommending that her brother Maurice's widow be employed as housekeeper at Derrynane: "I feel now delicate in mentioning her to you as I have that feeling about me (it is pride I believe) not to have any of my family living at your expense when I brought you no *fortune*"[2]. Owing to the poverty of her widowed mother Mary's education was defective. She did not know French, and resented the superior airs of the family governess who had a very good knowledge of that language which was considered essential to a lady's education. Mary's brother Richard shared this feeling of inferiority which he expressed in writing to congratulate O'Connell in 1815 on his escape from death in the duel with D'Esterre. Despite the fact that he had held a commission in the British Army and was currently an officer in the Kerry Militia, Richard ended his letter with the apology: "Make allowances for my manner of writing. You know my education was rather limited".[3] There was no need for this self-deprecation since the letter was well written. Likewise, Mary wrote intelligent letters which, politics apart, are more interesting than her husband's.

Despite Hunting-Cap's wealth and Morgan O'Connell's success in business, life in Iveragh was modest. The Big Houses of the barony were physically small, Derrynane being a very large rambling farmhouse, the original part dating from shortly after 1700. The only house which the more fertile parts of Ireland would have described as a 'gentleman's residence' was the handsome late Georgian Castlequin (now a ruin), overlooking Cahirciveen and built by the Mahony family, probably in the early nineteenth century. An insight into the ruggedness in living standards of even so long-established and so prosperous a family as the O'Connells is gained from a letter in which

2. Maurice R. O'Connell, ed., *The Correspondence of Daniel O'Connell,* (Irish University Press, 1972-74), iii, no. 1268, Mary O'Connell to O'Connell, 4 December 1825.
3. *Ibid.,* ii, no. 515, Richard O'Connell to O'Connell, 4 February 1815.

O'Connell tells his future wife that on hearing of their match, his sister Ellen expressed delight: "She was always afraid" she said, "that I would marry a proud woman of fashion who would look down on my family and despise this wild country".[4]

O'Connell's six sisters married, all but Ellen by family arrangement, at least one having to marry a man she disliked.[5] The five parentally approved husbands were Catholics of modest landed property, one (William Finn) a son of a wealthy Carlow merchant who was sometime owner of Finn's *Leinster Journal* in Kilkenny. At least two of these husbands were of ancient family—Jeremiah McCartie of Woodview, Newmarket, Co. Cork and Daniel O'Sullivan of Reendonegan (the house is today just barely standing), Bantry, Co. Cork. Ellen kicked over the traces and married her kinsman, a Daniel O'Connell who was a Protestant attorney in Tralee of unsavoury reputation. Her parents were all the more chagrined at her rebellion because another kinsman, also named Daniel O'Connell—he owned both the Great and Small Skelligs—was interested in her but she gave her heart to the attorney. Her marriage was the only one of the six that it known to have come unstuck. As a grass widow she kept house for Hunting-Cap at Derrynane, and ended her days nursing the sick poor with the Presentation Sisters in Cork city.

O'Connell's brother Maurice, his companion at school in St. Omer and Douai, became lieutenant in Count Walsh de Serrant's regiment in the British Army, in what was known at 'Pitt's Irish Brigade'. This brigade was organised by the boys' uncle, General Count Daniel O'Connell, a royalist refugee from the French Revolution, and included many Irishmen who had been army officers under Louis XVI. Maurice died of fever on active service in San Domingo in 1797.

The next brother, John, acceded to Hunting-Cap's wishes by marrying a Co. Cork heiress, Elizabeth Coppinger. John lived as a 'country gentleman' at Grenagh (it still stands) near Killarney. His pack of staghounds were famous, and he amused himself even more destructively by fighting eighteen duels. However, he faced up to his responsibilities as a landlord during the Famine. He died bankrupt in 1853, but fortunately for his family his wife's property was tied up so that he could not squander it.

O'Connell's third and youngest brother, James, was a disciple of Hunting-Cap, more humane than his uncle though probably less cultured (Hunting-Cap's letters were Augustan prose spiced with apt quotations from the Latin classics). James pleased his uncle by marrying a girl with a dowry of £2,000, a daughter of O'Donoghue of the Glen, scion of perhaps Kerry's oldest family. The marriage took place no doubt in Killarney but it was honoured by an *aeríocht* (a community festival) at Derrynane, and by a song composed by the Iveragh poet, Tomás Ó Súilleabháin, *Fáilte Shéamais 'ac Mhurchada* (Welcome to Morgan's son James).

James looked after the pennies and nursed the lands he inherited from

4. *Ibid.*, i, no. 72, O'Connell to Mary O'Connell, probably early September 1802.
5. *Ibid.*, i, no. 148, Jeremiah McCartie to O'Connell, 26 June 1805.

Hunting-Cap into a large estate. Though close-fisted he was good-natured and reluctantly lent money to his recklessly extravagant politician brother, accompanying each loan with warnings of doom which were invariably ignored. From about 1824 he lived at Lakeview near Killarney, replacing the modest old house there in 1870 with a much more ambitious one. Its special feature is the view from the reception rooms looking south over the magic of the Lower Lake. This uncharacteristic expenditure justified itself sixty years later when the money had run out and James's decendants turned the house into a successful hotel.

James was a Tory in politics but he switched allegiance in 1868 on learning that he would receive a baronetcy if Kerry returned two Liberal M.P.'s in the general election of that year, Gladstone's decision to disestablish the Church of Ireland being the big issue. James worked hard in the Liberal interest and collected his prize in the following year.

Both the brothers John and James and their uncle, Count O'Connell, disapproved of the attempt to repeal the Act of Union. However, John compromised somewhat by subsidising the successful election of his son Morgan John for Kerry in 1835. This son continued to represent Kerry until 1852. In 1865 he married Mary Anne Bianconi, daughter of the coaching magnate. As Mrs. Morgan John O'Connell she wrote that historically valuable hotchpotch, *The Last Colonel of the Irish Brigade.*

O'Connell's relations with his wife and children have been ably described by Professor Helen Mulvey in an essay in the recently published first volume of his correspondence. Consequently, the present writer need only deal with those children when they grew up. There is, however, one aspect of O'Connell's life which needs further treatment since new knowledge has become available—his widespread reputation for sexual immorality. In her essay Professor Mulvey writes:

> On the subject of O'Connell's marital fidelity, on the accusations of Ellen Courtney and the later statements of Sir James O'Connor and W. B. Yeats, the letters [between O'Connell and his wife] have nothing explicit to say. But the substance and tone of the correspondence as a whole are powerful evidence of O'Connell's fidelity and devotion to his wife and of his deep happiness in every aspect of his relationship with her[6].

The letters do indicate that he sowed wild oats as a young man before his marriage but the charge is, rather, one of sustained adultery. No historian has found reliable evidence of infidelity but any statement to that effect is met by the popular rejoinder that everybody knows he was unfaithful. A solution to the mystery has now been suggested by the scholars of folklore. They depict O'Connell as the principal folk-hero of modern Irish history, and therein lies the root of this widespread belief. Diarmuid Ó Muirithe, who has studied the folklore on O'Connell, states:

6. *Ibid.,* i, xxix.

All over the country the people told stories of his fabulous virility. Rathkeale in Co. Limerick stands indicted as the only town that didn't provide a woman for his bed. His mistresses were legion and they included Queen Victoria. . . These stories are products of the folk-mind. The heroes of old were ever famous for their sexual energy[7].

This combination of history, correspondence and folklore points to the (disappointing?) conclusion that O'Connell was a faithful husband.

Of the eleven children born to O'Connell and Mary seven survived. They comprised four sons, Maurice, Morgan, John and Daniel, and three daughters, Ellen, Kate and Betsey. Considering the greatness of their father and the intelligence and resourcefulness of their mother the children were not very distinguished.

Maurice, the eldest son and the heir to the family property was a brilliant student at Clongowes but he was lazy and failed to win a scholarship into Trinity College, Dublin. He studied at Trinity and in due time qualified as a barrister but did little professional practice. His father had him elected for Clare in 1831, and from 1832 until his death in 1853 he represented Tralee.

In 1832 Maurice made a romantic marriage, eloping in his yacht with Frances Scott from her home, Cahircon, on the Shannon estuary in West Clare. They were married in a Catholic ceremony in Tralee and a Protestant one in Kenmare. The Scotts were Cromwellian Protestant landlords of means but they sold out in the Encumbered Estates Court after the Famine. Cahircon is now a convent of the Salesian Sisters, and their other home, Knappogue in East Clare, a tourist banqueting castle.

Maurice and Frances had four children but then their marriage broke up. The O'Connell property was entailed so that the lazy and extravagant Maurice could not squander the capital. He spoke Irish[8] and was popular in Iveragh. He had illegitimate children, for at least one of whom his father was erroneously held responsible. In his *Four Years of Irish History 1845–1849* Charles Gavan Duffy maintains that Maurice sympathised with the Young Irelanders in their quarrel with O'Connell in 1846 but there is good reason to believe that Duffy is mistaken.[9]

O'Connell's second son, Morgan, was a lively and cheerful young man who went abroad to seek his fortune. When only fifteen-and-a-half years old he

---

7. "O'Connell in Irish Popular Tradition," Thomas Davis lecture delivered on Radio Telefís Éireann, 13 April 1975.

8. As a very small child Maurice O'Connell spoke Irish at Carhen (O'Connell, *Correspondence*, op.cit., i, nos 144 and 146). In his autobiography the famous war correspondent of the Crimea, William Howard Russell, says of his visit to Derrynane in 1845: "And there was Maurice O'Connell . . . talking Irish with boys and colleens, who laughed at his jokes as if they were at a fair or a wedding" (John B. Atkins, *The Life of Sir William Howard Russell,* London, 1911, i, 33).

9. Maurice R. O'Connell, "O'Connell Reconsidered, " *Studies,* LXIV, no. 254, (Summer 1975), pp 110-112. In addition to the factors dealt with in this article there is the speech made by Maurice O'Connell in the Repeal Association on 14 June 1847, just a month after his father's death. In this speech Maurice attacked the Young Irelanders for having opposed his father on the subject of moral versus physical force; and he called on Repealers only to support those candidates in the forthcoming general election who believed in moral force (*Nation,* 19 June 1847).

enlisted as an officer in the Irish Legion recruited to aid Bolivar in winning freedom for South America from Spanish rule. There is a portrait of him at Derrynane, probably painted by John Gubbins of Co Limerick. It depicts a comely, sensitive, earnest youth in the uniform of the Irish Legion. This force was organised by John Devereux of Co Wexford, an insurgent in 1798, who won O'Connell's enthusiastic backing for his expeditionary force for South America. Charges were made that Devereux was an adventurer who hoped to make a fortune—which he seems to have done—by organising this force. Mr Eric T. D. Lambert, who is writing the history of the Irish Legion, considers that these charges contain a substantial amount of truth. O'Connell's correspondence shows that Devereux, however mistakenly, enjoyed his full trust.

O'Connell gave Morgan a letter for Bolivar which the young man delivered in person at Barranquilla, a Caribbean port in (modern) Colombia. O'Connell commenced his letter:

> Illustrious Sir,
> A stranger and unknown, I take the liberty of addressing you. I am encouraged to do so by my respect for your high character and by my attachment to that sacred cause which your talents, valour and virtue have gloriously sustained—I mean the cause of Liberty and national independence.

The letter offered Morgan's "humble but zealous exertions" and went on to compare Bolivar with Washington, "your great prototype".[10]

In his letter home reporting his presentation to Bolivar, Morgan wrote:

> He is a thin spare man about the height of my uncle Rick, very fine forehead, dark eyes and a very mild melancholy cast of countenance. He is a man of very reserved manners but, when he wishes, can be as merry as another.[11]

Morgan left South America for home in September 1821, fifteen months after his arrival there. In a letter to Hunting-Cap O'Connell said of Morgan's departure:

> The war is over in Colombia and, as he never intended to remain there unless with the chances which a continued warfare would give of exalted promotion, and especially as land, not money, is the mode of remunerating all services, he determined to come home.[12]

And what to do with Morgan now! O'Connell wished to make him an attorney but Mary would have none of it.

> Now, love, to answer you on the subject of Morgan's becoming an attorney. I totally and entirely disapprove of it. It is a profession I never wished for any son of mine . . . [Morgan]

10. O'Connell, *Correspondence,* op.cit., ii, no. 837, O'Connell to Bolivar, 17 April 1820.
11. *Ibid.,* ii, no. 851, Morgan O'Connell to O'Connell, 25 August 1820.
12. *Ibid.,* ii no. 930, O'Connell to Hunting-Cap, 5 January 1822.

is too fond of liberty ever to submit to the control of any person for a period of five years, much less consent to be bound to a *desk* . . . It would be lost money to give him any other profession but the army.[13]

O'Connell could only reply that "your advice with respect to Morgan is decisive".[14] The young man wanted to enter the British service but O'Connell objected.[15] Count O'Connell recommended the Austrian Army as the most suitable,[16] and Morgan became a cadet in its 4th Regiment of Light Cavalry. Considering that he was a veteran of the French Army and had been promoted to the rank of a retired lieutenant-general after the Restoration, it is surprising that the Count did not suggest the French Army for Morgan. Unfortunately, in his letter on the subject he gives no reason for recommending the Austrian. Morgan was commissioned a lieutenant in the 6th Regiment of Light Cavalry while serving at Güns in Hungary in December 1826.[17] He does not seem to have made a success of his military career because he soon returned to Ireland where his father had him returned for Co. Meath in the general election of December 1832. He continued to sit for Meath until 1840 when he was appointed Assistant-Registrar of Deeds, and was Registrar from 1846 until his retirement in 1869. He had little interest in politics, and just did as his father directed. In 1840 he married Kate, daughter of Michael Balfe, a Catholic landlord in Co. Roscommon: they had no children.

The third son, John, was the only one who had a serious interest in politics and who really applied himself. Educated at Clongowes, as were all O'Connell's sons, and at Trinity College, Dublin, John became a barrister in 1837. As he had been an M.P. since 1832 and was needed by his father for regular attendance in parliament he had no chance of building up a legal practice. In 1838 he married Elizabeth, daughter of Dr James Ryan, a medical practitioner of Bray, Co Wicklow. M.P. for various boroughs almost continually from 1832, John retired from political life in 1857 on becoming Clerk of the Hanaper, a government post carrying a salary of £800 a year. When he died in 1858 his funeral was reported by the *Dublin Evening Post* as the largest seen in Dublin since his father's eleven years previously.[18] Immediately after the funeral a committee was established under the chairmanship of the Lord Mayor to organise a national collection in aid of John's eight children who were left inadequately provided for.[19] £5,000 was raised, partly in church and other local collections and partly in donations from prominent Dubliners. The donors included John Gray, the Protestant nationalist and owner-editor of the *Freeman's Journal,* which published an editorial in support of the fund.[20]

13. *Ibid.,* ii no. 1011, Mary O'Connell to O'Connell, 20 April 1823.
14. *Ibid.,* ii no. 1014, O'Connell to Mary O'Connell, 1 May 1823.
15. *Ibid.,* ii, no. 957, O'Connell to Mary O'Connell, 15 April 1822.
16. *Ibid.,* ii, no. 978, Count O'Connell to O'Connell, 5 August 1822.
17. *Ibid.,* iii, no. 1355, Morgan O'Connell to O'Connell, 1 January 1827.
18. *Dublin Evening Post,* 29 May 1858.
19. *Ibid.*
20. *Freeman's Journal,* 29 May 1858.

Politically John was easily the most important of his father's sons because he played the leading role in the Repeal Association during the last year of his father's life, and he tried, but failed, to keep that Association alive after his father's death. He spoke too often and too long in that body, and he provoked much hostility. The obituaries in the press reflect that hostility where they say they will refrain from dealing with the more controversial aspects of his career but they tend to agree that he was sincere, able, well informed and very hardworking. Webb's *Compendium of Irish Biography,* published in 1878, sums him up with the sentence:

> An amiable and conscientious man, he was generally respected but he was quite unable to sustain the role of leader of the Repeal agitation after his father's decease.

Two years later, in 1880, John's bones were dug up by the redoubtable Charles Gavan Duffy. In his semi-autobiographical histories, *Young Ireland* (1880) and *Four Years of Irish History 1845–1849* (1883), Duffy described John as jealous, unscrupulous, narrow-minded and incompetent, as trading on his father's popularity and cajoling the Catholic clergy into opposing the Young Irelanders. Duffy invented the thesis in these books that O'Connell was senile in his last years—a thesis that does not stand up to critical examination—and he used the thesis to accuse John of having induced his allegedly senile father to quarrel with the Young Irelanders and drive them out of the Repeal Association. Duffy's books became the standard history of the Young Ireland period, and consequently John O'Connell's reputation went down for the count. Today, however, Duffy is no longer regarded as a reliable historian, so that John's reputation is due for reappraisal.

In his famous book, *The Fall of Feudalism in Ireland,* Michael Davitt demolished what was left of John's reputation after Gavan Duffy had done with it, in the passage (p. 47):

> It is related that Mr. John O'Connell, M.P., eldest /sic/ son of the Liberator, read aloud in Conciliation Hall [meeting place of the Repeal Association], Dublin a letter he had received from a Catholic bishop in West Cork, in 1847, in which this sentence occurred, "The Famine is spreading with fearful rapidity, and scores of persons are dying of starvation and fever, but the tenants are bravely paying their rents". Whereupon John exclaimed, in proud tones, "I thank God I live among a people who would rather die of hunger than defraud their landlord of the rent!" It is not, unfortunately, on record that the author of this atrocious statement was forthwith kicked from the hall into the sink of the Liffey.

An examination of the debates of the Repeal Association for the Famine period—September 1845 until the end of the Association in June 1848—reveals no letter from a West Cork bishop and no statement of John's

21. Alfred Webb, *A Compendium of Irish Biography,* (Dublin, 1878), P.382.

O'Connell, his sons, John and Daniel, and party on their way to the Four Courts.

even remotely resembling the comment attributed to him by Davitt.[22] It is difficult to believe that any reasonable man would have made such an absurd statement, all the more so in John's case because his comments during the Famine on landlord-tenant relations were consistently anti-landlord. One may safely conclude that John almost certainly never made this statement.

O'Connell bought a partnership for his youngest son, Daniel Jr., in a new brewery in Dublin to which he gave his name. The young Dan did not prosper as a brewer, and ended his connection with the firm in 1841. Though M.P. for Dundalk 1846–47, Waterford City 1847–48 and Tralee 1853–63, he does not seem to have made any mark in politics. In 1863 he left Ireland to become a Commissioner of Income Tax in London. In 1867 he married Ellen Mary, daughter of Ebenezer Foster, member of a private banking family in Cambridge, England. They had ten children.

In 1825 O'Connell's eldest daughter, Ellen, married Christopher Fitz-Simon, a small Catholic landlord but the representative of an ancient family. They had twelve children. In 1823 the Catholic Association was planned at a dinner party in his ancestral home, Glencullen in the Dublin mountains. The house remains in the family, and the table at which the Association was planned is still in the diningroom. According to Fitz-Simon family tradition, Irish was spoken in the glen into the second half of the nineteenth century. Ellen was a good linguist and had some literary talent, publishing a book of poetry in 1863. *Derrynane . . . and other Poems.*

The most formidable of O'Connell's daughters was his second whom he always called 'Saucy Kate'. She married her kinsman, Charles O'Connell, a small Catholic landlord in Iveragh, and had eight children. She lived up to her father's description to the end of her long life. At a tea party in Mallow in the late 1880s a Protestant lady said to her: "We claim St. Patrick". Happily unaware that Patrick was saint by tradition Kate replied with a sweet smile: "And which of your Popes canonised him?"

The youngest of the three surviving daughters, Betsey, married Nicholas Joseph French, member of a modest Catholic landowning family in Co Roscommon. She had six children but was widowed fairly young. She suffered from a serious emotional disturbance which took the form of moral scrupulosity, and there was a question about 1848 of committing her to a mental home. In 1839 she informed her father of her scruples and he wrote to her two very anxious letters counselling her to seek and obey directions from her confessor.[23] When William J. FitzPatrick was about to publish his two volumes of O'Connell's correspondence in 1888, Betsey was embarrassed at his including these two letters. She withdrew her objection, however, when he headed the letters 'To his Daughter' and did not mention her name.

Historians have charged O'Connell with nepotism because of the number of

---

22. The Repeal Association debates were examined as reported in the O'Connellite *Pilot*. This newspaper gave these debates the fullest coverage. I am indebted to Miss May O'Mahony for making this examination.
23. William J. FitzPatrick, ed., *The Correspondence of Daniel O'Connell*, (London, 1888), ii, pp 187-92.

government posts he obtained for his family. The charge is technically true but unfair. He had four relatives appointed—his son Morgan and his three sons-in-law. The four salaries (they were not concurrent because one son-in-law died five years before another was appointed) totalled £3,200. This sum was less than the remuneration of the Master of the Rolls, a judgeship O'Connell was offered but refused. At almost any time after Emancipation the British Government would gladly have given O'Connell any job he wanted in order to get him out of politics. Since he had risen to power as a popular leader he might well have thought it dishonourable to take a well-paid government post, but there would have been no dishonour in leaving politics to apply himself exclusively to his practice at the Bar. Had he done so, he could have earned a great income, perhaps treble the amount in state salaries paid to his relations.

It is also charged that he sought to advance his family by bringing so many of them into parliament. This group consisted of his four sons, two sons-in-law, a nephew and a brother-in-law. Several of these relatives had little interest in politics, and attendance in London for half the year could be ruinous to any business they might have conducted in Ireland. Until 1911 M.P.'s were not paid any salary. But these relatives were very useful to O'Connell. As a political leader he had to have men in the House of Commons whose votes he could command; and he could use his personal popularity to have his relations elected when he would have had greater difficulty in procuring the election of others. He decided whether or not his relatives should stand for parliament in accordance with political needs; and he moved his sons from one constituency to another like pawns on a chessboard. In politics O'Connell's relatives were made to serve him, not he them.

Few popular leaders in any land, but particularly in Ireland, have been equipped so well as O'Connell was, by their family and family background. They provided lineage, wealth, success and an intimate knowledge of humble people. His wife, an intelligent and resourceful woman, gave him domestic security and strong moral support. In contrast to all that had gone before were his children, particularly his sons. These young men lacked the ability, and with the possible exception of John, the energy and ambition of their father's and grandfather's generations. They were a drag on their father financially but then they and their sisters could claim (though they never did) that he had sacrificed their prospects by subordinating his enormously profitable legal practice to politics in the fifteen or twenty years before Emancipation. Perhaps it was as well that he had docile sons. Had they possessed political ideas and ambitions separate from his they might have made serious trouble for him in his later years.

Chapter 3

The Folk-hero and Tradition

Gearóid Ó Tuathaigh

Historical fashion very often deals harshly with the reputations of 'great men'. Fresh evidence and changing perspectives may call for major revaluation of the contributions of accepted 'leaders' to the history of their time. Daniel O'Connell has not been immune to the slings and arrows of such revisionism. Since his death the nature and measure of his contribution to Irish history has been a lively battleground for successive generations of historians, not to speak of political propagandists. However, in all this revision and controversy there is, happily, some common ground. Not even his most grudging critics will deny that O'Connell was the towering giant of Irish politics in the first half of the nineteenth century. Nor will it be contested that he was the most loved Irish popular leader of the entire century. In his own time and since, he features in the songs and folklore of the people. Indeed, the folk tradition has paid him its highest compliment by fixing him immovably in the mould of folk-hero.

Predictably, the hero's birth is recounted as an event of special significance. According to a West Cork story the Kerry mountains pealed out their thunderous echo at his birth-hour.[1] Another story has it that O'Connell's parents were childless until the prayers of a needy congregation, for which they had provided a church, moved the Almighty to bless them with their heart's wish, a child. The child, of course, was Dan, and he was born with a cross on his back.[2] We have here all the stock elements of the tradition of the folk-hero—the portents of greatness, the preternatural and the fantastic. Indeed, folklore invests even O'Connell's ancestry with significance. From south Kerry there is a story that the O'Connell family fortune was based on the discovery of hidden treasure.[3] Another tradition traces O'Connell's pedigree into the prehistoric past of Ireland.[4]

Not surprisingly there is a rich store of stories relating to the hero's youth Almost without exception, they depict young Dan as the 'Counsellor' in-the-making. The ready wit, the silver tongue, the ingenuity, daring and guile, allied to an innate sense of 'fair play' for the underdog, all of these traits are already

1. Cited by Diarmaid Ó Muirithe in *Daniel O'Connell in Irish Folk Tradition,* a radio talk which is to be published shortly. Mr. Ó Muirithe kindly allowed me to consult the text of his talk before its publication. I am extremely grateful to him.
2. Caoimhín Ó Danachair, 'Donall Ó Conaill i mBéalaibh na nDaoine,' *Studia Hibernica,* 1974, p. 41. This paper is richly illustrated with folktales on O'Connell, and the present writer has drawn freely on these illustrations.
3. Ó Danachair, op. cit. p. 40.
4. Ó Muirithe, op. cit. p. 3.

evident in the youthful O'Connell. When the advice of the young Solomon is casually sought in legal disputes he confounds not only esteemed veterans of the Bar, such as John Philpott Curran, but also folk-heroes renowned for their clever speech, such as Eoghan Rua Q Súilleabháin.[5] Here, as an example, is a story collected by the late Máirtín O Cadhain in the Cois Fhairrge area of Conamara:

> Two men were out fishing when one of them fell out of the boat. The other man, in saving his companion, stuck the hook in his eye, causing him to lose the eye. The one who had lost the eye sued for compensation, but several courts failed to resolve the issue. One day, as the case was being tried in court, a group of youngsters, including young O'Connell, were playing beside the Courthouse. O'Connell called the other boys together and seated himself on a hedge, as if he were the judge and the other boys the jurors. "My judgement", said O'Connell, "is as follows. Let them go out in the boat again to the same place, and let the man who lost his eye be thrown into the sea. If he succeeds in saving himself let him be granted due compensation for his eye; if he doesn't, then he'll drown". One of the counsellors in the case overheard this interlude, and he went in and related the story to the judge. The judge decided that this would be his own verdict also. But, of course, the plaintiff would not be tempted to take such a risk.
> The judge then asked that the 'wise boy' be brought to him. This was done and the boy was sent to school, and a counsellor was made of him. And he was 'counsiléar na sgeiche'.[6]

Undoubtedly, the richest store of folktales about O'Connell relate to his exploits as a lawyer, as 'the Counsellor'. Here the wit and daring of the precocious youth reach triumphant maturity. The court, as Dr. Ó Danachair has rightly pointed out, was the great theatre of early nineteenth century Ireland.[7] It was also a place of contest in which the odds were heavily stacked against the underdog, where the Catholic peasant very often faced the landlords and the dependents of the landlords as the magisterial forces of law and order. When a counsellor came along who was prepared to champion the rights of the underdog, and, more importantly, one with the ability to win, to humble the mighty, then it is hardly to be wondered at that the peasants took him to their hearts and made him their hero. From the four corners of Ireland there are stories which illustrate the superb legal mind, the generous heart, and the verbal dexterity of O'Connell. His most famous case, the defence of the Doneraile conspirators, has passed into literature through the pen of Canon Sheehan. There are however less dramatic examples, and ones which show that O'Connell's talents were not necessarily or always on the side of innocence. Here is one example:

> Some fellow was apprehended for a crime and brought to justice. He left his cap at the scene of the crime, and the policeman got his cap. The accused man got Dan to plead for him. In court the policeman identified the man and referred to the incriminating cap. The judge examined the cap. O'Connell, silent for a while, then asked the judge if he might

5. See, for example, Ó Danachair, op. cit. pp 41-42.
6. *Ibid.* pp 42-3. The translation is my own.
7. *Ibid.,* p. 45.

examine the cap. The judge handed the cap to O'Connell, who recognised the cap as
belonging to the accused. There was no name on the cap. Dan looked closely at the cap
and as he did so he spelt out the accused man's name. He turned to the policeman and said
"Did you see the man's name in the cap?" The policeman said he did. "Now", said
O'Connell to the judge, "he's swearing to the name in the cap and there's no name at all in
it". The case was dismissed.[8]

These jousts of wit and words were not confined to the courtroom. Hapless
victims of injustice or deceit, wherever they might be, could always depend on
O'Connell to save the day for them. Here is a west Mayo version of a common
tale[9]:

There was an Irish harvestman in England who went into a shop. He was looking around,
not sure what he wanted (or indeed if he wanted anything), when the shopkeeper addressed
him. "What are you looking for", said the shopkeeper. "Nothing", said the harvestman,
"or, rather, what I'm looking for you don't have in your shop". "I'll bet you I have", said
the shopkeeper. "Done", said the harvestman. "How much?" said the shopkeeper. "As
much as I've earned this year", said the harvestman, tumbling it out of his pocket. The
shopkeeper counted out an equal sum and when the harvestman mentioned the article he
required the shopkeeper had it in stock. The poor harvestman had no choice but to
concede the victory, and to leave the shop weeping and lamenting.
Who should he meet on the street but Dan O'Connell, who asked him why he was so upset,
He told Dan his story. "Well", said O'Connell, "here's my advice. Cut off your small toe
and send it to Ireland in a letter. When it has arrived in Ireland go back to the shop and ask
the shopkeeper how much would it cost you to buy a measure of tobacco from your small
toe to the tip of your ear". The harvestman followed these instructions. In due course the
shopkeeper produced a tape and after he had measured the harvestman he quoted a price.
"Not so fast" said the harvestman, taking off his shoe and showing his foot, "my small toe
is over in Ireland". The shopkeeper sought to dismiss this with ridicule. But O'Connell,
who was in attendance, stepped forward and said: "He did this on my advice. You took
this man's hard-earned money from him, and you will now have to pay up every ounce of
tobacco until it reaches his toe in Ireland". The shopkeeper knew the game was up, and he
had to pay over the harvestman twice as much money as he had originally taken from him.

This story contains an element often found in O'Connell folktales, that is, his
ability to overcome what is accepted as the inevitable treachery and hostility of
the English. Here is a lively example, in poor verse, of O'Connell in 'enemy'
territory:

One day through the street as brave Daniel was walking
A party of cockneys for to view him they stood;
In order to humbug the monarch of Ireland
One pulled out a note and said "Sir, is that good"?

For to answer the question brave Dan was not lazy,
The note to his pocket he conveyed in a thrice,
When asked to return it, he says to the fellow
"Sir, I am a lawyer that's paid for advice."[10]

8. Department of Irish Folklore, University College, Dublin. (D.I.F.).
9. D.I.F. Recorded by Antoine Ó Luingseacháin. The translation is my own.
10. D.I.F. These verses come from a poem called 'O'Connell and the Tinkers.'

There was also treachery of a more serious nature, and here O'Connell often had to rely on the help and warnings of his fellow-countrymen in order to survive. The story of an Irish servant-girl who warned him of an attempt to poison him is particularly well-known:

A Dhómnaill Uí Chonaill, an dtuigeann tú Gaeilge?
Tuigim, a chailín, céard is léar duit?
Tá nimh in do chupán a mharódh na céadta,
Gairm thú a chailín is bhéarfaidh mé spré duit.[11]

There are countless other tales ot treacherous attempts on O'Connell's life, but always there is a young boy or girl from Ireland at hand to give timely warning or advice.[12]

It would be misleading to suggest that O'Connell never meets his match in wit or craft in the folk-tradition. The following tale from Donegal clearly illustrates that this was not so:

An old woman living on the side of the road owned a fine fat calf. One fair day a cattle-jobber bought the calf from her for £5, but left it with her until he would be passing back that way later in the day. But the old woman made the same bargain with two other jobbers, so that she got £15 for her trouble. When the three jobbers assembled on their way home there was great confusion and argument between them as to who was the rightful owner of the calf. The old woman went and sought O'Connell's advice. O'Connell admitted that she was in dire straits, and he took her case on the understanding that if he won it she would pay him £1, if not, he would waive his fee. He then confided to her that she had really no case, and he suggested that her only hope lay in convincing the judge that she was not of sound mind. This she could do by throwing her coat over her head and saying Bow-Wow-Wow, when asked why she had sold the same calf three times. She did as she was instructed, whereupon the judge turned to the three plaintiffs and reprimanded them sternly for even trying to do business with a simpleton. The case was dismissed. Outside the courthouse O'Connell met the old woman and requested his fee. She quickly threw her coat over her head and said Bow-Wow-Wow to him. O'Connell knew he had been beaten at his own game.[13]

In countless other stories O'Connell has to give best to precocious youngsters who, when questioned as to their identity, frequently announce that they are said to be the children of Daniel O'Connell.[14] There is one aspect of these stories which is especially worthy of note. Within the folk-tradition O'Connell is never forced to concede victory to his own or the people's traditional foes—the oppressive landlord or magistrate, the treacherous Englishman, the perjuring Peeler, the religious bigot or the grasping merchant. Against such foes he invariably triumphs. When he meets his match it is usually in an essentially good-natured context, and the victor is usually of his own breed

11. D.I.F. 'Daniel O'Connell, do you understand Irish? I do, my girl, what is the matter? There's poison in your cup that would kill hundreds: Bless you, my girl, and I will give you a dowry.'
12. Ó Danachair, op. cit. pp 50-52.
13. Ibid., pp 58-9. The translation is my own.
14. Ibid.

and, as indicated, often of his own seed—the poor but canny widow, the clever youth, the quick-witted peasant, the servant whose apparent simplicity hides a certain sly cunning when the occasion demands.[15] It has recently been suggested that these folktales "mirror the new democracy their subject had created almost singlehanded".[16] Certainly the pattern followed in contest-stories, as noted above, seems clear evidence of increasing self-confidence and self-esteem among the hitherto depressed peasantry. Here is undoubtedly a key element in the dynamic of popular politics in the Emancipation and Repeal agitations.

Finally there is the inevitable store of stories celebrating the physical characteristics of the folk-hero. He is credited with being almost indestructible; all the efforts of his enemies to do away with him—by dagger, bomb and pistol—are quite unavailing.[17] His cloak, and even his swaddling clothes, were said to have curative powers.[18] And then, of course, there is the quite staggering sexual prowess with which O'Connell is credited. In the best folk tradition his natural children, who turn up at frequent intervals, defy counting, not to speak of credibility.[19]

Strange to say, there is a relative scarcity of folklore relating to the O'Connell of the history books; the Liberator, the O'Connell of Emancipation and Repeal. True, there are a few stories celebrating O'Connell's success in Parliament.[20] But these do little more than buttress his reputation for ingenuity and verbal skill. In short, they simply involve the transplanting of the courtroom victor to the palace of Westminster. The intimacy of the folktale had no use for the abstractions of Emancipation or Repeal. It was as if the sacred drama of such 'high' politics required a different, a more formal idiom. Popular poetry provided this idiom.

By the early nineteenth century popular Gaelic poetry was but a faint echo of the vibrant instrument it had been a century or even a half-century earlier. The most popular genre of popular poetry—the *aisling* or dream-poem—depicted Ireland as a sorrowful maiden in bondage, awaiting her deliverer from over the water. The dramatic changes which this deliverer would accomplish had usually a strong millennial ring to them.[21]   By the early nineteenth century the *aisling* poems had largely degenerated into cliche-ridden echoes of the eighteenth century images and conventions. O'Connell was easily integrated into this genre of poetry. He was the new deliverer, and

15. *Ibid.* pp 57-59. The clever servant stories are particularly amusing.
16. Ó Muirithe, op. cit. p. 9.
17. Ó Danachair, op. cit. pp 50-52.
18. *Ibid.* See also Ó Muirithe, p. 3.
19. For an interesting antidote to the folklore on O'Connell's sexual prowess see the essay by Dr. Helen Mulvey in the introduction to volume i of *The Correspondence of Daniel O'Connell* edited by Maurice R. O'Connell, i, 1792-1814. (I.U.P. 1972).
20. Ó Danachair, pp 60-62.
21. For a fuller account see my Gaelic Ireland, Popular Politics and Daniel O'Connell, *Journal of the Galway Archaeological and Historical Society, 1975 pp. 21-34. The author expresses gratitude to Rionach Ní Fhlathartaigh, M.A. for allowing him to consult copies of folksongs on O'Connell in the mss of the Department of Folklore, U.C.D. Iníon Ní Fhlathartaigh has published two articles on these songs in Comhar,* Lúnasa and Meán Fomhair 1975.

the poets from Kerry to Antrim and from Waterford to Donegal celebrated his arrival to win back her rights for Cáit Ní Dhuibhir. Here is a good example from West Cork:

Go moch roimh Ionnradh Phoebus i Lios gCéin sea bhíos-sa,
I gcoill chluthmhair aoibhinn fé dhíon-ghuth na n-eon;
Chualadh an ceisneamh taobh liom ag an mbé agus i sínte
Garda ina timpeall agus í aca fé yoke;
Luigidh de bhúr ngreamanna, choíche beidh sibh scartha liom
Tá O'Connell ag pléidh le fada dhúinn, ag glanadh na slighe romhainn:
Is geallaim feasta dom cháirdibh go mbeidh cránta is bodaigh fill
Go fánach gan fághaltas san áitreabh so fós.[22]

Even in poems other than the *aislingí* this theme of deliverence recurs again and again. Here is O'Connell's local poet-laureate in Kerry, Tomás Rua Ó Suilleabháin:

Sé Dónal binn Ó Conaill caoin
An planda fíor den Ghael-fhuil:
Gur le feabhas a phinn is meabhair a chinn
Do scól sé síos an craos-shliocht;
Beidh Dónal coíche ar a dtí
Go nglanfar cruinn as Éilge iad,
Nuair a bheidh an dlí fúinn féin aris,
Ar theacht Emancipation.[23]

In Galway, the blind poet Raftery gives his reasons for advising people to pay the Catholic rent:

Beidh ceart an dlí díbh i dtír is i dtalamh
Ní baolach dúinn feasta faid is mhairfeas Ó Conaill.[24]

Another Munster poet, Diarmuid Ó Mathúna, sees deliverance coming with Repeal:

Éigse Mumhan, éistig liúm
Tá an garda chúinn ar bharr na tuinne
Tá Reipéil rianta 'mblian a cúig
Tá 'cimeád cúil dúinn Dónal Ó Conaill.[25]

22. D.I.F. Recorded by Proinsias Ó Ceallaigh, Baile Mhuirne, C. Cork. "Early in the morning I was by Lios Cein, in a lovely wood under a canopy of birdsong: I heard the bewailing near to me from a maiden stretched out, a guard around her and she under arrest. 'Let go'. Ever shall yet be parted from me, O'Connell is stating our case for many a day and clearing the way before us: And I promise my friends that sows and churls will be scattered without a stake in this place yet".
23. James Fenton (ed.), *Amhráin Thomáis Ruaidh*, pp 95-6. (1922). "It is sweet and kind Donal Ó Conaill who is the true plant of Gaelic blood. With his expert pen and lively intelligence, he soundly thrashed the voracious breed. O'Connell henceforth will not let up until they are banished entirely from Ireland. When the law will once again be in our own hands with the coming of Emancipation."
24. Dubhglas de hÍde (eag.), *Ábhráin agus Dánta an Reachtabhraigh* (1969), p. 61. "You will have right and justice on the land. There is no danger to us so long as O'Connell lives."
Cited by Padraig Ó Héalaí, *Filíocht na Mumhan sa Naoú Céad Déag*, in Leachtaí Cholm Cille 3, (Má Nuat 1972), p. 48.
25. "Worthies of Munster, listen to me; Our protector is coming on the crest of a wave: Repeal is destined in the (forty) fifth year: Daniel O'Connell is keeping goal (i.e. manning the gap) for us."

Finally, a Co. Meath poet, Aodh MacDomhnaill, likened O'Connell to Moses:

Ó Conaill ina lár is Ó Briain ar a láimh
Mar Mhaoise ag sárú Éigipt.[26]

Among the deliverer's virtues his incorruptibility was especially prized by the poets. From West Cork again we have the following verse of praise:

Tá Dómhnaill Ó Conaill i mbun chúil ag Gaedhealaibh
Agus go deimhin ní baoghal dóibh go dtógfaidh sé breab;
Mar suidhfidh Parliament arís in Éirinn,
Agus beidh ar gcamthaí a 'pléireacht ar Shliabh na mBan.[27]

Or again,

Mo ghrá mo bhráthair Dómhnall, an prionnsa fóghanta nár breabadh riam.[28]

An interesting proof of the strength of poetic convention is the way in which some of the poets depict O'Connell as winning victory by the sword or by force, in clear contradiction to his oft-stated views on the need for non-violent methods of agitation. Here tradition triumphs over reality. When O'Connell won the Clare election in 1828, Raftery spoke of

Gunnaí is lámhach is teinte cnámha,
Beidh againn amárach agus tá sé in am
Ó fuair Ó Conaill buaidh ar an námhaid
Aipeóchaidh bláith a's beidh meas ar chrainn.[29]

Diarmuid Ó Mathúna, when forecasting Repeal in the poem cited earlier, advises his reader to

Glan do phíce, a's bíodh sí ar faor
Dinidh sgéal do líon gach baile.[30]

26. Colm Beckett, 'Donall Dílis ó Chontae Chiarraí' in *An tUltach*, Nollaig 1975, p. 5.
    "O'Connell in the centre and O'Brien at his side, and he (i.e. O'Connell) like Moses overcoming Egypt."
27. D.I.F. Recorded by Proinsias Ó Ceallaigh, Baile Mhúirne, Co. Cork.
    "Domhnall Ó Connaill is in the goal for the Gael, and there is no danger of his taking a bribe: Because a Parliament will once again sit in Ireland, and our people will disport themselves on Sliabh na mBan."
28. *Ibid.* from the poem Go moch roimh lonnradh Phoebus cited n. 22 above.
    "My treasure is brother Daniel, the good prince who was never bribed."
29. de h-Íde, op. cit. p. 123.
    "Guns and shooting and bonfires we will have to-morrow: and it is time for it. Since O'Connell has won a victory over the enemy, flowers will bloom and trees will be fruitful."
30. See n. 25.
    "Clean your pike and see that it is sharp, Spread the word to every townland."

And a Limerick poet, in praising O'Connell for fighting for justice for Ireland states:

Gheobhaimid le toradh claidheamh (sic) é is claoidhfimíd na Sasanaigh.[31]

Not all poets, however, succumbed to these militaristic conventions. Aodh Mac Domhnaill, for example, expected an O'Connell victory . . .

Ní le gunnaí nó púdar,
Ach le briathra breá cumhra
Mar bholadh na n-úlla.[32]

In a lament written after O'Connell's death a Clare poet put the record straight:

Ní raibh dorta fola nó dearbhughadh éithigh
Id linn ar an saol nuair a bhí tú ar fáil
Na flaithis geala go bhfuair t'anam gléigeal
Nuair a chuaigh tú dhá éileamh ar Rí na nGrást.[33]

And another Clare lament, by Seamus Mac Cruitín, spoke of O'Connell's triumphs having been accomplished . . .

Gan chréacht, gan chosgar, gan fuiliú.[34]

The unanimous acclaim with which the Gaelic poets treated O'Connell poses an interesting problem regarding cultural and political consciousness in pre-famine Ireland. O'Connell, as is well-known, deliberately and consciously turned his back on the remnants of Gaelic culture, most notably the language. He justified his belief in the necessity (and the desirability) of adopting English in place of Irish on strict utilitarian grounds:
"Therefore, although the Irish language is connected with many recollections that twine round the hearts of Irishmen, yet the superior utility of the English tongue, as the medium of all modern communications, is so great that I can witness without a sigh the gradual disuse of Irish".[35] It is possible, of course, that O'Connell was here

31. D.I.F. Recited by Denis Condon, Galbally, Co. Limerick.
"We will get it at the point of a sword, and we will vanquish the English."
32. Beckett, op. cit. p. 5.
. . . "Not with guns or gunpowder, but with fine sweet words like the scent of apples."
33. D.I.F. Recorded by Michael Ó Laoidhleis, Cill Mhichil, Co. Clare.
"There was no bloodshed or false oaths in your time when you were at hand (i.e. O'Connell): The bright heavens were the reward of your shining soul when you came before the Almighty."
34. Ó Muirithe, op. cit. p. 17.
. . . "Without wound, without destruction, without bloodshed."
35. Cited by Gerard Murphy in *Daniel O'Connell: Nine Centenary Essays.* ed. by Michael Tierney (1949) p. 4.

oversimplifying what was, for him, a more complex psychological problem.[36] He clearly enjoyed himself in the company of the poets and peasants of his native Uíbh Ráthach; he was not unconscious of the beauties of the Irish language, nor was he without interest in the history and antiquities of Ireland.[37] Yet for all these instincts he was by intellectual choice an utilitarian, and he had little time for the concepts of cultural nationalism being expounded in his own time by Thomas Davis. Despite this attitude he retained the unswerving loyalty of the Gaelic poets. We may well wonder how this was so.

The fact is that by the early nineteenth century the Gaelic scribes were themselves resigned to the inevitable 'disuse of Irish'. In the *aisling* poem convention demanded that the 'liberation' of Ireland be expressed in the defeat and humiliation of 'bodaigh an Bhéarla' and 'sliocht Luther is Calvin',[38] and in the restoration to the natural place of honour of the native (i.e. Catholic) Irish-speakers. By the early nineteenth century an odd scribe could still be found trying to accomodate O'Connell to the poetic convention, and absurdly forecasting that O'Connell would restore Gaelic culture at the point of a sword.[39] But the majority of the poets faced the grim reality, however much it grieved them. Some sought refuge in macaronic songs: others, like the Clare poet, Séamus Mac Cruitín, turned to writing derivative verses in broken English.[40] Indeed the stark reality of the tragedy facing the Gaelic poets of the early nineteenth century is captured by MacCruitín himself in a most moving poem, significantly entitled 'Ag cur slán le Gaoidhilge':

Is dóiligh liom gan sult gan scéal
caint comhluadar seanGhael
'S a sleachta díl doilíseach fann,
i dtuathaigh iargúil Éireann.
Mairg riamh dár n'uaisle thréig
Le huabhar, seachmall ná sithléig,
an teanga cháidh do chuireadh mian
re héacht a n-eachtraibh imchian.

In the closing lines we hear very clearly the sorrowful tolling of the bell:

Mo shlán go brách a bród sa laoi
le héigse suadh agus seanchaí.[41]

36. See Ó Tuathaigh article, op. cit. For an interesting and personal view see Máire Cruise O'Brien, 'The Gaelic Background in *Irish Times*, 6 August 1975.
37. R. Dudley Edwards, *Daniel O'Connell and his World* (1975) pp 84-88.
38. The phrases translate as 'the ruffians of the English tongue' and 'the seed of Luther and Calvin'.
39. See, for example, *Amhráin Thomáis Ruaidh* n. 23 above.
40. P. Ó Fiannachta, *Leas ar ár Litríocht* (Má Nuad 1974), pp. 185-6.
41. P. Ó Healaí, op. cit. pp 52-3.
    "I find it hard without pleasure or story, the conversation of the company of the Gael. While their beloved descendants are sorrowful and weak in the lonely districts of Ireland. Alas, that our nobles over deserted—through pride, confusion or neglect—the sacred language which inspired with the stories of heroic deeds in the past. Farewell for ever, to its pride in verse, to the poesy, sages and storytellers."

So far as O'Connell was concerned the significant point is that the poets, almost without exception,[42] accept his indifference (in terms of political action) to the 'cultural' dimension of liberation. They accept that he is busy winning rights for the people and they applaud his leadership. But they seem to accept that a battle on the linguistic front was not part of his political obligation. Indeed, for the majority of Gaelic writers in the early nineteenth century it was probably the case, as Professor Dudley Edwards has written, that

"In so far as O'Connell's priorities favoured anglicisation as an essential part of Irish emancipation, he merely spoke as the articulate thinker for the ordinary people of the south and west".[43]

If the *aisling* forecasts of a language revolution were in conflict with the real world of pre-famine Ireland, the same cannot be said of the references to sectarian conflict. The sectarian tone of much of the Gaelic poetry of the late eighteenth and early nineteenth centuries is quite blistering. Here, for example, is a typical piece from Raftery

Le féachaint ins na síontaibh seo is baolach don aicme
Nach dtroisgeann an Aoine 's nach ngéilleann do Chaitlicigh
Na flaithis ní bhfuighe siad gan séala na hEaglaise,
Do réir mar duirt Peadar 's a Mháistir;

Sgríobh Pastorini go dtiocfaidh an bealach-sa,
Lá gach aon mhí go mbeadh cruinniugh 'ins gach baile aca,
Ag Cluain Meala beidh díbirt ar New Lights a's Orangemen,
'S i mBaille Locha Riach 'seadh léigheadh a mbeatha dhoibh,
Ó chailleamar Clayton tá Daly 'na leabhaidh 'gainn,
Do lucht Bíoblaí bréige ná géilligí feasta,
Nach n-umhlaíonn do shagart ná bráthair.[44]

The Galway poet Peatsaí Ó Callanáin is another good witness:

Is é Hanraí an tOcht a thionscail seo
De réir mar a deir na húdair,
Cromail, Creanmar, Leaitimear,
Ceailvin agus Liútar.
A chuir spíonadh is fán ar Chaitlicigh,
Le feall is persecution,

42. For a contrary view see Breandán Ó Buachalla (ed), 'A speech in Irish on Repeal' in *Studia Hibernica* no. 10, pp 84-95.
43. R. Dudley Edwards op. cit. p. 88.
44. de h-Íde, op. cit. pp 58-9.
    "To look forward in time, one fears for the crowd who do not fast on a Friday or give allegiance to Catholics. Without the seal of the Church they will not enter heaven, as it is said by Peter and his Master. Pastorini wrote that it would come to pass that on a day in each month there would be a rounding up of them: In Clonmel there would be a banishment of New Lights and Orangemen, and in Loughrea their lives will be read out to them. Since we lost Clayton we have Daly in his place; To those of the false Bibles do not yield in the future, to those that show no respect to priest or brother."

Ach beidh Oscar thíos ag raith orthu,
Dhá lascadh lena shúiste.[45]

The Munster poets were scarcely more ecumenical,[46] and the Orange songs gave as good as they got in metrical bigotry.[47] Indeed, in the realm of political poetry the popular ballads in English are quite in harmony with the sectarian remnants of the Gaelic tradition. The 'Banished Defender' of the early nineteenth century sets the typical tone:

Poor Catholics of Erin give ear unto these lines I write,
I've fled to the mountains, for ever I am banished quite,
For the sake of my religion I was forced to leave my native home,
I've been a bold Defender and a member of the Church of Rome.

The reason that they banished me, the truth I mean to tell you here,
Because I was a head leader of Father Murphy's shelmaliers,
And for being a Roman Catholic I was trampled on by Harry's breed,
For fighting in defence of my God, my country and my creed.[48]

Another Catholic fugative, 'a patriot so bold' defiantly proclaims that

'No heretic of Calvin's breed will ever me control'[49]

A Munster ballad has encouraging words for Catholics:

When Luther planted the Reformation,
With cunning schemes he first began;
He lit a candle kept long time blazing
But now it's faded, and it's powers are gone.
We have heard the text of the divine sages,
That when the date of those years are gone,
One true Catholic, without a weapon,
Would banish legions from Slieve na Mon.[50]

The Orange balladeer has a rather different version:

Come all ye blind-led Papists, wherever that ye be,
Never bow down to images, for God you must adore,
Never bow down to images for God you must adore,
Come, join our Orange heroes, and cry Dolly's Brae no more.[51]

45. Seán Ó Ceallaigh, *Filíocht na gCallanán* (1967), p. 65.
    "It was Henry the Eight that started it, as reported by the authors: Cromwell, Cranmer, Latimer, Calvin and Luther. Who scattered and damned Catholics, through deceit and persecution. But Oscar* down below (i.e. the devil) will take it out on them, flogging them with his flail."
    *It was believed in the stories that Oscar, being a pagan, went to hell.
46. See P. Ó Héalaí, op. cit.
47. For examples see G. Zimmermann, *Irish Political Street Ballads and Rebel Songs* (Geneve 1966), pp 295-316.
48. *Ibid.*, p. 173.
49. *Ibid.*, p. 193.
50. *Ibid.*, pp 206-7.
51. *Ibid.*, p. 312. For other examples see E.R.R. Green "Songs of the Orangemen" in *The Bell* xiv no. 6 (September, 1947), 35-44.

True, much of this partisan verse was quite amusing, but the essential fact of sectarian tension which lay behind it was unmistakable.[52]

The poets and balladeers had little difficulty in fitting O'Connell into this landscape. For the Catholic poems he was the hero who would "keep those Brunswickers down".[53] In the Orange mythology, of course, he was something of an anti-Christ:

Dan O'Connell he may boast of his great big rebel host,
He can swear they're ten million in number,
But half of them you'll find, they are both lame and blind,
But we're the bould Orange heroes of Comber.[54]

So far as O'Connell's own views are concerned, he was a consistent and convinced advocate of religious toleration. He was gratified when Protestants joined with him in the Emancipation and Repeal campaigns. And yet it is hardly surprising that these essentially tolerant views should have been largely forgotten or ignored by the poets. The objective conditions of popular agitation in early nineteenth century Ireland dictated to a large extent the sectarian language of popular politics. Evangelical Protestantism was coming into collision with a revivalist and reorganising Catholic church, increasingly manned by Maynooth priests.[55] More fundamental still was the fact that O'Connell's campaign for 'civil rights' was essentially an assault on the citadels of Protestant privilege, an attempt to force the Protestant minority to concede full civil rights to the Catholic majority.[56] It would have been remarkable indeed if the balladeers had described this struggle in terms other than sectarian. Very often, when O'Connell turned his considerable powers of invective against the intransigence of the 'Orange faction' it must have seemed that he too had forgotten his views on religious tolerance. In general however it was the poets who simply appropriated O'Connell and fitted him into their own poetic conventions and general world-view.

Finally, if any further evidence were needed to prove how totally O'Connell had become absorbed into the folklore, we need look no further than the tributes and tears which came swelling forth from a famine-stricken people on hearing of O'Connell's death in 1847. The poet Aodh Mac Domhnaill spoke of:

Dónal cróga seolta Ó Conaill,
Fear chosg gach donais de shliocht Gael,
Dá áthrach óna thuras don Róimh
Ó chathair Ghenoa go flaitheas Dé.[57]

52. For a brief statement on sectarian tension see L. M. Cullen, 'The Hidden Ireland: re-assessment of a concept'. *Studia Hibernica*, no. 9, pp 7-47. Also, Brian McNamee, 'The Second Reformation in Ireland'. *Irish Theological Quarterly*, xxxiii, 1966, pp 39-64.
53. A reference to the 'Brunswick clubs' founded to oppose Catholic Emancipation.
54. Cited by Ó Muirithe. op. cit. p. 15. The pagination here is, of course, that of the ms. of the unpublished text.
55. See McNamee. op. cit.
56. For a sympathetic view of the 'colonial' mentality see M. Hurst, *Maria Edgeworth and the Public Scene*. (London 1969).
57. Beckett. op. cit.. p. 6. "Brave. skilful Daniel O'Connell, the obstacle to all harm for the Gael, Transported. on his trip to Rome, from Genoa to Paradise."

From his faithful constituency, Clare, Séamus Mac Cruitín lamented the passing of

Ó Conaill cáidh an flaith gan bhéim.[58]

The composer of a lament entitled 'Erin's King, or Daniel is no More' surveyed O'Connell's achievement:

In ninety-eight he viewed the state
Of this lovely island, I declare,
With grief oppressed he came from the south
And he was elected in the County Clare.
They first seduced him and then abused him
But he confused them till they gave o'er.
The oath of allegiance he refused to take,
But our noble Dan is now no more.

The Emancipation without hesitation
To our lovely isle he soon brought o'er;
Our clergy crowned him with a wreath of glory
When that he sailed to old Erin's shore.
Our chapel bells they do ring melodious
When no scorpion dare cross the door;
Quite broken-hearted from us he departed,
The Pride of Kerry and Old Erin's shore.

To Mullaghmast and likewise Tara,
As a modern Moses he led us, you see,
Tho' we were pursued by proud and haughty,
In the land of promise he left us free.
A shout is gone from Dingle to Derry
Along the Boyne, the Liffey and the Nore,
And all repeat in mournful accents,
Our noble leader brave Daniel is no more.[59]

And, let the last word lie with the anonymous author of yet another lament, The Kerry Eagle:

Now to conclude may his soul rest in Heaven I pray
For his motto was peace, and his country he ne'er would betray,
The whole world, I'm sure, can't produce such a man
Let us all live in peace, and remember brave Dan.[60]

The Irish folk tradition, in song and story, gives ample evidence that the common people did indeed remember brave Dan.

58. Ó Muirithe, op. cit. p. 17. "O'Connell the sacred hero without blemish."
59. Zimmermann, op. cit., pp 232-3.
60. Ibid. pp 235.

Chapter 4

O'Connell in the House of Commons

Oliver Mac Donagh

I

O'Connell was a member of that rare species, men who enter parliament late with a considerable reputation and actually enhance it. He was heavily handicapped in the race. In 1830 a man of fifty-five was on—if not over—the threshold of old age. Certainly, he was an unpromising entrant for a new career which was in certain ways the obverse of his old. Moreover, O'Connell was an object of fear and loathing to the British political classes whose stronghold he was breaching. As a popular agitator, he seemed to personify the force which threatened their hereditary domination. As Irish, as catholic and as a working junior counsel, he was regarded as an intruder upon a company of gentlemen. As a public man, his intemperate vilification and open passion were adjudged 'low'. In short, he had ranged against him the peculiar combination of insolence and frightened ruthlessness which marks a privileged order under threat.

But in other respects O'Connell was fortunate in the timing of his entry upon the parliamentary stage. In terms of British politics, 1830 represented one of those formative moments when one system is in final disarray, and its successor is still obscurely in the making. The eighteenth century political system, in which the use of crown patronage and influence in the house of commons provided the basis of government, had lost its mainspring before the Napoleonic wars were ended; and the decay was not only further advanced, it was also universally apparent after the death of Lord Liverpool in 1827. Viewed in this light, the Clare bye-election of 1828 had a significance quite beyond either the immediate catholic question or Irish disaffection. It seemed to sound the doom of the effortless ascendancy of the nobility and gentry in parliamentary politics which had characterised the preceding century and more. It was this aspect of the result which most deeply impressed and concerned men like Peel and Wellington. What was to follow no one knew. But it was clear that some degree or other of power-sharing with the commercial and professional classes was inevitable, that the representative principle would make some advances in the parliamentary system and that party would have both to shift its base from self or family interest towards ideology, and to act in future as the supplier of the guaranteed support in the house of commons

43

which a government needed to survive. As a conventional British radical on all these matters, O'Connell had at once a clear programme to push and a considerable body of potential allies.

In terms of Irish politics as well, 1830 marked a formative moment. The constitutional implications of the act of union were by now fully apparent. On the one hand, the protestant interest, as a whole, had moved over to support of the union; a quasi-colonial government for Ireland, in the form of a lord lieutenancy and all the surrounding apparatus of administration had, contrary to many of the original expectations, been retained; and successive British cabinets had opted for a species of 'indirect rule' based upon a privileged position for and the near-monopoly of office and favours by the loyalist minority. On the other hand, the catholic relief act of 1829 had weakened and, in a limited sense, even broken into this redoubt; O'Connell had established independent sources of power, both by capturing county seats and by gathering and organising intimidatory masses; and, in the process of attaining these objectives, he had succeeded, more or less, in associating the catholic church with agitation, hostility to British rule and pressure for denominational parity and 'justice' in Ireland. Thus, he occupied, in 1830, an interesting bridgehead. It was clear that advance in some direction or other would be attempted. In which direction to move, and how and with whom, were still dark questions. But never since 1801 had Irish circumstances been nearly so uncertain or unfixed.

II

O'Connell—and this was doubtless an ingredient of his success there—did not approach parliament in any spirit of diffidence or awe. Thirteen years earlier, when he first had encountered the high politics of London, he had written privately to his wife, "the truth is—and I would not say it to another human being but you—I felt in our conversations that it was not difficult to exceed in intellect and sound views men of high names . . . Darling, do not smile at my vanity, but . . . I felt how cruel the Penal Laws are which exclude me from a fair trial with men whom *I look on* as so much my inferiors".[1] O'Connell had not changed since 1817; and with his superb assurance and plasticity, he immediately attained a position of authority in the commons. In his first full session under the whigs, 1831, on the seventy-seven sitting days, he spoke 283 times. Some of these were mere interjections, but more were considerable, often very considerable, speeches. Almost all were powerful or telling. By now, he had both caught 'the feeling of the House' to a nicety and focussed the Irish chief secretary, E. G. Stanley, clearly in his sights.

If we look at O'Connell's performance in the 1831 session in some detail, we can get not only a fair measure of the range of his participation in parliamentary business but also an understanding of the range and nature of

1. M. R. O'Connell (ed.), *The correspondence of Daniel O'Connell*, ii. 147.

his parliamentary tactics and technique; for he came to the house of commons fully formed in these respects. The later 1830s and the 1840s brought novelties in his approach, but these were mere logical or necessary developments or modifications of his initial stands. Moreover, there is point in looking to the beginning of whig rule to introduce O'Connell as a parliamentarian. Only when the liberals were in power was he a true believer in—or at any rate a true practitioner of—'the parliamentary method'. Under conservative rule, he instinctively assumed that progressive legislation would dry up, and the power of the state would be thrown behind the protestant faction in Ireland, and that Irish 'reform' would be either hopeless to expect or unpalatable in form. For good measure, Peel (who was almost as deeply antipathetic to O'Connell as O'Connell was to him) was master of the tories almost to the end of O'Connell's period in the house of commons. During phases of tory government, therefore, O'Connell turned towards extra-parliamentary agitation and attempts to organise pressure from without. His attendances at parliament during Peel's second ministry, 1841–1846, were meagre and his performances perfunctory. Only when, as we shall see, in late 1845 the prospects of the liberals' return brightened was 'the parliamentary method' once more in the ascendant with him.

The meaning of the parliamentary method for O'Connell was immediately apparent in his approach to the dominant critical issue of the 1831 session, parliamentary reform. He was of course committed to a full radical programme, down to universal male suffrage, the secret ballot, triennial parliaments and equal electoral districts. Lord John Russell's bill fell very far short of this. Yet O'Connell accepted it—and on suggestive and prophetic grounds: firstly, as an instalment, and secondly, on trial as to its capacity to provide, by other than radical means, radical political ends. Later, he observed,

This measure gave none of these [the radical demands] . . . but it was in other respects so liberal and so extensive that it . . . would demonstrate one of two things—either that further reform was not necessary . . . or that it would give all these things at a future period, . . . safely, certainly and rationally.[2]

His entire handling of such issues as repeal was already foreshadowed.

Other expressions of O'Connell's radicalism also have revealing accompaniments. He was second only to Joseph Hume in pressing for reductions in public expenditure, and especially for the abolition of useless offices, both to save money and to limit government support resting upon patronage. On the other hand, his drive for municipal reform in Ireland was soon to take the form of pressing for the sharing of power and office with protestants and tories rather than curtailing local authority or suppressing posts. He warmly supported freedom of expression, and this arose peculiarly as an issue of 1831 over curbs upon the press. O'Connell's opposition was formulated in terms of counter-productivity. The *Republican* and the *Poor*

2. Hansard, 3rd series, iii, 181 (8 Apr. 1831).

Man's Guardian were 'ridiculous and disgusting trash'. They would be the only gainers from a prosecution. 'It was an excellent puff for ... seditious publications, and the author must be much obliged to him [the Minister] for having pitied the sorrows of a poor old libeller who must otherwise have starved.'[3] Through all this, too, ran O'Connell's characteristic combination of, on the one hand, absolute and universal goals and, on the other, expedient acceptance of half-measures, contingent toleration of substitutes, selective pressure and disingenuous argument, if it seemed more likely to attain the end.

    Foreign affairs were pressed into the background in 1831, but the aftermath of the continental revolutions of 1830 occasionally engaged parliament's attention. It is interesting to note that whereas O'Connell was hostile to the new Orleanist regime in France, he warmly supported the Belgian and Polish struggles for independence. The probable explanation of this opposition to Louis Phillippe is the anti-clericalism of the Second Monarchy: for long he had distinguished the French *libéraux* from true liberals in this regard. Otherwise, he would surely have approved the apparent diminution of privilege and despotism in France. His approbation of the United States in debates during the same session indicates that his old feeling that the western world was engaged in a supernatural conflict between the forces of tyranny and the forces of freedom was far from dead.To an extent, his attitude towards the Belgians and Poles was determined by just this consideration: the revolts were classic cases of 'the cause of poor downtrodden Man'. But they were also peculiarly close to Ireland's situation, illustrations of 'this lesson, that one nation cannot continue with impunity to wrong and oppress another.'[4] In both instances unions with more powerful alien states had been forced upon them; and in both cases catholic peoples had been subjected to heretical or schismatic overlords. Thus here already the three themes of O'Connell's liberalism, nationally considered, seem to converge. He was at once a universal liberal, an enemy of coercion and a believer in religious no less than racial self-determination.

    When attention turned towards Ireland, much of the debating times of the house and of O'Connell's interventions were devoted to affairs of the moment, such as the Newtownbarry affray or the Doneraile conspiracy. But although O'Connell was generally muted upon the larger political question, he did incidentally argue for repeal of the act of union on some occasions. It is interesting to note that he substantially repeated the pattern of arguments he had used for parliamentary reform. Firstly, he asserted his fundamental principle: 'if the union were not repealed, Ireland would indeed soon cease to be part of the British Empire. It was necessary to the welfare and domestic happiness of Ireland that she should have a domestic legislation'.[5] Almost in the same breath, however, he was hinting already at a 'justice for Ireland' experiment: let them see whether a liberal, reforming government could and would provide Ireland with the same benefit as she might hope to gain with

3. *Ibid.*, iv, 423 (28 June 1831).
4. *Ibid.*, iv, 247 (22 June 1831).
5. *Ibid.*, iii, 21 (Apr. 1831).

parliamentary independence. 'the object of those who advocated Repeal of the Union was, to obtain cheap government, and a just administration of the laws... The Repeal of the Union was merely a means to attain an end, and those who advocated that measure expected now to obtain their object without going through that ordeal... they were now willing to try the effect of a reformed House of Commons...'[6] In turn, this line of argument was accompanied by a demand for equal treatment for Ireland under the act of union, for identifying practices in Ireland and Great Britain; the relationship was not truly a marriage but a form of subordination. This handful of sentences seems to fix at the very outset the range of O'Connell's dialectical and tactical manoeuvres. At the same time, his emphases and alternatives were deeply idiosyncratic. As we have seen, his 'moves', like the opening gambits of a chess master, were essentially the same, no matter what the contest he is engaged in.

The other striking characteristic of O'Connell's observations upon the larger aspect of Irish government in 1831 was his relentless and comprehensive hostility to the influence of the ascendancy and the protestant interest—or, to use his own omnibus term, 'orangism'. The converse of this drive was, in part, the entry into power and office of a counter-balancing number of catholic and (where they could be found) protestant liberals, and in part a surprising predilection for direct British rule as against sub-government by the loyalist minority. For example, a recurrent theme in O'Connell's speeches during the year was denunciation of the yeomanry as a partisan force, ill-led, ill-conducted, cruel and vindictive, and the desirability of replacing them by regular British troops. Again, while he repeatedly attacked Irish offices monopolised by the 'orange faction', he often favoured, not their abolition, but the replacement of their beneficiaries. At the same time (even at the cost of open conflict with Hume) he argued for the retention of the lord-lieutenancy in Ireland. Thus, although O'Connell's formal demand was for self-government, in both the parliamentary and the executive senses, for Ireland, his 'provisional position' would appear to have been a threefold demand for the reduction of the power, privileges and rewards of the ascendancy, for the advancement of catholics and for the maintenance of British and central authority in Dublin as the best mode of assuring the attainment of his other objects.

Thus we find a basic similarity of approach in O'Connell's handling in parliament of the major matters of concern. On constitutional reform, he stood on the simple principle of full democracy (for adult males) and a moderate form of direct popular government. He also supported the radical line, invariably clear-cut and based on general political assumptions, on almost all other issues. In foreign relations, his starting point was the conflict which he assumed to exist between enlightenment and the *ancien régime*. So far as Ireland went, his basic programme was a single amending measure, requiring perhaps no more than a sentence or two in a statute, the repeal of the act of

---

6. *Ibid.*, iv, 652-3 (4 July 1831).

union. But in most cases he was not only ready but even eager to shape or accept half-loaves.

III

1831 was in several respects an unusual session for O'Connell. In the first place it was dominated by a single British issue, the reform bill, to a greater extent than any other in which he was engaged. Secondly, O'Connell acquiesced in this domination, and it seemed quite natural to his contemporaries, Irish and British alike, that he should have subordinated the Irish question to the achievement of the great reform. Thirdly, when the year began he was heading for a collision with the whig government. In February, he was prosecuted for promoting unlawful organisations. Yet a month later the prosecution lapsed and he was in substantial parliamentary alliance with the whigs; and before the year was out, when the reform bill seemed in great danger, he instituted the National Political Union to bring together all Irish refromers, whig, radical, liberal and nationalist. Thus the year would seem at first sight to have been quite extraordinary in O'Connell's preoccupations and fortunes alike.

But this apparently bizarre course of events and succession of attitudes should not deceive us. There was an underlying consistency throughout. It is clear that O'Connell hoped and wished to come to terms with the whig government as soon as they took office in November, 1830. He was willing to cooperate with and support them in return for legislative concessions, executive favour and a more equitable distribution of Irish offices. This, in his eyes was a much more promising tactic—at any rate, at that juncture—than defiance, conflict, the organisation of agitations and outright opposition in the house of commons. But initially the whigs, and in particular the Irish chief secretary, Stanley, were far from contemplating any bargain with O'Connell. On the contrary, anxious to establish itself as more royal than the king in this regard in the estimation of the British public, the government sought to destroy him politically. The introduction of the reform bill changed all this. The whigs now needed O'Connell's support to keep their measure alive, while he saw Ireland's prospects as vastly enhanced in the reformed parliament which would follow the passage of the bill. It would be too much to speak of even a tacit alliance as yet. But already the shadowy outlines of the Lichfield House compact were beginning to be discernible.

Thus 1831 should be seen as part of the larger pattern of O'Connell's parliamentary hopes and performance. 1832 was a year of ebb rather than flow in the incoming tide of 'liberal alliance'. O'Connell was rebuffed by the whigs when their Irish parliamentary reform measure neither enlarged the Irish franchise nor gave Ireland the twenty-five additional seats which he—justifiably—regarded as a most moderate demand. Moreover, the Irish

The Irish Truant.

executive, still dominated by Stanley, proved hostile once again, now that the English reform act was safely on the statute book. O'Connell's response was to attempt to put new pressure on the whigs by three departures. Firstly, he began to organise a separate parliamentary party, initially the 'National Council'. Secondly, he tried to make common cause, possibly even a common front, with the Irish (as distinct from the British) tories. Finally, he stood for repeal of the union at the general election of 1832 and insisted on a repeal pledge from the popular candidates in Ireland if they were to have his endorsement.

In the following year, the next wave of the incoming tide slowly gathered and began to break. He had been rebuffed by the Irish conservatives, but partially successful both in forming a distinct parliamentary group and in wringing a repeal pledge from Irish members—these developments, of course, interacted with and supported one another. Even his partial success, however, brought its own problems. The attempt to form an independent 'party' raised new issues of discipline and produced a challenge to his leadership from the 'left', and this last eventually forced him to introduce a doomed motion in favour of repeal in 1834. Moreover, the whigs, so far from being brought to heel by his monoeuvres in 1832, were bent on carrying a draconian Irish coercion bill. From all these dangerous nettles, O'Connell plucked the flower, safely. The crushing defeat of the repeal motion absolved him from further trafficking with repeal (and conflict with the whigs on this issue) for the immediate future; his marshalling of his forces during this debate and still more during his protracted obstruction of the coercion bill in 1833 confirmed his mastery of his 'party'; and the success of his obstruction in amending the coercion measure both taught the whigs in general that he and the Irish constituted a formidable force in the house of commons, and split them in two on the issue of Irish government. Although the comparison has never (so far as the present author knows) been made, O'Connell's parliamentary performance in 1833–4 anticipates in both general form and detail and tactics Parnell's house of commons strategy and *modus operandi* in the early 1880s. Nor does it seem much inferior to Parnell's as an exercise in political skills.

Although on the surface an alternative to the 'liberal alliance', O'Connell's parliamentary course in 1832–4 should rather be seen as a variation in the method of consummating it. Even so sanguine a politician as he could not really have expected a *volte face* by the Irish tories; nor did he seriously contemplate at this stage a mass agitation for repeal. Essentially, nothing had changed for him since 1830—an understanding, or even better an actual compact, with the whigs still seemed to offer most hope of gain at least cost or danger. He had no intention of using his house of commons 'tail' (the thirty or so M.P.s whose votes he could, generally speaking, deliver) as a permanent opposition to a liberal government. He meant to—and did—use them instead to increase his bargaining power. By mid-1834 O'Connell's tactic of demonstrating to the whigs the value of his co-operation, and contraiwise the awkwardness of his opposition, was beginning to bear fruit. The cabinet divided on the issue of Irish church reform, Melbourne replaced Grey as prime minister and the most reactionary elements in the whig leadership began their move out of the party. But this was a limited success. The potential alliance failed to become actualised immediately, the more conservative members of the new cabinet, chiefly Melbourne himself, and the king, William IV, were hostile to both Irish reforms and co-operation with O'Connell.

The general election of December 1834–January 1835, however brought home to the whigs the disastrous consequences of postponing a decision on allying with or resisting O'Connell. They and the radicals between them emerged from the contest with some 300 seats, almost exactly equal to the strength of the conservatives. O'Connell, with sixty or more members in some degree or other subject to his influence, held the balance of power. On the other hand, the result brought home to O'Connell the danger of admitting to power, through indiscriminate hostility towards the whigs, a tory government, hell bent (as he saw it) on restoring protestant ascendancy and coercion in Ireland, and blocking Irish reform. The outcome was the Lichfield House compact of 1835 whereby, in effect, O'Connell agreed to maintain the whigs in office in return for certain reforms, a certain influence over Irish legislation and, above all, a change in both the conduct and the personnel of the Irish administration. By no means all of this was specified, even informally. But such were the tacit understanding and undertakings on which the alliance was built. At last O'Connell's parliamentary strategy had been consummated.

It is by no means easy to reach a verdict on the wisdom or otherwise of this strategy. It has been generally condemned, at least implicitly, by Irish political historians. Certainly, the returns, particularly in terms of legislation, seem meagre; and the 'collaborationist' strain which was herewith introduced into Irish parliamentary politics was to be attended with many pains and immeasurable bitterness. But much of the criticism is mis-directed or unhistorical or both. Presumably the alternative assumption is that O'Connell should have maintained his 'party' as an independent opposition. But in a situation where the major British parties were nearly equal in numbers this would have meant, sooner or later, restoring the tories to office—and that in a phase of conservative revival in the constituencies. In terms of O'Connell's immediate objectives, the alliance was not unprofitable. The whigs were effectively, though not formally, committed to Irish municipal and local government as well as church and tithe reform, and to abandoning coercion and other Irish departures which O'Connell strongly resisted. More important still, with Mulgrave as Lord-lieutenant and Thomas Drummond as under-secretary, and a steady influx of liberal and catholic public servants, legal and police officers and magistrates, they were providing the first Irish executive for a century and a half which worked against protestant ascendancy. It was this which really mattered for O'Connell in the 1830s; and although this change was necessarily impermanent, it did produce a lasting shift in power and influence in Ireland. The clock could never be turned back to 1830; the future struggles for parity would have to take place on higher ground.

IV

The Lichfield House compact was to govern O'Connell's parliamentary conduct for the next six years, although from being an unqualified alliance in 1835–8, it dwindled to a conditional alliance in 1838–41. But this was a mere tactical variation on O'Connell's part; practically, his relationship with the government did not change. This did not mean that he and his 'party' invariably voted with the whigs. On radical motions such as those in favour of the ballot or against flogging in the army, they sided against the ministry—and, of course, the tories. On a few Irish issues, notably the poor law, their opposition was bitter and sustained. But the essential point is that none of these votes threatened the government's existence. Where that was at stake O'Connell either found reasons for supporting Melbourne or was discreetly absent. It is true that O'Connell attempted, particularly in 1839–41, to increase the pressure on the whigs to reform in Ireland by threatening to withdraw parliamentary support and also to shift his major effort from the house of commons to the Irish country-side. But the menaces were neither seriously meant nor effectual. Fundamentally, this was because both he and the government were aware that the real stumbling block was the tory-dominated and obdurate house of lords; and that there was no hope of rallying British opinion to support an assault on the upper chamber at this stage—especially if the *casus belli* were Irish.

By 1841 there were many indications that O'Connell and the whigs were weary of each other, though they went on cohabiting dully and irritably like a disenchanted middle-aged couple who could yet think of no more appealing course. They were also both weary of office and association with office; and the house of commons vein which O'Connell had set out to follow as far at it would go in 1830 had petered out. When in 1831 he denounced Newtownbarry or excoriated the 'orange' yeomanry, the commons was shocked into attention by so unfamiliar a standpoint and so strange a passion. By 1841, the respective parties were all too accustomed to the arguments and counter-arguments—it was mere routine marching—and the Irish and the parliamentary system had fallen supinely into a species of symbiotic relationship.

Thus even before the general election of 1841 took place O'Connell was losing interest—temporarily at any rate—in 'the parliamentary method'. In the event, a mere eighteen repealers were returned and there was no serious attempt to work with the whigs and liberals at the polls. O'Connell was no longer placing emphasis upon the parliamentary party or the house of commons: conservative governments had to be challenged out-of-doors. In the long and legislatively fruitful session of 1842 he and the repealers were ineffectual and directionless in the house of commons. Thereafter, O'Connell was absent for some two and a half years, apart from one attendance at the house during the course of his appeal against his conviction in the state trials of 1844. After 1841, his 'party' had been reduced to a handful, some of them rogues or buffoons, working without steady support from any quarter of the commons; and

O'Connell must have been aware that in these circumstances he stood only to lose in power and influence by appearing in the chamber. This was certainly borne in upon him with a vengence in mid-1845 when he allowed Smith O'Brien to persuade him to return to the arena for the passage of the Queen's colleges bill. The venture proved disastrous. It was clear that under Peel's government, with the whigs listless and divided and a firm conservative majority, 'the parliamentary method' as practised by O'Connell would bring nothing but reverses and humiliation.

Correspondingly, O'Connell's interest in parliamentary politics revived when the prospect of a new 'liberal alliance' opened up. Early in 1844, he had privately indicated that he was willing to resume, substantially, the Lichfield House compact. Precipitately, he promised support for Lord John Russell in a common anti-corn law front when the whigs looked like returning to power at the end of 1845—very possibly, he saw the cycle which began with the junction on the reform bill in 1831 re-commencing. Ironically, when the whigs did regain office in mid-1846 (and without a clear majority) it was too late for O'Connell to exploit the opening. He was enfeebled in mind and body, without a significant body of supporters in the house and patently bankrupt in political alternatives. Only the shell was left. When eight months later, a dying man, he last addressed the house, his final broken rambling was heard in pitying silence and awkward murmurs of pretended agreement. The marvellous years of invention, virtuosity and resource, when O'Connell had carved out all the first brave tracks in unknown country, were drawing at last their tardy and reluctant tribute.

Chapter 5
O'Connell and the English Radicals

Fergus D'Arcy

The contribution of Daniel O'Connell to English radical politics has not been the subject of any detailed published study to date.[1] That he made a contribution of some significance however it may be measured or assessed, can hardly be denied. At the purely superficial level of the 'language of politics' it was O'Connell who gave us the term 'Tory Radical', if G. J. Holyoake is to be believed;[2] furthermore it was O'Connell, according to another account, who was the first to apply the term 'The Charter' to the programme of radical reform that was the basis of the Chartist movement.[3] It hardly surprises that one with O'Connell's gift of language should have commanded the attention of radical politicians and the transient popularity of English mass audiences. One who could describe Lord Eldon as 'a man who took a look at his conscience and wept' was bound to be a favourite with the crowd of radical Westminster.[4] O'Connell and the English radicals shared common problems and were confronted with a common enemy in the monopoly and abuse of power. In the pursuit of their respective aims they found each other indispensible at times: O'Connell found radical support vital in his Catholic Emancipation campaign in the 1820s; without O'Connell and his Irish parliamentary colleagues the Reform Act of 1832 would not have been carried. Yet, for all their professions of mutual regard and recognition of sharing common problems or facing a common enemy, the personal and political relations of O'Connell and English radicals were more often strained than harmonious. O'Connell often felt badly done by them; yet, it needs to be said that despite his support of radical causes and his professions of radicalism he himself often enough gave cause to doubt his sincerity; and much more serious in the long term, those radicals from whom he sought or expected help for support in his campaign for Repeal of the Act of Union turned out to be those who were least disposed to give it, while those radicals who were prepared to support Repeal were the very ones he

1. The theme 'O'Connell and Radicalism' is of sufficient extent to form the subject of a book, and individual aspects of it, such as O'Connell and the Benthamites, O'Connell and the colonial reformers, O'Connell and the poor laws, all beyond the scope of the present essay, are in themselves sufficient for individual monographs. I wish to thank Professor Maurice O'Connell for his kindness in permitting me to consult the manuscript of the remaining unpublished volumes of his edition of *The Correspondence of Daniel O'Connell* and Professor R. D. Edwards, Miss K. Holland and the staff of the Archives Department, University College, Dublin for providing the facilities.
2. G. J. Holyoake, *The Life of Joseph Rayner Stephens, preacher and political orator* (London, 1881), p. 184.
3. S. S. Sprigge, *The life and times of Thomas Wakley* (London, 1899), p. 313.
4. *The Times,* 26 May 1829, on the occasion of a celebration at the Crown and Anchor tavern to mark the twenty second anniversary of the election of Sir Francis Burdett for Westminster.

ultimately rejected. Relationships with radicals which began in mutual respect and admiration in the early part of the nineteenth century ended ultimately in futility or mutual incomprehension.

O'Connell's earliest significant acquaintance with England came in January 1797 when he registered as a student at Lincoln's Inn. It was ironic that a conservative Catholic youth should be converted to radicalism in England, having only just fled from France and the menace of its revolution; but according to John O'Connell, his father attended the trial of Thomas Hardy in the autumn of 1794 and emerged from that experience a convert to 'popular opinions and principles'.[5] His reading over the next few years included some of the most radical writings of the age. An entry in his journal for 8 December 1795 shows him reading William Godwin's *Political Justice*. In early January 1796 he had acquired the second volume of this work and he confessed:

> I admire this work more, beyond comparison more, than any I ever met with ... it has made me a happier and I think a better man.[6]

Around that time he was also reading Paine's *Age of Reason,* Wollstonecraft's *Vindication,* and Smith's *Wealth of Nations*[1]. Nevertheless, for a man of O'Connell's stature virtually nothing is known of his intellectual development at this critical stage, beyond the meagre fare provided by the journal. When he returned to Ireland at the end of the eighteenth century there is no evidence that he returned as a fire-breathing radical determined on democracy. The condition of the Catholics, rather than any secular radical cause, became the preoccupying political issue for him. There is no indication of any willingness on his part, up to 1829, to engage in any common enterprise with English radicals, and up to 1816 there is no evidence that he had any interest in or knowledge of the activities of English radicals. The evidence, instead, is all the other way: English radicals were aware of Ireland and aware of O'Connell before he was aware of them.

As early as 1803 William Cobbett had given space in his *Political Register* to the publication of articles denouncing the government of Ireland[8] and two years later he himself took up one aspect of the Irish Question with his patron, William Windham:

> in that miserable country the Holy Gospel is made a scandalous job ...(and) were it not for the abused Roman Catholic priest the people of more than one half of Ireland would 'live without God in the world'.[9]

Two years later when the Irish Insurrection Bill was about to become law Cobbett in his *Register* questioned the necessity for so extreme a measure and

5. J. O'Connell, *The life and speeches of Daniel O'Connell, M.P.* (2 vols., 1846), i, 11-12.
6. A. Houston, *Daniel O'Connell: his early life and journal, 1795-1802,* (London, 1906). p. 106).
7. *Ibid.,* pp 110, 127.
8. G. D. H. Cole, *The life of William Cobbett* (London, 1947), p. 84.
9 *B. M. Add. Mss* 37853 ff 170-171, William Cobbett to William Windham, 14 June 1805.

deplored the fact that while coercive legislation was enacted nothing positive was done to alter a situation which made coercion necessary:

> Is there no way of conciliating the good will of the people of Ireland? . . . Are they to be ruled by nothing but stripes? . . . When one considers the heartburnings which exist among the Catholics and which are constantly kept alive by the collection of tithes alone, then one is not astonished at the necessity of an insurrection bill.[10]

When that bill had passed the Commons he observed:

> We may rail against the Irish as long as we please; we may call them rebels and half savages till we are tired; no one can prevent us from despising or hating the Irish but I think it is too much for us to blame them if they should happen most cordially to hate us in return.[11]

Cobbett was not alone. The doyen of English radicals, Major John Cartwright, held sympathetic opinions towards the Irish even before the Act of Union. During the 1798 rebellion he wrote to his nephew Edmund, then a captain in the West York militia, on the morality of volunteering for service in putting down the rebellion:

> Are you then sufficiently acquainted with the measures and the system of government that have been pursued in Ireland, to say decidedly whether or not the resistance of the people be justifiable or the contrary? If on this point you are in the dark, to volunteer to Ireland in the service of the Government is to leave it to chance whether the acts you commit are to be justifiable homicide or murder, Can you run such a risk?

For his own part, the Major could not:

> I have to say, that in my judgement, no nation ever had a juster cause for resistance to oppression than the Irish.[12]

Even before the Act of Union Cartwright appreciated the fact that both countries and peoples were governed by the same ruling class and he remarked that "if Ireland be reduced to slavery by means of an English army, Irish armies will be made to return the favour and to subjugate the people of England".[13] As it happened, some forty years after the crushing of the 1798 rebellion by English soldiers, the Newport rising of John Frost and the Chartists was put down by Irish officers and men.[14]

It was Cartwright's conviction that Ireland would not get justice until the entire kingdom got more representative institutions and any attempt to get

10. J. M. & J. P. Cobbett, *Selections from Cobbett's political works* (6 vols., London, 1835), ii, 275-277.
11. *Ibid.,* ii, 284.
12. F. D. Cartwright (ed.), *The life and correspondence of Major Cartwright,* (2 vols., London, 1826), i, 281, Major John Cartwright to Captain Edmund Cartwright, 25 June 1798.
13. *Ibid,* i, 281-282.
14. M. O'Connell, ed., *The Correspondence of Daniel O'Connell,* no. 2665, Daniel O'Connell to Richard More O'Ferrall, 29 November 1839.

Catholic Emancipation first was beginning at the wrong end. He said as much in a letter to Lord Fingall in 1812 and he called upon the Irish peer to join in the cause of parliamentary reform. He got no good of Fingall, however, who insisted on confining his political efforts to the narrower issue.[15] When Cartwright next appealed to the Irish for aid in the cause of radical reform it was significant that he should have addressed himself not to Fingall but to O'Connell.

O'Connell, whose own activities in Ireland were known to Cartwright from 1815 at least,[16] first showed a practical interest in the cause of parliamentary reform in the following year. On 10 December 1816 at a meeting of Catholics in Dublin he was about to propose an address to the people of England calling for support but he was prevailed upon by O'Gorman Mahon and others not to do so, on the peculiar ground that "England was at this moment in a state of too great agitation for any address".[17] Exactly one week later, at an aggregate meeting of Catholics assembled for the purpose of adopting a petition for Emancipation, O'Connell had determined to speak on, and propose a motion in favour of parliamentary reform, but he backed down and "sacrificed his judgement for the sake of unanimity".[18] It was a decision forced on him by the delicacy of upper class Catholics who wanted no connection with English radicals and radicalism. It was one of the first of many compromises that made O'Connell a flexible politician but that also earned him a reputation among English radicals for unreliability.

Cartwright himself had heard of O'Connell's interest in reform and he wrote to him on 24 December and again on 4 January 1817 to urge O'Connell to push the cause in Ireland, and to recruit the aid of the Catholic clergy in particular.[19] O'Connell responded positively by attending a reform meeting in Dublin on 13 January at which a short-lived Reform Club was founded. At this meeting O'Connell made one of the earliest speeches which seemed to mark him out as a radical reformer declaring

the great body of the people should be voters. No distinction had been made by the God of nature between them and the first peer of the land

and he supported a petition calling for universal suffrage, equal distribution of seats and annual parliaments.[20] Nothing much came of this meeting, however, nor did anything come of a meeting he had already with Cartwright in the summer of 1817 on a visit to London.[21] Insofar as any relationship was sought to be developed between English radicals and Irishmen the initiative

15. Cartwright, *op. cit.*, ii. 22-24, Major John Cartwright to Lord Fingall, 24 February 1812.
16. M. O'Connell, *op. cit.*, ii. 57-8, no. 570, John Hancock to Daniel O'Connell, 13 August, 1815.
17. *Dublin Evening Post*, 14 December, 1816; hereafter cited as *D.E.P.*
18. *D.E.P.*, 19 December 1816.
19. M. O'Connell, *op. cit.*, ii, 127-8, no. 678; ii. 129-130, no. 680, John Cartwright to Daniel O'Connell, 24 December 1816; 4 January 1817.
20. *D.E.P.*, 14 January 1817.
21. M. O'Connell, *op. cit.*, ii, 146, no. 700, Daniel O'Connell to Mary O'Connell, 10 June 1817.

continued to come from the former. In 1819, a few weeks before the Peterloo Massacre, the radical orator Henry Hunt chaired a great reform meeting at Smithfield in London which adopted an "Address of the People of Great Britain to the People of Ireland". The Address pointed out how "a system of unprincipled misrepresentation has for centuries detained us in mutual ignorance and alienation from each other" and it proposed a 'Political Union' of the people of the three kingdoms, in the cause of 'universal civil and religious liberty'. The Address claimed that the people of Ireland could never achieve Emancipation without uniting with British radicals in a common campaign for religious and civil rights.[22]

As was to be the case so often in the future, English radical overtures were greeted with suspicion. On this occasion the *Dublin Evening Post* hoped that "a proper and sensible answer will be returned, declining the honour of the fraternal embrace of John Bull".[23] Unlike the *Post* O'Connell was delighted with the Address, and yet, like the *Post*, he was not prepared to act on it. And then on 16 August 1819 came Peterloo: from Ireland there came no resolutions of sympathy, from O'Connell no comment, from the *Dublin Evening Post* only the caution:

> As an answer to those who would involve the People of Ireland in the proceedings of the English Reformers we recommend the following details ... they afford a warning written in characters of blood, of the inevitable consequences which would result to this country if the People were spirited on to imitate the conduct of the Reformrers in England.[24]

As to the Address which Hunt had issued before the events in Manchester, O'Connell answered the radical orator indirectly in an "Address to the Catholics of Ireland" issued on 22 October 1819 in which he explained his inaction. Up to that point, O'Connell declared, the Irish Catholics "have pursued the strict line of gratitude and prudence" and they have done so because of the way in which their claims had been received by the House of Commons in the previous session; the majority against these claims had been merely nominal and, by implication, any imprudent act might delay the time when that hostile majority in parliament would become a minority. While England was caught up in political turmoil Ireland had been kept tranquil. He went on:

> Let not our conduct be mistaken. Let it not be imagined that we are insensible to the blessings of universal liberty or careless of the unjust state of the parliamentary representation—quite the reverse—but we deemed it right in gratitude to our Protestant neighbours, in duty to ourselves and our children to abstain from any conduct which might endanger the advantages of our present situation.[25]

22. *D.E.P.* 27 July 1819.
23. *Ibid.*, 27 July 1819.
24. *Ibid.*, 19 August 1819.
25. *Ibid.*, 28 October 1819.

He hastened to add that no one was more favourable to reform that he, but he felt it would be folly to jeopardise a "most propitious moment" for gaining Emancipation by joining in a crusade for "an uncertain reform". Events were to show that Emancipation would prove as uncertain a reform as extension of the suffrage. O'Connell concluded his address by adding that were their petition rejected he for one would encourage "a peacable but determined agitation for Reform, without which we must, if we are now rejected, ever despair of Emancipation".[26]

Although nothing came of O'Connell's efforts for Emancipation in 1819 he did not follow the course he described in his October Address, and this despite yet another plea from Cartwright.[27] The cause of parliamentary reform found no promoter in O'Connell or in anyone else of political weight in Ireland between 1819 and 1829.[28] Emancipation continued to be the great cause and came to be the means of increasing contact between O'Connell and the advanced section of English politicians. It was in this cause that O'Connell came to know and admire Burdett and Brougham, and, at the same time, it was his own foundation of the Catholic Association and his inauguration of mass agitation from 1824 that brought him a degree of fame previously unknown.

O'Connell had conceived an admiration for the radical Whig Henry Brougham as early as 1817 at which time Brougham, although only at the beginning of his career as an M.P., had already a formidable reputation as an opposition speaker and scourge of the Tory administration.[29] O'Connell was greatly disappointed at not being able to meet him when in London that summer.[30] It was an admiration destined to turn sour when Brougham came to office in the first Reform Ministry in the 1830s in which he fully supported coercive legislation for Ireland out of loyalty to his prime minister, Grey, and in desperation to remain in office.[31] It was a desperation matched only by O'Connell's own anxiety to keep the Melbourne Whigs in office in the later 1830s. Brougham had no particular interest in Ireland or in Catholic Emancipation as such, accepting the need for Emancipation simply as one constituent of Whig liberal dogma, and it was only from 1823 when O'Connell attracted a new attention that Brougham began to attend to him.[32] For all that, Brougham's support of the cause was important for O'Connell as the Whig lawyer had access to people in power in a way which men like Cobbett and

26. *Ibid.,* 28 October 1819.
27. M. O'Connell, *op. cit.,* ii, 319-320, no. 902, John Cartwright to Daniel O'Connell, 25 Apr. 1821.
28. Apart from Lord Cloncurry's support for parliamentary reform; W. J. FitzPatrick, *The life, times and contemporaries of Lord Cloncurry* (Dublin, 1855), p. 327.
29. Brougham's reputation as an opposition speaker, already great in 1816 from his attacks on the Holy Alliance and Castlereagh's foreign policy, was greatly enhanced in 1817 by his chairmanship of a committee of inquiry into the education of the 'lower orders' and its revelations of widespread alienation and embezzlement of educational charities and endowments: S. Maccoby *English Radicalism 1786-1832* (London, 1955), pp 312, 343-344; F. Hawes, *Henry Brougham* (London, 1957), pp. 106-108.
30. M. O'Connell, *op. cit.,* i, 146, no. 700, Daniel O'Connell to Mary O'Connell, 10 June 1817.
31. Hawes, *op. cit.,* pp. 247-248.
32. This is borne out in the Brougham-O'Connell correspondence which becomes significant only from 1823, for which see M. O'Connell, *op. cit.,* ii, passim.

Hunt had not. Unlike Burdett and O'Connell himself in 1825, Brougham was not prepared to witness the disfranchisement of the forty shilling freeholders and he fought hard against Littleton's bill for this purpose.[33]

Francis Burdett, whose relationship with O'Connell was at times to be of critical importance, had visited Ireland in 1817 and was pleasantly surprised; to his wife he wrote:

> they are the simplest, kindest, gayest of people I ever was amongst, and strange as it may sound of the savage Irish, the most polite, really polite.[34]

O'Connell, despite an earlier attempt, did not meet Burdett until his visit to London in 1825 when the radical baronet presented a Catholic petition in the Commons and carried a motion for an Emancipation bill on 1 March 1825.[35] Initially repelled by Burdett's reserve, O'Connell found him to improve much on acquaintance.[36] As with Brougham, O'Connell's relationship with Burdett, fruitful in the 1820s became embittered and barren in the 1830s. This was partly because Burdett became increasingly conservative in his attitudes and associates and because O'Connell came, for a time at least, to wield a degree of power within the Commons which Burdett found unacceptable. Burdett voted for coercion in 1833,[37] and declared himself opposed to Repeal in the same year.[38] Against this, Burdett professed himself disgusted at the violence of O'Connell's language and came to resent that O'Connell's support was essential to the very existence of Whig government.[39] The disputes between Burdett and O'Connell need not be followed through their progressive degeneration; suffice it to say that O'Connell had the last word: when Burdett, whose political view had become increasingly unacceptable to the radical electorate of Westminster, abandoned that constituency for the comparative safety of conservative Wiltshire he was denounced by O'Connell who remarked, "I never knew before that Wiltshire was like Morrison's Pills, fit for all diseases".[40]

In his dealings with Burdett in the middle 1820s, and particularly in his agreement to the supplementary provisions of a state payment of Catholic clergy and the disfranchisement of the forty shilling freeholders O'Connell made a concession which not only caused a bitter controversy on his return to Ireland later in 1825, but which greatly damaged his reputation among the extremer radicals in England. William Cobbett was especially outraged. It was O'Connell's creation of the Catholic Association and his commencement of mass agitation which revived Cobbett's interest in Ireland. Writing to express

33. Maccoby, *op. cit.*, pp 395-396.
34. M. W. Patterson, *Sir Francis Burdett and his times, 1770-1844* (2 vols., London, 1931), ii, 447.
35. *Annual Register*, 1825, p. 51.
36. M. O'Connell, *op. cit.*, iii, no. 1172, Daniel O'Connell to Mary O'Connell, 21 February, 1825.
37. *Hansard*, 3rd series, xvi, 1283, (29 March 1833).
38. *Ibid.*, xv, 585-586 (12 February 1833).
39. Patterson, *op. cit.*, pp 636-639.
40. *The Pilot*, 17 November 1834, O'Connell speaking at the Stockport Reform Festival on 13 November 1837.

his admiration for O'Connell in December 1824 Cobbett urged him to issue an address to the people of England calling on them to support Emancipation,[41] and Cobbett duly published it in his own *Political Register*.[42] In turn, Cobbett's *History of the Protestant Reformation,* whatever its merits as history, did much to engage sympathy for the cause outside parliament. This was especially important in view of the fact that Emancipation was one of the few, if not the only, issue on which the Commons tended to be in advance of the feeling in the country in the nineteenth century. Cobbett, as parliamentary reformer, could not understand why O'Connell, whom he thought was also a parliamentary reformer, was now agreeing to a measure of disfranchisement. He expressed his dismay in a bitter open letter on 19 July 1825 to the Catholics of Ireland.[43] O'Connell for his part was publicly to confess his folly and regret. Speaking in Louth in July 1828 he declared:

> I am now to speak of a transaction which makes me blush and the consideration of it should be a lesson to all . . . Though a blush mounts to my cheek at the recollection of my folly, it is a comfort to me to feel that my motives were honest. It has been a lesson to me never to give up one particle of principle . . . I did agree to give up the forty shilling freeholders, because I thought them the property of their landlords. I have seen them become an independent body of men and I would as soon lose my life as one single particle of their political rights.[44]

Later that evening he remarked "From the earliest period of my life—I am now, I ever shall be a Radical Reformer." Cobbett was not the only one who had been distressed by O'Connell's willingness to sacrifice the 'freeholders', for Henry Hunt, too, later found in it an occasion for attacking O'Connell.

The disappointment of men like Cobbett and Hunt lay in the fact that O'Connell's willingness to compromise called into question his claim to be a 'Radical Reformer'. Beyond his appeal to and recruitment of the Irish masses in the cause of Emancipation from 1824, and his own professions of radicalism, nothing O'Connell had done up to 1829 had given proof of his genuineness in this regard. The achievement of Emancipation changed all this.

His election for Clare, his 'address of the one hundred promises' with its advocacy of universal suffrage, shorter parliament and secret ballot, his maiden speech in the Commons and his critical contribution to the passing of the great Reform Act, all seemed in earnest to mark the arrival of a radical reformer. He became, for a time, a symbol of hope and achievement to middle and working class radicals alike, was sought after for meetings and legal advice on political organisation, and came to play a central part in many of the major movements and moments of the next decade.

From the moment of his stand for Clare old disagreements with some of the English radicals were made up. Henry Hunt came along to a meeting of

41. M. O'Connell, *op. cit.*, iii, no. 1146, William Cobbett to Daniel O'Connell 28 December 1824.
42. J.M. & J.P. Cobbett, *op. cit.*, vi, 464-469.
43. *Morning Register*, 27 July 1825, citing *Political Register*.
44. *Morning Register*, 16 July 1828. He had expressed his regret as early as 9 July 1825 at a meeting in Dublin. See *Dublin Evening Post*, 12 July 1825 also 26 July 1825.

Emancipation supporters at the Crown and Anchor in July 1828 and heartily
supported O'Connell's decision,[45] and in May 1829 a reconciliation with
Cobbett was effected at a meeting of Westminster electors at which O'Connell
for the first time in his career outlined to an English audience his own political
opinions and aims. The declamatory oratorical style which was alternately to
enthrall and outrage English audiences was evident on this occasion: 'First
then, Englishmen, I appear before you as a reformer, a radical reformer'', and
he went on to make a rousing speech for parliamentary reform.[46] Within
twelve months he was the chairman of the meeting which set up the
Metropolitan Union of Radical Reform. Here before an audience of ten
thousand, attended by some of the greatest popular radicals of the age, Carlile,
Hetherington and Hunt, O'Connell spoke on the cause of reform: "the
principle of universal suffrage was the only rational, just and honest principle.
Of the grades of society in representation he knew nothing', and he called for
law reform, shorter parliaments and secret ballot.[47] The meeting ended with his
election as one of the members of the council of the new body. In the following
year further popular renown came with his support of the Reform Bill in
parliament and in particular from his speech on the subject on 8 March 1831.
Even the *Times* was compelled to praise it.[48] In 1832 came new heights of
popularity when he addressed great meetings of reformers at Birmingham and
Wolverhampton.[49] In June 1832 he received a tumultous reception when he
addressed a meeting of the National Union of the Working Classes in London
and called for an Irish reform bill equal in scope to the English one.[50] Two
years later he was prominent at public meetings and in parliament in defence of
the Tolpuddle Martyrs and in denunciation of the treatment they had
received.[51] His concern with this case, given his legal ability and reputation,
was especially valuable,[52] and though he shared Robert Peels's view that any
interference by the legislature with the judicial process was to be avoided, on
the grounds of humanity he voted in favour of the radical Thomas Wakley's
motion for pardon.[53] There followed, in the autumn of 1835, his round of
speeches in England in a campaign for reform of the House of Lords, in which
he addressed very great audiences. In November 1837 at Stockport in
company with Richard Cobden he reaffirmed his radicalism by reasserting his
commitment to universal suffrage, shorter parliaments and the ballot.[54] In
addition he expressed his wish to see the abolition of the corn laws.

   Within parliament he seemed to act consistently with his speeches outside.

45. *The Times*, 3 July 1828.
46. *Ibid.*, 26 May 1829.
47. *Freeman's Journal*, 11, 13, 15 March 1830.
48. *The Times*, 9 March, 1831.
49. *Freeman's Journal*, 24 January; *D.E.P.*, 19 June 1832.
50. *D.E.P.* 19 June 1832.
51. *True Sun*, 19 April 1834, *Morning Register*, 22 April, 1834, *Hansard*, 3rd series, xxii, 735-738 (14
    April 1834); xxiii, 123-127 (28 April 1834); xxviii, 1237, 1268 (25 June 1835).
52. J. Marlow, *The Tolpuddle Martyrs* (London 1971), pp 114-115.
53. *Hansard*, 3rd series, xxviii, 1273 (25 June 1835).
54. *Tyne Mercury*, 14 September 1835 for his reception in Newcastle; *The Pilot*, 14 September 1835 for
    his Manchester speech; *Pilot*, 17 November 1837 for Stockport.

In May 1830 he moved for leave to bring in a bill to secure triennial parliaments, secret voting and universal suffrage, only to be defeated by 319 to 13.[55] In 1833 and again in 1835 he spoke in favour of George Grote's motion on the ballot.[56] In 1839 he supported Attwood in his request that the House receive the first national petition of the Chartists,[57] and in 1842 he supported the radical T. S. Duncombe on the second national petition.[58] Again, in April 1842 he spoke and voted in favour of Sharman Crawford's motion for leave to bring in a bill embodying the six points of the Charter,[59] and two months later spoke in favour of Ward's motion on the ballot.[60]

During all this period his language was sometimes that of an extreme radical. In 1839 during a debate on Chartism and the question of a Birmingham police force he attacked the House of Lords for its resistance to reform, and remarked:

what prospect had the working classes who had no votes for electing members of parliament of finding redress? They had no representatives ... you have deprived them of the franchise and you suppose that they will be contented and satisfied under that system? They would not deserve the name of Englishmen if they were satisfied. They are a slave class and you are a master class, and so long as this state of things existed it was their right and duty to be dissatisfied.[61]

In November 1840 in correspondence with the reformers of Leeds he repeated these views even more vigorously. he described the Reform Act of 1832 as 'a swindle' as a result of which the English people

though favoured beyond those of other portions of the Empire, are still divided into two unequal classes—a master class and a slave class ... yes, the majority of the English people are practically slaves—shame upon them for continuing so.[62]

However, the rhetoric of politics can be misleading: it is as well to recall that Robert Southey before, and Benjamin Disraeli after this time, could both use language every bit as graphic and provocative without for a moment ceasing to be extremely conservative[63] and to remark that for all the pointedness of language and radicalism of stance in parliament O'Connell was inconsistent, unreliable and opportunistic to a degree that alienated support. Despite the great energy and eloquence, the actual achievement, in the context of English radical politics, was meagre. Relations with English radicals which began in great hopes ended in ultimate futility. As the 1830s passed he found it increasingly difficult and finally impossible to straddle the widening gulf

55. *Hansard,* new series, xxiv, 1206-1244 (28 May 1830).
56. *Ibid.,* 3rd series, xvii, 661 ff (25 April 1833); xxviii, 461-463, (2 June 1835).
57. *Ibid.,* xlix, 259-260 (12 July 1839).
58. *Ibid.,* lxiii, 85 (3 May 1842).
59. *Ibid.,* lxii, 937-943, 982 (21 April 1842).
60. *Ibid.,* lxiv, 348, 407-409 (21 June 1842).
61. *Ibid.,* xlix, 961 (29 July 1839).
62. *The Pilot,* 23 November 1840.
63. R. Southey, *Letters from England* (London, 1807), B. Disraeli, *Sybil* (London, 1845).

between middle and working class aspirations, and the middle class parliamentary radicals with whom he worked disappointed him in their failure to support him on the one vital issue of Repeal of the Act of Union.

On all Irish matters other than Repeal there was a hard core of parliamentary radicals varying in number from twelve to twenty who consistently voted for liberal measures for Ireland. Joseph Hume, Joseph Brotherton, John Easthope, John Fielden, George Grote, George Strickland, John Leader, Thomas Duncombe, Thomas Wakley, Matthew Wood, William Molesworth, Henry Warburton, John Roebuck are the chief of that group who steadily supported measures such as church reform or municipal reform and who spoke and voted against coercive legislation in the 1830s and 1840s. Yet however radical they might be on Irish or non-Irish issues and however steadfast their opposition to repression, at Repeal of the Union they all stopped.

In the famous debate on Repeal between 22 and 29 April 1834 not one English M.P. spoke in support and not one English M.P. voted in support. This is contrary to the commonly held view that there was one English member who voted for Repeal.[64] This is not so; the member in question, J. Kennedy of Tiverton, did not vote in favour of Repeal but simply in favour of O'Connell's motion for a committee of inquiry into the Act of Union and its effects. He shortly afterwards explained that the was in fact against Repeal.[65] Only one radical member bothered to speak in this debate, Joseph Hume. Of all the middle class radical members between 1822 and 1847 Hume was the one closest to O'Connell and the one with the greatest sustained interest in Irish problems. On this occasion he confessed that

> Ireland has not been fully or fairly dealt with. Notwithstanding all this, however, he did not intend to vote for Repeal of the Union because he felt that that measure instead of bettering the condition of Ireland, would add to her sufferings and at the same time be productive of injury to England.[66]

It was not the first time that Hume had spoken on the question. In 1830 he found himself in agreement with Robert Peel that "to promote the separation of the two countries would be most injurious".[67] Ten years later he returned to the subject and in open letters to his Kilkenny constituents he repeated his conviction that "Repeal would be disastrous to both countries".[68] If Hume, who for a long time was friendly with O'Connell and under an obligation to him for his Kilkenny seat and who was deeply interested in Ireland, could not favour Repeal it hardly surprises that the remainder of the parliamentary radicals could not support O'Connell on this. They were not very interested in Irish questions and their basic difference was aptly enough expressed by the

64. D. Gwynn, *Daniel O'Connell* (Cork, 1947) p. 207.
65. *Hansard*, 3rd series, xxiii, 286 (29 April 1834); 695 (7 May 1834).
66. *Ibid.*, xxiii, 238-250 (29 April 1834).
67. *Hansard*, new series, xxiii, 706-707, (22 March 1830).
68. *The Pilot*, 2, 25 November 1840.

Birmingham M.P. G. F. Muntz, onetime vice-president of the Birmingham Political Union, during the three-day debate on the Irish Arms Bill in 1843. He prefaced his contribution to the debate with the observation that

> he had not the slightest intention to take any part in the present debate merely respecting the Arms Bill, of which he knew nothing, such a measure not having been connected with the government of England.[69]

If no English M.P., radical of otherwise, supported Repeal during the great debate of April 1834, did any English M.P. support Repeal at any stage in the first half of the nineteenth century? Between the Act of Union and 1850 three English radical M.P.s indicated support in principle for Repeal and it happens that these three were extreme popular radicals, spokesmen for the working classes and the poor, William Cobbett, Henry Hunt and Thomas Wakley. Hunt expressed his support for the measure in 1831, declaring that "the people of Ireland were the best judges of their own grievances".[70] Cobbett expressed his support in February 1834 during the debate on the King's Speech, the final three paragraphs of which criticised the Repeal agitation. Referring to O'Connell, Cobbett inquired:

> Why should not the Repeal question be agitated as well as the Reform question? Let not the honourable and learned gentlemen despair. He would live to see the Repeal of the Union carried. . . .[71]

Ten days later he remarked that during the previous session he

> did not know whether the Repeal would be productive of good or evil; but since then he had seen the question so much agitated and he had seen his Majesty's ministers so angry upon the subject that he had begun to suspect that the Repeal would be a good thing. He had attended with the greatest care to all the arguments both for and against the question and he was now of opinion that a Repeal of the Legislative Union would be a good thing for England and Ireland.[72]

Thomas Wakley, who was returned for Finsbury in January 1835, voiced his attitude to the subject during a debate on Irish municipal reform in 1837 in the course of which he said

> if the advantages of the English Municipal Bill are to be withheld from them (the Irish) it will be but an act of justice to proclaim with one voice that the Act of Union was an insult, a reproach and a mockery, and that it ought not to continue to exist.[73]

Eleven years later, when Feargus O'Connor introduced a Repeal motion in the

---

69. *Hansard*, 3rd series, lxx, 139 (19 June 1843).
70. *Ibid.*, ii, 488 (14 February 1831); see also iv. 652-653 (4 July 1831).
71. *Ibid.*, xxi, 98 (4 February 1834).
72. *Ibid.*, xxi, 354 (14 February 1834).
73. *Mirror of Parliament*, i, 99 (8 February 1837).

Commons Wakley still supported Repeal and was the only Englishman to cast a vote in favour of it. His action and attitude was in sharp contrast to that of the Benthamite radical John Bowring who observed that he had

> intended to address the House on this subject, but he could gather from various indications on the part of the House that they were anxious to proceed to more practical measures and he would not therefore trespass further upon their attentions.[74]

Significantly, the only others in the first half of the nineteenth century to support Repeal were the Chartists. It was ironic therefore that O'Connell who gave the support of a great name, exceptional energy and talents, and not a few votes to middle class reformers and their movements on issues which *they* held to be vital, received from them in return indifference, incomprehension or hostility to the most vital political issue for him, and that he should have got support for that issue from those extreme radical reformers whom he alienated by his own inconsistency and expediency.

That O'Connell laid himself open to charges of inconsistency on some issues of principle it would be fruitless to deny. His earliest professions of radicalism included the advocacy of annual parliaments.[75] Yet, in the Commons in July 1831 in the course of speaking in favour of triennial parliaments he denied he had ever advocated annual parliaments.[76] His position on the question of universal suffrage changed too. Having advocated this measure from 1817 he appeared to change his mind on it in the later 1830s. In the Commons in July 1839 on the occasion of Thomas Attwood's presentation of the first Chartist petition O'Connell declared:

> I candidly admit that I am a thorough Radical Reformer, therefore I am for the utmost practical extension of the suffrage. I am not for an universal suffrage because I consider it totally inapplicable to the existing state of society ... I don't think that apprentices or servants should have a vote, or anyone over whose opinion a direct dominion could be exercised.[77]

Yet, unaware of any contradiction, he went on in the same speech to advocate the ballot. Then, on speaking on the occasion of the second Chartist petition in May 1842 his opinion would appear to have altered:

> I am—though I may be mistaken—a decided advocate of universal suffrage. And I rest that opinion on the failure of every man I ever heard discuss this question and on that particularly of the Right Honourable Member for Edinburgh, Mr. Macaulay, to say where the line should be drawn which determines that servitude should end and liberty commence.[78]

74. *Hansard,* 3rd series, xcv, 784, (7 December 1848)
75. *D.E.P.,* 14 January 1817.
76. *Hansard,* 3rd series, iv, 653 (4 July 1831).
77. *Ibid.,* xlix, 235 (12 July 1839).
78. *Ibid.,* lxiii, (3 May 1842).

A Ship in Distress.

Speaking at Leeds in January 1843 and referring to his desire to see an extension of the franchise, he once again entertained doubts:

> It is a matter of some difficulty to define the limits to which the franchise can be extended so as to be free from the perpetration of any fraud . . . Anxious then as I am that it should be extended to every man who has arrived at the age of discretion and is unsullied by crime, I am nevertheless still more anxious the right should be possessed without the power of using it improperly . . . we will for the present be content to make the qualification for the franchise a fixity of residence . . . It is therefore that I am for the present for household suffrage.[79]

As late as August 1843 he was still adhering to household suffrage.[80]

That O'Connell could subordinate principle to the exigencies of power politics is something his parliamentary speeches and voting on the factory question appears to indicate. On this issue in particular, apologists of the time, and since then, have been anxious to deny the imputation and to rationalise the matter. O'Connell took an interest in the question of the hours of employment of children in factories from the earliest part of his parliamentary career. In February 1832, when Michael Sadler introduced a petition calling for the limitation of these hours, O'Connell made his first contribution, remarking that

> the case of these individuals reminded him strongly of that of minors in law . . . the present was an opportunity wherein sound policy and humanity were legitimately connected in legislating on behalf of these poor children.[81]

A year later when the Whig Morpeth raised the question of the desirability of legislation on the matter, O'Connell on his own admission

> could not remain silent on this important question notwithstanding the maxim of non-interference between master and servant. There was, however, a maxim in law that minors should be protected and the law was bound to protect them. It was truly horrible to read the evidence adduced of the nature and extent of infant labour in factories.[82]

In March 1833, on the occasion of Lord Ashley's presentation of a petition for a Ten Hours' Bill, he again felt compelled to speak:

> it was a question of humanity and religion that ought not to be neglected. The objection to the present system was that it not only destroyed the health of the children, but prevented them from having any religious education.

O'Connell's most emphatic intervention on the subject came in July 1833 when the Whig lord, Althorp, tried to get amendments made to Ashley's Factory Bill then in progress through the House. Althorp was worried that

79. *The Pilot*, 25 January 1841.
80. *Ibid.*, 23 August 1843.
81. *Hansard*, 3rd series, ix, 1095 (1 February 1832).
82. *Ibid.*, xv, 392 (8 February 1833).

Ashley's measure "was carrying his protection to too great lengths as regards the age of the children" so that its effects "might be found to increase the power of foreigners to compete in the British market and so cause a decline of the manufacturing interests".[83] O'Connell objected to Althorp's delaying of Ashley's legislation:

> there ought to be no more delay ... And what was it they were delaying about? It was whether a child could work more than a negro in the West Indies ... The King was bound to protect all his subjects under twenty one years ... The principle was clear ... Why not legislate at once? Oh! there might be a counter-balancing evil. If the child's labour were stopped a yard of calico might not be spun ... the protection ought to last until twenty one ... but, at all events, let them not go below eighteen. Let them therefore get rid of all this hypocrisy.[84]

Ashley wanted the statutory limit fixed at eighteen years, Althorp wanted it fixed at fourteen. Althorp's amendment was carried, though O'Connell voted against it. Ashley thereupon passed his bill over to Althorp, and it was as Althorp's measure that it became law.[85] Three years later the President of the Board of Trade, Poulett Thompson, tried to amend the Act to allow the employment of twelve and thirteen year olds. O'Connell did not speak in the debate, but he voted for the amendment and his vote, with that of his sons, was sufficient to carry the day.[86] In doing so he saved the Whig government, with which he was in alliance, from defeat. Three years later, when that alliance was yielding little value to Ireland, another factory regulations bill came up for discussion. An amendment to its first clause was moved, raising the age at which the parties would come under its operation from eighteen to twenty one. Poulett Thompson opposed it but O'Connell once again joined forces with Ashley and supported it [87]

This kind of voting laid him open to charges of inconsistency and expediency and served to alienate him from the English working classes and their leaders, especially the Chartists. With the Chartists O'Connell had a short flirtation and a long hostility. Having attended the foundation meetings which drew up the Charter early in 1837[88] he was estranged from the movement by autumn 1838 at the latest, and from 1839 he began to commit himself and Ireland to the Corn Law Leaguers, and in the early 1840s to the Complete Suffragists.[89]

As regards Repeal of the Union, O'Connell in rejecting the Chartists and supporting the Leaguers took the wrong side. Given the intransigence of the

83. *Ibid.*, xix, 221 (5 July 1833).
84. *Ibid.*, xix, 233 (5 July 1833).
85. *Ibid.*, xix, 906-913 (18 July 1833).
86. *Ibid.*, xxxiii, 788 (May 1836).
87. *Ibid.*, xlviii, 1070–1073 (1 July 1839).
88. W. Lovett, *The life and struggles of William Lovett in search of bread, knowledge, and freedom* (London, 1876), pp 111-115.
89. M.O'Connell, *.cit.*, nos. 2597, 2598. Daniel OConnell to Richard Cobden, 23 March 1839, Daniel O'Connell to Joseph Parkes, 30 March 1839; H. Richard, *Memoirs of Joseph Sturge* (London, 1864), pp 297-311.

House of Lords, the composition of the Commons, the disunity and ineffectiveness of the parliamentary radicals, O'Connell's expectation of support from a body of radicals who were hostile, uncomprehending or indifferent to Ireland, was for his own sake, unfortunate. The Chartists became and remained the only group in England in the 1840s to admit the full extent of Irish claims to justice by supporting them on the vital issue of Repeal.

Something of the well-intentioned incomprehension of the middle class parliamentary radicals can be seen from a famous reform meeting at Leeds in January 1841. The radical J. A. Roebuck, professing himself in all sincerity the friend of Ireland and the friend of O'Connell nevertheless implicitly censured O'Connell for seeking Repeal:

> Ireland is not sufficiently represented (in parliament), neither is Yorkshire nor is Leeds. The mischief is not in the separation in the sea that divides us . . . Ireland and England are but one—the enemy is the same to both.[90]

In one of the finest speeches of his career O'Connell replied to this, pointing out that though they had a common enemy it was about all they had in common; that if Yorkshire had been singled out from the rest of the kingdom by being given a reform bill in 1832 of lesser extent than enjoyed by the kingdom as a whole, and that if Yorkshire had been singled out for coercive legislation, it too might soon seek a separate legislature. Nothing O'Connell could say had the slightest impact on Roebuck, however. Eleven years after O'Connell's death Roebuck arrived in Galway and delivered himself of the following sentiments:

> I believe, from the bottom of my heart, that if there be anything disagreeable to Ireland you have only to make your statements of grievance to the English House of Commons in order to be attended to . . . There can be no hope for England or Ireland without the perfect union of the two countries . . . I can say with truth that the people of Ireland have no better friends than the members of the English House of Commons who wish you all well.[91]

Roebuck is not unique. Richard Cobden who received very great support from O'Connell in his famous campaign to repeal the Corn Laws gave something less than justice to O'Connell in return:

> I found the populace of Ireland represented in the House by a body of men, with O'Connell at their head, with whom I could feel no more sympathy or identity than with people whose language I did not understand. In fact, *morally* I felt a complete antagonism and repulsion towards them. O'Connell always treated me with friendly attention, but I never shook hands with him or faced his smile without a feeling of insecurity; and as for trusting him on any public question where his vanity or passions might interpose, I should have as soon thought of an alliance with an Ashantee chief.[92]

90. *The Pilot*, 25 January 1841.
91. R. E. Leader (ed.), *Life and letters of John Arthur Roebuck* (London, 1897), p. 272.
92. J. Morley, *The life of Richard Cobden* (12th ed., London, 1905), p. 491.

The relations between O'Connell and English Radicals proved to be unsatisfactory through most of the period from the Act of Union to his death in 1847. English Radicals appreciated O'Connell's great political gifts and entertained great expectations of the contribution he could make to their cause. Likewise, to the extent that they were free from the more obvious prejudices of the ruling elite, he expected their support for his cause. Nevertheless, ultimately the hopes and expectations on both sides were destined to disappointment. That disappointment arose chiefly from differing priorities. For the parliamentary Radicals the defeat of monopoly of power and privilege was the great end of their endeavours, for him merely the means to a better deal for Irish Catholics in particular and Ireland in general. If sacrificing the forty shilling freeholders would secure advantage for Irish Catholics, or if keeping the Whigs in power from 1835 would secure advantage for Ireland, then he was prepared to do both. Such compromises understandably led the parliamentary Radicals to distrust him. Conversely, their inability to consider the cause of Ireland in his terms meant inevitably that no benefit to his country would derive from his association with the vast majority of them. Only the most extreme of the parliamentary Radicals, spokesmen for the working classes, Hunt, Cobbett and above all Wakely, were prepared to take an Irish view of Irish problems; and outside parliament it was only among working class politicians that any real sympathy for Ireland could be found: yet, alliance with this sector O'Connell was not prepared to promote, and would in any case have been unable to promote after his vote on the factory question and his support of the Whigs in the 1830s.

93. *The Pilot*, 8 July 1846, speech at Repeal Association on 6 July 1846.

Chapter 6
Macaulay's O'Connell

Owen Dudley Edwards

The career of Daniel O'Connell is emphatically an epoch, not only in the history of his island, but in that of the world. The name of Andrew Jackson alone may be coupled with his as a symbol of the transition of political activity from the élites to the masses.[1] Yet that democratisation of politics in the United States which is called Jacksonian was a phenomenon of which Jackson was far more symptom than cause, far more exploiter than agent. As a political symbol his place is secure; as a political innovator, his claims pale by contrast with those of many of his enemies and allies. Moreover, the very size of the country ensured that his fellow-citizens could enthusiastically support him from diametrically opposing assumptions as to what his views on many questions were, indeed as to what nature of man he was. O'Connell's Ireland, more than half of contemporary Jacksonian America in population, but merely the equal of the state of Maine in extent, knew its O'Connell and knew what he stood for. It might not always know how far he would pursue in action what he advocated in theory, but it was not likely to produce O'Connellites differing as dramatically in their images of the chief as did the Pennsylvanian and Georgian Jacksonians. The popular conception of Daniel O'Connell was fundamentally based on detailed knowledge of him. The popular conception of Jackson was fundamentally based on much vaguer considerations—military glory, mannerisms, aphorisms, opposition to widely-feared bogeys. Here, in fact, despite the specific contrast of political careers, Jackson's popularity seems to resemble that of a third contemporary of Irish origin—the first Duke of Wellington.

The important part of O'Connell's career was passed in an Ireland integrally part of the United Kingdom, and for the half century after his death the memory of O'Connell was necessarily deeply affected by his place in British as well as in Irish popular culture. Despite the attention which twentieth-century national piety had paid to nationalist expression in Irish writing during the

1. Oliver MacDonagh, "The Contribution of O'Connell" in Brian Farrell ed., *The Irish Parliamentary Tradition* (Dublin, 1973), pp 163, 275, for which point MacDonagh is indebted to Farrell. I have benefited also from the ideas of Thomas N. Brown, Lawrence J. MacCaffrey and David N. Doyle, as orally expressed in my presence, on this matter. J. W. Ward, *Andrew Jackson: Symbol for an Age* (New York, 1955) superficially examines the problem but for a real insight into Jacksonianism see Marvin Meyers, *The Jacksonian Persuasion* (New York, 1957). George Dangerfield, *The Era of Good Feelings* is essential to understand the origins of the Jackson years. Glyndon G. Van Deusen, *The Jacksonian Era* (New York, 1959) keeps a balanced head. Arthur M. Schlesinger, Jr., *The Age of Jackson* (Boston, 1945) is invaluable as an unconscious illustration of the irrational hold of Jacksonian myths despite the lapse of a century.

preceding century, it was in fact British cultural products that saturated the mass of the Irish population, whether they went to school or met the scholars. We are now rightfully questioning the justice of the long indictment of O'Connell in Irish nationalist historiography, whether its antecedents be the dissents of Thomas Davis, the romances of Charles Gavan Duffy, or the cruelties of John Mitchel. Yet a deeper problem may lie ahead, more daunting because less visible. The British image of O'Connell subtly underlies the posthumous Irish image; while easily controvertible when opposed by obvious Irish facts or myths, much of it survives unquestioned, *ipsis Hibernicis Hibernior,* because of its extent in dissemination, of its unconscious acceptance by Irish writers and readers, and above all of its invincible respectability. There is an interesting contrast with the fate of American interpretations of O'Connell. The Americans have often brought profound perceptions to their work; but they often fail with Irish audiences by sheer cultural difference of presentation. British images, on the other hand, can win acceptance not because they are necessarily close to O'Connell but because they are in tune with Irish cultural norms and goals. The Ireland of the twentieth century is a much more 'British' country, whether under independence or union, than was the Ireland of O'Connell's day. The revolution in cultural communications by itself supplies testimony on this point; London was the metropolis of that revolution.

The pioneers in the making of this image have receded from our gaze. It is doubtful whether one enthusiastic reader of the pages of Mitchel or the modern versions of Gavan Duffy ever pauses to think how little of the force and depth of their attacks on O'Connell would remain were it not for Thomas Carlyle. It is likely that few even of those who can quote relevant passages know how much of the respectable O'Connell has been engraven on our consciousness by the subtle selectivity of Gladstone. And it is questionable whether anyone at all can assess the place Macaulay's O'Connell has in our view of him. The problem is most acute in the last case. It is a fairly simple matter to assemble the Carlyle attacks and to perceive their personal impact on the writings of Young Ireland and its disciples Griffith, Pearse, Connolly and later writers. Gladstone's most notable contributions were made during political flashpoints when a ready audience in Ireland attended to the reports of his utterances. But Macaulay, far the most widely read of the three, a prescribed English text for Irish school state examinations to the end of the Victorian era, supplies us with only a handful of scattered references, of which but a few have been singled out either by themselves or in Gladstone's plagiarisms. Yet the question is a vital one. Macaulay, the great popular writer of his generation, produced a more vivid impact on the culture of the nineteenth century than any other historian or essayist we could name. Macaulay's Ireland must have been a major component in the Victorian image of Ireland. And in the view of Ireland which he communicated, Macaulay was deeply affected, probably far more than we can ever know, by his personal impression of Daniel O'Connell.

The re-evaluation of Macaulay is as thoroughly under way at the moment as is that of O'Connell.[2] At long last, scholars are asking themselves what Macaulay achieved instead of indulging in exercises of self-congratulation at his expense; we are witnessing the same development with respect to O'Connell.[3] It is ironic that Macaulay himself summed up the mental condition which dictated the mass of influential writing about both of them in the century after their deaths: "Just so we have heard a baby, mounted on the shoulders of its father, cry out 'How much taller I am than Papa?'"[4] Those who make mock of Macaulay's schoolboy would do well to remember Macaulay's baby.

If we are to get a sense of O'Connell's impact on Macaulay, we must first disabuse ourselves of the notion that the latter formed his ideas early and retained them inviolate. His would-be friends, such as the Trevelyans and Sir Charles Firth,[5] have done even more than his foes to suggest as much, and have in addition given him the dubious if improbable accomplishment of having written his history from the perspective of the high and narrow Whig historiography of the late nineteenth- and early twentieth- centuries. It was not until Sir Herbert Butterfield produced his *George III and the Historians*, a work which far transcends its subject in significance, that the distance separating Macaulay from his *soi-disant* heirs was made clear. As for the earlier matter, any schoolboy[6] who will but follow the character of Halifax as treated in Macaulay's essay on Hallam (1828), and that on Sir William Temple

2. Trevelyan, *The Life and Letters of Lord Macaulay* (London, 1876, revised and enlarged edition, 1908). Thomas Pinney, ed., *The Letters of Thomas Babington Macaulay*, i-ii (Cambridge, Eng., 1974) go down to the end of 1833. Dr. Robert Robson is editing the Journals. John Clive, *Macaulay—The Shaping of the Historian* (New York, 1973), brings its subject down to 1839. I have had the advantage of listening to Professors Clive and Pinney, and Dr. Andrew D. Hook, at a symposium on Macaulay at the University of Edinburgh in 1974, and my present essay owes a little to my own paper on Macaulay's view of Ireland, delivered then. Dr. Pinney's remarks on the Trevelyan *Life* and his textual analysis of examples of the Macaulay MSS and Trevelyan's printed text demonstrated conclusively that Trevelyan as a copyist and editor is quite untrustworthy. I have therefore drawn on the letters published by Trevelyan, covering the years after 1833, for nothing more than corroboration of other evidence. I must also express my thanks to my colleagues Roger Highfield (otherwise of Merton College, Oxford) and Robert Patterson of the University of South Carolina for much helpful assistance when I was doing a little work on Macaulay during my terms as a visitor to its faculty; and also to Roger Jellinek of the *New York Times* for very stimulating editorial guidance.
3. A penetrating and authoritative modern study of O'Connell is R. Dudley Edwards, *Daniel O'Connell and his World* (London, 1975) and I have found it of immense value. Professor MacDonagh's essay (see n. 1), is a masterly performance. Professor Maurice R. O'Connell's edition of his ancestor's letters and his own scholarly essays are doing excellent work in establishing the realities. Of more popular recent comments, Raymond Moley's study, and the birth centenary supplement to the *Irish Times* (Terence de Vere White, ed.) offer useful food for reflection. Maureen Wall's lectures on O'Connell when I was a student of hers were gems of lucidity and originality. My father asked me to think about O'Connell and Macaulay, and I am most grateful to him and my mother for their gentle encouragement of my Macaulay enthusiasm over many years. I have learned a great deal from my graduate student Douglas Riach, whose Ph.D. dissertation was on "Ireland and the campaign against American Slavery" (Edinburgh, 1976).
4. The editions of Macaulay's works are so numerous, that to be of assistance to the general reader it seems best to cite them by chapter and heading (in the case of the *History*), by title and paragraph number (in the cases of the essays and speeches), and by title and line (in those of the poems). Macaulay, "Sir James Mackintosh's History of the Revolution" (published *Edinburgh Review* July 1835), para. 24. See Clive, *Macaulay*, 481.
5. Firth, *A Commentary on Macaulay's History of England* (London, 1938). A posthumous and fragmentary work, whose editor, Godfrey Davies, was neither willing nor able to make needful emendations, it is a little unfair to blame its author for a book he never passed for the press, yet his criticisms of Macaulay's omniscience and imprisonment by the prejudices of his age are balanced by little awareness of the same fault in himself. G. M. Trevelyan was widely regarded as a modern version

(1838), and his *History of England* (1848–1855), will at once perceive a massive capacity for reappraisal. I select this as the most obvious example: Halifax is the hero of the first part of the *History*.

That Macaulay was influenced by his times and his life as a party politician is a commonplace observation, normally accompanied by commonplace aspersions. Macaulay himself was characteristically early in the field with his justification:[7]

> Gibbon has remarked that he owed part of his success as a historian to the observations which he had made as an officer in the militia and as a member of the House of Commons. The remark is most just. We have not the smallest doubt that his campaign, though he never saw an enemy, and his parliamentary attendance, though he never made a speech, were of far more use to him than years of retirement and study would have been.

Macaulay, therefore, was not only influenced by those events

> *quaeque ipse . . . vidi*
> *et quorum pars magna fui*[8]

(as he might have been tempted to put it): he took pains to ensure he was. If experience must of its nature be his prison (and the vast range of his reading and imagination brought much light through the bars of that prison), then experience would also be his springboard. And in Macaulay's public life, Ireland meant O'Connell. The year of O'Connell's death was the year of Macaulay's parliamentary defeat, primarily on an Irish issue. Although re-elected without his solicitation in 1852 he never again played any part of note either in Commons or Lords from 1847 to his death in 1859. The first public question to arouse his active attention was Catholic emancipation, from 1826 to 1829: and that, as he never failed to underline, was O'Connell's victory. Elected to Parliament in 1830, he sat in the successive Houses with O'Connell as a fellow-member to 1834, when he sailed for India to be 'the least Indian of Indian civil servants' (in Gladstone's characteristic phrase).[9] He returned in 1839 and joined Melbourne's cabinet as Secretary at War. He was in opposition from 1841 until 1847 and so, of course, was O'Connell—when he was not an absentee by reason of disgust or imprisonment. And even when O'Connell was not physically before him, his shadow fell everywhere:[10]

> Go where you will on the Continent: visit any coffee house: dine at any public table: embark on board of any steamboat: enter any diligence, any railway carriage: from the moment that your accent shows yout to be an Englishman, the very first question asked by your companions, be they what they may, physicians, advocates, merchants, manu-

---

of his great-uncle, but on certain questions such as character of Marlborough he had in fact a vigorous bias against him. As a matter of detail, Macaulay's first reported impression of O'Connell was of the older man following "me out of the house to pay me the most enthusiastic compliments" on his second speech on the Reform Bill (Macaulay to his sister Hannah, 6 July 1831, in Pinney ed., *Letters*, ii. 63).
6. I am basing this on primary source-material, using a sample of one.
7. Macaulay, "Mackintosh", para. 2.
8. *Aeneid*, ii. 5-6.
9. Clive, *Macaulay*, 290.
10. Macaulay's speeches were prepared by himself for publication, where he wanted them preserved, but few were in his view definitive texts. I have quoted only from his version. Speech on the State of Ireland, delivered in the House of Commons, 18 February 1844, para. 16.

facturers, or what we should call yeomen, is certain to be "What will be done with Mr O'Connell?" Look over any file of French journals; and you will see what a space he occupies in the eyes of the French people.

Everywhere, that is, except in India. Ireland offered many significant parallels and contrasts with India to the British essayist and administrator; but it is highly noteworthy that Macaulay should have been absent from Westminster during the heyday of the Lichfield House compact. He returned to find the Irish leader the ally of his sworn chieftains rather than their enemy; his very speech preliminary to his election in Edinburgh in 1839 found the government of Ireland one of the strongest cards he had to play against the supporters of Peel; but he writhed under the paradoxial indignity of a Whig government being maintained in existence by the whims of the Queen respecting her bedchamber attendants.[11]

One of the most important points about Macaulay's view of O'Connell lies in their similarity. Both men were educators of mass audiences, albeit with eyes confidently fixed on present and future middle classes. O'Connell was highly conscious of a poor rural clientele, politically, and favoured a far wider suffrage than did Macaulay. But both men subscribed to the concept of improvement. Both men were mass communicators—one by speech, the other by writing. And the values they wished to inculcate in those audiences, who psychologically meant so much to both of them, were those of an educated middle-class. The term seems repulsively purblind to us now, living as we do in an era all too aware of how greedily the middle-classes came into their kingdom, and conscious as we must be of the terrible indictment of middle-class destruction of spiritual values so eloquently drawn up after their fashions by Karl Marx and Oscar Wilde. But it was very much the dawn of middle-class rule of which O'Connell and Macaulay were the heralds. They preached a joy in the idea of improvement. It could take the form of winning their audience by ascribing to it, not the qualities they knew it to have, but those they intended it to acquire. Seen in this light, O'Connell seems less of a flatterer of his supporters. Seen in this light, Macaulay's 'every schoolboy knows' becomes a tactful method of conveying the rudiments of culture.

Both men were superb communicators in their chosen fields—and not in each other's. Macaulay's speeches made no concessions to the concentrative powers of his hearers. O'Connell's writings made no concessions to the intellectual powers of his readers. The one aimed above, the other below, their true marks. But in their spheres they were unrivalled. Both were aware that they moved in social circles beyond the ken of those masses whom they addressed. Both were anxious to enlarge those circles to a degree which allowed for some measure of participation. Both were cultural dictators: the listener was intended to feel impelled to find a voice, in the service of O'Connell, the reader to find a pen, in the service of Macaulay, or rather, in the causes each was propounding. Both were great vulgarisers. Macaulay's zeal to

11. Speech at Edinburgh, 29 May 1839, paras 12, 14.

maximise a cultural audience was as much an impassioned protest against the self-service of élitist scholarship as was O'Connell's ambition to maximise a political audience a devout anger against the self-service of élitist government. This was only to be done by giving those audiences a confident partnership in the business of communication. To this end both were perfectly ready to vulgarise by vulgarity. The cloying respectability which was one unlooked-for effect of their improving missions has said its plenty in criticism of O'Connell's achievements as a vulgarian. Neo-élitism replied to Macaulay also, but perhaps the freedom by which he held his readers requires a little more celebration. Take his means of showing how Louis XIV maintained the magic of monarchy while in permanent public view[12]:

> He took his very emetics in state, and vomited majestically in the presence of all the *grandes* and *petites entrés*.

One of the most persuasive aids in their evangel of improvement was laughter. If O'Connell's thunderous hilarity be not attested to by this volume then it has seriously failed in its job, but I may be forgiven for repetition by stressing how much learning, legal learning in particular, was shown so productive of fun as well as profit by him. Both in his own actions, and in the folklore he evokes by them, he drove home the lesson that there was laughter and triumph to be gained by technical mastery—and after that, the kingdom was yours. That coach-and-four could only be driven through Acts of Parliament by the application of knowledge of Acts of Parliament. Concomitant with this was the anti-élitist reassurance that, once self-improvement had enabled one to storm the palace, the emperor had no clothes anyway. Time and again, Macaulay uses the same means to make the same point. Would the publishers and reviewers impose on the audience to persuade it to devour bad verses?; then he, Macaulay, would show that the verses were bad, officially so that he might denounce puffing but more surreptitiously to cultivate the ordinary reader's standards of criticism and show that the treacherous critics could not maintain their monopoly. The assault on Robert Montgomery's poems is so rich in gems that selection is a solecism ("as is always the case with the good things of good writers, much prettier in its place than can even be conceived by those who see it only detached from the context").[13]

There are a thousand stylistic felicities which recall the other vulgariser in the speeches of O'Connell, in the writings of Macaulay. Compare O'Connell's orotund ironies with the mature Macaulay[14]:

> That Fuller's plot is less celebrated than the Popish plot is the fault rather of the historians than of Fuller, who did all that man could do to secure an eminent place among villains.

The delight of both men in forceful and exceptionally stimulating apposition is

---

12. Macaulay, essay on Dumont's *Mirabeau* (published *Edinburgh Review*, July 1832: Macaulay did not include this essay in his *Critical and Historical Essays*; it was posthumously republished in his *Miscellaneous Writings*), para. 24.
13. Macaulay, "Mr. Robert Montgomery's Poems" (published *Edinburgh Review* April 1830), para. 20.
14. Macaulay, *History of England*, ch. XVIII. "Fuller's plot".

too universal a trait to lend itself to a single illustration. Naturally, the tricks of
the trade differed. O'Connell's oratory was distinguished by a vigorous use of
alliteration, as might be expected from a native of late eighteenth-century
Gaelic Kerry; Macaulay is fun to read aloud, but that is not the primary
function of his work, and hence he relies far less on so pre-eminently oral a
device. A more subtle quality is evident in the use of image and metaphor.
O'Connell preached non-violence by a deliberate employment of military
terminology to excite his audience and to underline his message by the very
contrast of his style and content. Macaulay is rather too militaristic a writer to
have much concern with that problem, but he did have some occasion to
testify to the insignificance of military engagements:[15]

> During the first half century after the commencement of the Reformation, the current of
> feeling, in the countries on this side of the Alps and the Pyrenees, ran impetuously towards
> the new doctrines. Then the tide turned, and rushed as fiercely in the opposite direction.
> Neither during the one period, nor during the other, did much depend upon the event of
> battles or sieges. The Protestant movement was hardly checked for an instant by the defeat
> at Muhlberg. The Catholic reaction went on at full speed in spite of the destruction of the
> Armada. It is difficult to say whether the violence of the first blow or of the recoil was the
> greater.

The brilliance of this passage is that it at once summons up the military events
in the eye of the mind, only to reduce them to insignificance by its argument.
And the consciousness of the descriptive quality of sound and word-
arrangement which O'Connell learned so well from his Gaelic origins finds an
echo here. It is hardly accident, yet it can be nothing more or less than instinct,
that the passage exhibits such perfect contrasting arrangement of
polysyllables: "movement . . .defeat . . .Muhlberg"; "reaction . . .destruction. . .
Armada". The evocative examples offered their own contrast with the German
and Spanish names, but Macaulay's exploitation of them conveys the
fascination with the alien which the imagery of O'Connell's orations so often
exhibits. O'Connell's Catholic upbringing, and Macaulay's classical education,
would have played their part in giving them so clear a sense of what could be
done with the values and stresses on strong and weak syllables.

One very significant relationship between them in ideology arises from this
passage. Macaulay is readily identified with a form of history as national self-
glorification. ("The history of England is emphatically the history of
progress.")[16] O'Connell stands in every modern history textbook as an apostle
of nationalism. Yet both communicators in fact did much to oppose certain
forms of nationalism. Professor MacDonagh appropriately quotes O'Connell's
journal entry, made when he was twenty-two: "I will endeavour to give liberty
to my country and increase the knowledge and virtue of human-kind."[17]
Macaulay would not have quarrelled with the sentiment, though he might have
sought a redefinition of the country. Both men were universalists, although in
politics Macaulay was notably less so than O'Connell. The Irishman's

15. Macaulay's "Ranke's History of the Popes" (published *Edinburgh Review*, October 1840), para. 28.
16. Macaulay, "Mackintosh", para. 29.
17. MacDonagh, "O'Connell", 166.

nationalism meant that since he had a country which was in formal status less than a country, it gave him an arena of interest which was much more. Macaulay's nationalism arose from no such sense of disadvantage. Hence we do not find his early attacks on slavery and its effects[18] being formally maintained in their own right after slavery was abolished within the British Empire, but he was glad to attack American slavery when he found an unexceptionable pretext. O'Connell would have found very little with which to quarrel in Macaulay's speech of 26 February 1845[19] in the House of Commons save that the orator apologised rather too frequently for discussing the affairs of another country when on the topic of the Sugar Duties he thundered against United States slavery and racial discrimination. (It cannot be pleaded that this was but a filial attempt to please an antislavery parent, as has been argued respecting some of Macaulay's earlier attacks on the peculiar institution: Zachary Macaulay had died in 1838.)

Where Macaulay showed some of O'Connell's universalist beliefs was in the literary sphere. His verses on the Armada written in 1832 offer a chauvinistic thrill superior to that of Young Ireland patriotic balladry at its fizziest; but, no man could better show the universal insignificance of a moment of national glory. It was not only a fondness for rhetoric which led him into the famous passage of the New Zealander suggesting the vigour of the Church of Rome might long outlive the centre of English civilisation; [20] he had previously been ready to declare that the intellectual empire of ancient Athens could, nay, would do so.[21] Education for O'Connell was a European affair by virtue of his geographical circumstances; Macaulay was his own educator to a great degree, and he elected for a European, as opposed to a merely Graeco-Roman and English, field. The moving passage commencing his essay on Bacon which celebrates our love of dead writers regardless of their questionable lives (beginning "The genius of Sallust is still with us. But the Numidians whom he plundered, and the unfortunate husbands who caught him in their homes at unseasonable hours, are forgotten"), includes two English writers, two Greek, two Roman, one Italian, one Spanish, and one French—Bossuet.[22] The European perspective of both men was necessarily highly selective, and Macaulay, in particular, lacked the fibre to come to terms with the dynamics

18. Notably his essay on "Social and Industrial Capacities of Negroes", *Edinburgh Review*, xlv. (1827), 383-423. The origin of the essay in a contemporary controversy, and its authorship by so youthful a pen, supply sufficient reasons to account for Macaulay's failure to reprint it. The failure of his friend Thomas Flower Ellis and of his sister Hannah Macaulay Trevelyan to reprint it in the posthumous *Miscellaneous Writings* may indicate some lack of sympathy on their part in 1860 with its subject. It has been reprinted in *Race*, xiii. (1971-2) with an introductory note by John Clive and Anthony Lester but it is very regrettable that no editor, ancient or modern, has elected to include it in any volume of Macaulay's writings, selected or otherwise. See also Clive, *Macaulay*, 110-11.
19. Macaulay, Speech on the Sugar Duties, House of Commons, 26 February 1845, paras 8-11. And see para. 17 for an interesting attack on the pro-slavery supporter of Irish Repeal, Robert Tyler, son of the President.
20. Macaulay, "Ranke", para. 3. In my youth every Jesuit schoolboy knew it. They were not made as familiar with para. 23.
21. Macaulay, essay on Mitford's History of Greece (published *Knight's Quarterly Magazine* November 1824, reprinted *Miscellaneous Writings*), last para. Ellis, preface to *Miscellaneous Writings*.
22. Macaulay, "Lord Bacon" (published *Edinburgh Review* July 1837), para. 3. Clive, *Macaulay*, 489-90.

of human self-destructiveness which would have enabled him to appreciate Euripides and Racine. But the European sense exists for both of them. Beyond Europe, their universalism was selective. Reading and experience told Macaulay of Indian realities of which O'Connell had little perception. Deeper commitment to universal philanthropy gave O'Connell some American awareness which Macaulay possessed only in the most rudimentary form. An eloquent passage in his essay on Barère, for example, takes on an unintended dimension of savage irony because of his failure to assign the source of a quotation uttered by his detested and detestable subject—it is in fact one of the best-known apophthegms of Thomas Jefferson.[23]

Despite the quarter-century of difference between the ages of the two men, they possessed strangely similar reactions to two European events—the French Revolution, and the Romantic movement of the 1840s. As to the first, theirs was a view which relatively few of their contemporaries took, for it came to terms with the several positions of Burke, Mackintosh, Bentham, Fox, and Lamennais. It is difficult to see what quarrel O'Connell would have had with Macaulay's statement of it.[24]

No doubt there would have been specific disagreements as to what constituted extreme cases, in which Macaulay would prescribe the medicine of the French Revolution, but they did agree, and thereby largely differed from most English politicians, in their positive response, settling for neither favour nor hostility. They also tended to view the Revolution and its legacy as a totality, rather than identifying with favoured persons or phases.[25] They were both pre-eminently conscious of the tyranny which the Revolution established, and of the tyranny which opposition to it produced in Britain and Ireland.

Their places as self-conscious children of the age of the democratic revolution throw into relief the tension in their natures between reason and romanticism. They were conscious disciples of the former, and they tried to press the latter into their services, sometimes being temporarily enslaved by it. Rationalism took them into specifically divergent channels. It made a

23. Macaulay, essay on Barère (published *Edinburgh Review*, April 1844, and the only essay published there of any length after 1832 to be excluded by Macaulay from the *Critical and Historical Essays*, but republished *Miscellaneous Writings* — presumably Macaulay's revulsion from its subject motivated his refusal to reprint it), para. 41. ("The tree of liberty', he said 'as an ancient author remarks, flourishes when it is watered with the blood of all classes of tyrants. ' . . . In the course of our own small reading among the Greek and Latin writers, we have not happened to fall in with trees of liberty and watering-pots full of blood; nor can we, such is our ignorance of classical antiquity, even imagine an Attic or Roman orator employing imagery of that sort". Later, Macaulay returns to the remark. "The tree of liberty must be refreshed from time to time, with the blood of patriots and tyrants. It is its natural manure" wrote Jefferson to Colonel William Stephen Smith, 13 November 1787, from Paris (Adrienne Koch and William Peden, eds., *Life and Selected Writings of Thomas Jefferson* (New York, 1944), 436).)
24. Macaulay, "Mackintosh", para. 16.
25. "Danton was brave and resolute, fond of pleasure, of power, and of distinction, with vehement passions, with lax principles, but with some kind and manly feelings, capable of great crimes, but capable also of friendship and of compassion. He, therefore, naturally finds admirers among persons of bold and sanguine dispositions. Robespierre was a vain, envious, and suspicious man, with a hard heart, weak nerves, and a gloomy temper. But . . . he was . . . disinterested. . . . his private life was correct . . . he was sincerely zealous for his own system of politics and morals. He, therefore, naturally finds admirers among honest but moody and bitter democrats". (Macaulay, essay on Barère, para. 5)

Benthamite of O'Connell, and an anti-Benthamite of Macaulay, albeit one who from time to time acknowledged much common ground with the Benthamites. It made for a pragmatic style in politics for them, with the difference that where Macaulay often asserted the pragmatic in terms of the ideal, O'Connell would assert the ideal and settle for the pragmatic. It was a qualified rationalism, in that it was largely restricted to public questions. Their religious beliefs had both been exposed to the winds of rationalism, and had emerged pruned but fortified thereby. The struggle for Catholic emancipation had given both of them so strong an awareness of religious bigotry as to leave them bitter and unrelenting opponents of sectarianism in all its forms. This was qualified in the case of O'Connell by his readiness to acknowledge and exploit the special relationship of Catholic priest and penitent; what is singular is that Macaulay, a forceful critic of the doctrines and intellectual effects of post-Tridentine Catholicism, drew from his experience of anti-Romanist agitation a strange tenderness when it came to dealing with that precise point. He wrote contemptuously in reply to Gladstone:[26]

> Here is a poor fellow, enlisted in Clare or Kerry, sent over fifteen thousand miles of sea . . . He fights for the Government; he conquers for it; he is wounded; he is laid on his pallet, withering away with fever . . . He pines for the consolations of that religion which, neglected perhaps in the season of health and vigour, now comes back to his mind . . . And because the state for which he dies sends a priest of his own faith to stand at his bedside . . . because the state for which he dies does not abandon him in his last moments to the care of heathen attendants, or employ a chaplain of a different creed . . . Mr. Gladstone finds that India presents "a melancholy picture", and that there is "a large allowance of false principle" in the system pursued there.

Within the sphere of positive religious conviction, O'Connell made his position clear enough. Macaulay's Christianity could resemble his in the formal character of its expression, but the depth of conviction occasionally flashed into light. The nature of O'Connell's leadership meant that he had to assert his religious conviction, whereas Macaulay's quiet rebellion against his parents turned him emotionally against frequent expression of the outward signs of religious conformity. But just as O'Connell's utterances can supply food for genuine religious appetites, Macaulay also produced occasional remarks whose contemplation is of major spiritual value. One's mind turns specifically to the last two paragraphs of his essay on the civil disabilities of the Jews.[27]

With respect to romanticism, their place is somewhat comparable to that of Sir Walter Scott. They were not romantics; they knew how to use romanticism to do some of the work they wished to set in hand; their effect was to induce much romanticism of temper in their audiences; they were from time to time drawn off their rational bases by their enthusiasm for their subject-matter. They had the power to make their audiences weep as well as to make them

26. Macaulay, "Gladstone on Church and State" (published *Edinburgh Review*, April 1839), para. 84.
27. Published *Edinburgh Review*, January 1831.

laugh, and learn, and act; it was a power they sometimes used to excess; it was a power which could turn on themselves. Sometimes the sorcerer can be self-enchanted, if much less frequently than the sorcerer's apprentice. But for much of the time they used romanticism as a tool. O'Connell's attitudes to Young Ireland might be compared to those of a car manufacturer who sees a group of his subordinates doing impressive framework design but then insisting that all other considerations of production be subordinated to outward appearance. Macaulay's most famous contribution to romantic literature, which won the applause of even Arthur Griffith in this connection, was in fact a scholarly exercise in informed speculation as to the nature of the lost folklore of early Rome and the manner in which forgotten bards might have exploited it.

We turn, now, to the most interesting point of similarity, that which made so many of the others matters of alarm and resentment to Macaulay rather than causes of identification. In the British establishment both were outsiders, and the antecedents whence they came were not merely those of another class, but of another civilisation, in O'Connell's case wholly, in Macaulay's case partly. The generation's difference was a big one. It is a long distance from Cahirciveen in 1775 to Rothley Temple, Leicestershire, where Macaulay was born in 1800, or to Clapham, where his family settled in 1802–03. It is a much shorter distance, emotionally speaking, from O'Connell's place and date of birth to Inveraray in 1768, where Zachary Macaulay was born. The Macaulay ancestors were no *douce* Lowlanders from whom accomplishment in law or letters might be politely presumed. Macaulay was ready enough, when seeking election in 1839 in Edinburgh, to throw in a graceful and appropriate reference to his lineage.[28]

To do him justice, his method of citation was faithful to his whole gospel of improvement and as such in harmony with the prophets of the new Scotland. But it was not an analogy we find him making in England. Scottish audiences would hear the word 'British' from him in contexts where he normally said English.[29] But that was the limit of his concession. Even as a candidate for the Edinburgh votes, he spoke of Scotland as 'your country'.[30] He was English. Macaulay won a place in Whig society which was given to virtually no other person so destitute of social background. One wonders if he suppressed his resentments at the snubs he must have sustained from scions of noble houses who surpassed him in status as thoroughly as he dwarfed them in intellect. O'Connell's situation was Macaulay's at one remove and in one respect. He was the Liberator; but he was also a Celt on the make. As Professors Dudley Edwards and MacDonagh have pointed out, he was acutely conscious of the barriers in the way of his social advancement.[31] It was only possible for him, himself, to become a parliamentary leader by creating an agitation which broke open the doors; but however much his agitation increased Irish Catholic

28. Macaulay, Speech at Edinburgh, 29 May 1839, para. 10.
29. E.g. in his speech delivered at the opening of the Edinburgh Philosophical Institution, 4 November 1846.
30   Speech at Edinburgh, 29 May 1839, para. 14.
31. R. Dudley Edwards, *Daniel O'Connell*, 21-22, 57-58 *et passim*. MacDonagh, "O'Connell", 162-63.

self-consciousness and visibility as an importunate and alien element, what he
wanted was acceptance for him and for Ireland. It is doubtful whether
Macaulay saw this, but at certain moments his friendlier view of Ireland
moved from the philanthropy of an outsider, to the anger of a fellow-sufferer[32]:

> You are ready enough to call Mr O'Connell an alien when it serves your purposes to do so.
> You are ready enough to inflict on the Irish Roman Catholics all the evils of alienage. But
> the one privilege, the one advantage of alienage, you deny him. In a case which of all cases
> most require a jury *de mediatate*, in a case which sprang out of the mutual hostility of
> races and sects, you pack a jury all of one race and all of one sect.

Earlier in that speech he had alluded to Catholic Emancipation[33]:

> In 1829, at length, concessions were made, were made largely, were made without the
> conditions which Mr. Pitt would undoubtedly have demanded, and to which, if demanded
> by Mr. Pitt, the whole body of Roman Catholics would have eagerly assented. But these
> concessions were made reluctantly, made ungraciously, made under duress, made from the
> mere dread of civil war. How then was it possible that they should produce contentment
> and repose? What could be the effect of that sudden and profuse liberality following that
> long and obstinate resistance to the most reasonable demands, except to teach the
> Irishman that he could obtain redress only by turbulence?

And the extent to which Macaulay himself had reason to be sensitive to
English nativism—even to a Leeds supporter he was "Mr Mackholy the
Scotchman"[34]—lent a vehemence to his exposition[35]:

> You, for your own purposes, inflamed the public mind of England against Ireland; and you
> have no right to be surprised by finding the public mind of Ireland is inflamed against
> England. You called a fourth part of the people of the United Kingdom aliens; and you
> must not blame them for feeling and acting like aliens. You have filled every public
> department with their enemies. What then could you expect but that they would set up
> against your Lord Lieutenant and your official hierarchy a more powerful chief and a more
> powerful organisation of their own? They remember, and it would be strange indeed if they
> had forgotten, what under the same chief, and by a similar organisation, they extorted from
> you in 1829; and they are determined to try whether you are bolder and more obstinate
> now than then.

Fragments of this speech were quoted from time to time in subsequent Irish
nationalist literature. Was the last sentence one of the remoter origins of the
last lines of Patrick Pearse's 'The Rebel'? Certainly it was a speech of anger;
party advantage was hardly sufficient to account for the understanding and the
underlying tone of identification which marked it. And it ended on a note of
emotion almost O'Connellesque[36]:

32. Speech on the State of Ireland, House of Commons, 19 February 1844, para. 17.
33. *Ibid.*, para. 12.
34. Quoted in E.P. Thompson, *The Making of the English Working Class* (Harmondsworth, 1968), 905-06.
35. Speech on the State of Ireland, House of Commons, 19 February 1844, para. 13.
36. *Ibid.*, closing lines.

I trust that the number and the respectability of those in whose company I shall go into the lobby will be such as to convince the Roman Catholics of Ireland that they need not yet relinquish all hope of obtaining relief from the wisdom and justice of an Imperial Parliament.

The super Yahoo was of course under conviction by now, with his Repeal crusade in ruins. Not only could Macaulay afford to be generous about him, but Ireland was in the comfortable condition of needing his services as a spokesman instead of being so alarmingly represented by its own.[37] But the judgement he passed on O'Connell in this speech transcended the immediate situation, perhaps because the situation enabled it so to do. Specifically he attacked the government for the brevity of notice and insufficiency of dissemination of the proclamation of the Clontarf meeting[38]:

The negligence of the Government would probably have caused the loss of many lives but for the interposition of the man whom you are persecuting. Fortune stood your friend; and he stood your friend; and thus a slaughter more terrible than that which took place twenty-five years ago at Manchester was averted.

And in his general summation he brought the full resources of his free range of comparative historical analysis into play to establish the fact asserted at the commencement of this essay[39]:

It was no common person that you were bent on punishing. About that person I feel, I own, considerable difficulty in saying anything. He is placed in a situation which would prevent generous enemies, which has prevented all the members of this House, with one ignominious exception, from assailing him acrimoniously. I will try, in speaking of him, to pay the respect due to eminence and to misfortune without violating the respect due to truth. I am convinced that the end which he is pursuing is not only mischievous but unattainable: and some of the means which he has stooped to use for the purpose of attaining that end I regard with deep disapprobation. But it is impossible for me not to see that the place which he holds in the estimation of his countrymen is such as no popular leader in our history, I might perhaps say in the history of the world, has ever attained.

Ireland had been a Whig card, in Macaulay's estimation, between 1839 and 1841; his satisfaction at its loss of turbulence, the diminution of its military establishment and its increased potential for improvement was, of course, characterised by Whig self-congratulation rather than by what would have been indiscreet if accurate tributes to O'Connell.[40] The Tories in reply played the No-Popery card, and Macaulay rekindled much of his earlier contempt for religious bigotry, with appropriate sentiments towards Irish Catholicism as a

37. O'Connell had been convicted immediately before the debate, but had not yet been sentenced. He took part in the debate.
38. Speech on the State of Ireland, House of Commons, 19 February 1844, para. 15.
39. *Ibid.*, para. 16.
40. Speech at Edinburgh, 29 May 1839, 3rd last and last paras. Speech on a vote of confidence in Melbourne's ministry, House of Commons, 29 January 1840, last 7 paras.

result.[41] But the Repeal agitation of 1841–43 carried implicitly with it a repudiation of the Whigs as well as of the Tories. Yet while it was under way, Macaulay produced two literary responses to it, of which one was amusingly derogatory and the other startlingly sympathetic, and both were in other contexts. His essay on Barère said of its subject's official addresses[42]:

> His peculiar style of oratory was now formed. It was not altogether without ingenuity and liveliness. But in any other age or country it would have been thought unfit for the deliberations of a grave assembly, and still more unfit for state papers. It might, perhaps, succeed at a meeting of a Protestant Association in Exeter Hall, at a Repeal dinner in Ireland, after men had well drunk; or in an American oration on the fourth of July. No legislative body would now endure it.

Macaulay's prejudice against universal suffrage resulted in an interesting linkage of Irish and American rhetoric; we may notice the Irish are exempted from the Exeter Hall and Fourth of July oratorical category when in their sober senses, so that Macaulay remained kindly, however bland his implication that Repeal intoxication was comparable to Protestant fulmination in its unfitness to inaugurate legislation.

In the *Lays of Ancient Rome* (1842) Macaulay asserted that the position of the Plebeians and of their elected Tribunes bore some resemblance to that of the Irish Catholics during the period 1792–1829.[43] Clearly he had O'Connell—the 'persecuted Tribune' as he called him in his speech of 19 February 1844 on Ireland[44] in mind in his references to the Tribunes of Rome and their oratory. Other aspects of the *Lays* also tie in with what we know of Macaulay's Irish frame of reference.

Macaulay bitterly resented the freedom with which O'Connell the super Yahoo hurled his alliteration against the Whigs.[45]

It was also in the month of February, 1833, that his indignation, still at fever heat, prompted him to tell the diarist Charles Greville "that if *he* had had to legislate on Ireland, he would have suspended the laws there for five years, given the Lord Lieutenant's proclamation the force of law, and put the Duke of Wellington in charge".[46] Professor Clive remarks on this "rapid transformation of the liberty-loving Commonwealthsman into the stern supporter of military force; though, remembering Cromwell's activities in

41. Speech on the State of Ireland, House of Commons, 19 February 1844, para. 13. Speech in support of the Maynooth College Bill, House of Commons, 14 April 1845, *passim*. Speech on the Church of Ireland, 23 April 1845, *passim*.
42. Para. 58.
43. Introductory matter to the lay "Virginia", para. 3.
44. Para. 17.
45. Macaulay, Speech against Repeal of the Union with Ireland, House of Commons, 8 February 1833, 2nd last para. Macaulay to his sister Margaret Macaulay Cropper, 23 February 1833, Pinney ed., *Letters* ii. 230. On the Yahoo-complex, the final sneers about "Irishmen . . *spaking* about the *repail*" are very suggestive—on the matter of accent, so notable a betrayal of Yahoo origins, Macaulay was secure and hence made much of the distance it gave him. See also Macaulay to Ellis, 7 March 1831, *ibid.* 6-7 Macaulay to his sister Hannah, 6 July 1831, *ibid.* 30-31.
46. Clive, *Macaulay*, 230.

Ireland, one might add that Macaulay here took over the tradition whole". In his essay on Sir William Temple, written five years later at the end of his Indian mission, Macaulay asserted as much.[47]

A world which has seen 'those fearful phenomena' becoming 'known to the nations of Europe' is in a position to ponder the dubious mercy of words such as 'extirpation' and 'eradication' to which Macaulay had referred in this essay.

Unhappily, it was the preachment of genocide which won its audience as regarded future British writers and Irish readers.

His Yahoo complex arose not from his conviction of his differences with Yahoos, but because of his awareness of common origin. But this unhappy product of his resentment of O'Connell placed him for once in the ugliest and most dangerous company, and his influence and power over his audience made him even more dangerous than his companions.

Yet if O'Connell induced that response, if the liberalism of the British humanitarian was not proof against anger towards the presumption of an 'uppity nigger' as in their hearts white liberals sometimes find the advocates of Black Power, if Macaulay's desire to speak for the Irish Roman Catholics was temporarily soured when through the inescapable phenomenon of O'Connell they spoke for themselves, if the gentle Yahoo found his assurance unpleasantly punctured by the omnipresence of the super-Yahoo, if party loyalties induced personal animosities whereby O'Connell as the voice of Gaelic Ireland became the origin of a belittling view of an earlier Gaelic Ireland, Macaulay as historically-minded observer of his age, Macaulay as democratiser of culture, gave essential testimony to the place of O'Connell in the advance of democracy. If later British writers missed the significance of this, and failed to see that democracy in fact developed on a mass basis earlier in Ireland than in Britain, it is not Macaulay's fault. In the growing climate of racism in the late nineteenth century, it was his negative response to O'Connell and his Ireland which was listened to, and his recognition of its achievement which was set aside. When democracy had become respectable, the real Whig historians ignored the important part of the story; Macaulay had not. Even where improvement, and rationalism, and party effect, might induce him to slight the contribution of men and ideas which won his hostility, he was too much of an enthusiast and too fascinated a student of the totality of human experience to persist in so doing. And while O'Connell's similarities might be embarrassing, there was a justification for Macaulay's great thesis of the Revolution of 1688, which he never fully realised, in the career and achievement of O'Connell. The influences of that revolution on the Americans, on the French and on Edmund Burke ('the greatest man then living')[48] were of overwhelming importance in the making of the mind of Daniel O'Connell and of the movement which he led.

They were, after all, fellow-crusaders in the cause of human freedom, above

47. Published *Edinburgh Review*, October 1838. Para. 28.
48. Macaulay, "Warren Hastings", para. 166.

all of cultural freedom. And as we think of the long despair in which O'Connell closed his career, it is only just to notice that the same years brought Macaulay to the end of his political life in the same cause where he had supported O'Connell twenty years before. O'Connell had been prepared to accept the Union if it could work; on 14 April 1845 Macaulay concluded his speech in favour of the increased Maynooth grant.[49]

> to this bill, and to every bill which shall seem to me likely to promote the real Union of Great Britain and Ireland, I will give my support, regardless of obloquy, regardless of the risk which I may run of losing my seat in Parliament. For such obloquy I have learned to consider as one glory; and as to my seat I am determined that it never shall be held by an ignominious tenure; and I am sure that it can never be lost in a more honourable cause.

On 23 April 1845 he declared against the maintenance of the Church of Ireland.[50] On 28 July 1847 he was defeated at Edinburgh for re-election, on precisely the point he had prophesised. After all, the Yahoos were not confined to his own Gaelic origins. Yet less than two years later he returned to Scotland to be inaugurated Rector at Glasgow University. And it is rather pleasant to think how delighted O'Connell would have been by the impudence as well as the constancy with which he gave his first statement in the country of his ancestors after he had received so signal an illustration of its persistent anti-Catholicism:[51]

> ... a man, never to be mentioned without reverence by every lover of letters, held the highest place in Europe. Our just attachment to that Protestant faith to which our country owes so much must not prevent us from paying that tribute which, on this occasion, and in this place, justice and gratitude demand, to the founder of the University of Glasgow, the greatest of the restorers of learning, Pope Nicholas the Fifth...

It continued, of course, for many sonorous and sparkling sentences of panegyric, and there, unconquered, insuppressible, in the truest sense carrying on the work of liberation of men's minds we may take our affectionate leave of O'Connell's Macaulay.

49. Speech in support of the Maynooth College Bill, last para.
50. He went out of his way to make such a declaration; the amendment for which he was voting merely called for the new funds needed for Maynooth to be taken from the funds applicable to "ecclesiastical purposes in Ireland".
51. Inaugural speech delivered at the College of Glasgow, 21 March 1849, para. 4-5.

Chapter 7

Daniel O'Connell, Cardinal Cullen and Expatriate Nationalism

David Steele

"Pigs and Papists will begin to look up again", observed O'Connell in 1840 to his old friend, P. V. FitzPatrick, when the time seemed ripe to apply more pressure for repeal of the Union after an interval dictated by tactical considerations.[1] The remark exemplifies one of O'Connell's signal attributes, the often grotesque mockery which he employed not only to discomfit and, at its most corrosive, to demolish opponents, but also to identify himself with the people of Celtic and Catholic Ireland whose betterment was the passion of his life. By this means, among others, the immensely successful lawyer, agitator, demagogue and parliamentarian, courted as well as feared and reviled by his English antagonists, maintained a community of feeling with those whom he once described, privately, with an utter lack of sentimentality that cannot fail to shock, initially: "I never will get half credit enough for carrying Emancipation" he commented, "because posterity never can believe the species of *animals* with which I had to carry on my warfare with the common enemy. It is crawling slaves like them that prevent our being a nation ..."[2] Nearly seventy years later, Michael Davitt—certainly not an uncritical admirer of his—made the same essential point when he tried to measure O'Connell's achievement: "Ireland has never produced a greater man ... and Europe very few that can truly be called his equal in the work of uplifting a people from the degrading status of religious and political serfdom to conditions of national life which necessarily created changes and chances of progress ... bound to lead on to the gain of further liberty".[3] Davitt is an outstanding instance of the expatriate Irish nationalist, a man dedicated to promoting, first by revolutionary and then by other methods, the freedom of both Ireland herself and the Irish abroad. The emigrant Irish and their descendants were for long vulnerable to crippling discrimination which could not be effectively combated until the mother country's stature had been enhanced and Irish Catholics everywhere accorded, as a result, a respect

1. M. R. O'Connell (ed.), *The Correspondence of Daniel O'Connell*, 8 vols. (Shannon and Dublin, 1972-), vi, no. 2748, O'Connell to FitzPatrick, 14 September 1840. Hereafter cited as the *O'Connell Correspondence*, Vols. iv-viii while yet unpublished, and were made available to me by kindness of Professors O'Connell and R. Dudley Edwards.
2. *Ibid.*, no. 2621, O'Connell to FitzPatrick, 14 May 1839.
3. Michael Davitt, *The Fall of Feudalism in Ireland* (London, 1904), p. 35.

commonly denied to them in the United States, Great Britain, Canada and Australasia. This is what Davitt had in mind when he paid tribute to O'Connell as "a Colossus who impressed the world with the greatness of Celtic personality".[4]

For O'Connell pride of race and devotion to Catholicism were fundamentally inseparable. Sending his sons to the Jesuits at Clongowes in 1815, he did so, he told the rector, because "I am most anxious that they should be strongly imbued with the principles of Catholic faith and national feeling."[5] While this combination of loyalties was his people's inheritance, its new strength and purposefulness in the nineteenth-century owed a lot to O'Connell. In the first place, it is not too much to say that he gave the Irish Catholic Church a political education necessary if her influence was to match the growth and liberalisation of Anglo-Saxon representative government. The lower clergy provided numbers of willing pupils, and he relied heavily on them. He had to work harder, and less successfully, to overcome episcopal caution. Not until two years after his death did the Irish bishops acquire an O'Connellite leader in the person of Paul Cullen. At the local celebrations to mark the centenary of O'Connell's birth, one of Cullen's protégés, Bishop James Quinn of Brisbane—a notable figure in the history of the Irish in Australia—singled out for high praise the Liberator's patient cultivation of the Irish Hierarchy: "no part of his hard task was more delicate or required more judgment, integrity and power, than to conciliate, and gain the approval and confidence of the ... Bishops".[6] The character of James Quinn's apostolate in Queensland—which led contemporaries to refer to that British colony, only partly in jest as 'Quinnsland'[7]—is evidence of the profound impression which O'Connell made on Irish Catholicism at home and abroad. Bishop Quinn's labours, and those of Irish prelates and clergy all over the English-speaking world, bore witness to Ireland's global mission. O'Connell's understanding of this historic role is another respect in which he enlarged Irish Catholic nationalism's vision of itself. "Ireland", he said in a speech of June 1841, "is fulfilling her destiny—that of Catholicising other nations".[8]

O'Connell loved his religion, he liked to say, "because it was Irish".[9] His sharp criticisms of Vatican policy, when it militated against Irish national interests, are well known. His ultramontanism was unusual then and significant for the future in distinguishing clearly between the Papacy's religious function and its conservative politics during the period. "I am attached to the centre of unity", he wrote of his attitude to Rome, "with the most ardent desire never to separate myself from it either in thought or word

4. *Ibid.*, p. 36.
5. *O'Connell Correspondence*, ii, no. 508, O'Connell to Fr. Peter Kenney, S.J., 4 January 1815.
6. *O'Connell Centenary Record, 1875, published by Authority of the O'Connell Centenary Committee* (Dublin, 1878), p. 604.
7. Sir C. Gavan Duffy, *My Life in Two Hemispheres*, 2 vols (London, 1898; repr. Shannon, 1968), ii, p. 218.
8. W. J. O'Neill Daunt, *Personal Recollections of the late Daniel O'Connell*, 2 vols (London, 1848), i, p. 293.
9. William Fagan, *The Life and Times of Daniel O'Connell*, 2 vols (London, 1847-8), i, p. 529.

or action."[10] At the same time, he was jealous of the independence of the Irish Church: "For we are, thank Heaven, a separate nation still and have preserved through ages of persecution—English persecution, political as well as religious—our separate existence and so much of our royal and national station as consists in a national hierarchy complete in all its parts . . ." The passage comes from a long letter of his in May 1842 to Cullen as Roman agent for Ireland's bishops protesting against a suspected inclination of the Pope's advisers to overlook the distinctive identity of Irish Catholics. "British!!! I am not British. You are not British", exclaimed O'Connell. He furnished Cullen with no fewer than sixteen reasons why repeal of the Union with Britain would be "an event of the most magnificent importance to Catholicity". Among those arguments he held out the prospect that the forcible recovery, with repeal, of lands bestowed upon the Anglican church at "the so-called Reformation" would provide, when other calls on their revenues by the Church had been met, for the erection of a seminary in Ireland to supply priests to "the vast regions of the globe where the English language is understood". The college of All Hallows, Dublin, was founded that year, but he seems to have envisaged a more ambitious project. Finally, he suggested, after repeal an Irish cardinal in Curia should be the channel of communication between his country and the Papacy. He deplored the 'anomaly' that Ireland, alone in Catholic Europe, had never been vouchsafed a cardinal. The religious and eclesiastical ambitions expressed in this document were not less important than the political aims bound up with them.[11]

Hyperpole was commonplace in the oratory of O'Connell and his disciples in Ireland and overseas. To the extent that they indulged in conscious exaggeration, it was done to raise the self-esteeem of a people badly in need of the encouragement. Bishop James Quinn assured his Irish-Australian audience that "the fact of being a member of one of the oldest, noblest and most chivalrous races in the world was something to be proud of".[12] In the course of the prolonged struggle for Catholic Emancipation O'Connell made good use of this appeal. He told a big meeting in 1823: "Irishmen never combat to be upon a *level* with, but always *above* their competitors . . . there was not a corner of the world but resounds with their achievements".[13] It followed that the dominant Anglo-Saxon Protestants in the United Kingdom and elsewhere were culpably blind in failing to recognise the true worth of the Celtic and Catholic Irish. In 1813 O'Connell asserted that "so dishonest and besotted a people as the English never lived", and again "As to English stupidity, it is really . . . proverbial . . . England . . . is ready to sanction any crime—to credit any delusion".[14] Addressing the O'Connell centennial banquet in Boston, General Benjamin F. Butler, a past and future governor of Massachusetts, set

10. *O'Connell Correspondence*, vi, no. 2369a, O'Connell to an unidentified correspondent in Rome, 1837.
11. *Ibid.*, vii, no. 2959, O'Connell to Cullen, 9 May 1842. Cullen was for long rector of the Irish College in Rome, and finally of the College of Propaganda in 1848-9.
12. *O'Connell Centenary Record*, p. 601.
13. John O'Connell, *The Life and Speeches of Daniel O'Connell*, 2 vols (Dublin, 1846), ii, p. 400.
14. *Ibid.*, i, pp 425-6.

out to whip up the religious and racial enthusiasm of the gathering. Although a Protestant of Scotch-Irish stock, he was an opportunist who carefully cultivated the state's large Irish Catholic vote. He recalled the hostile reaction Irish Catholics had encountered not long before during the first decades of their heavy immigration: "men ... who had come here searching for liberty ... were not fit to be citizens of a free republic". He ascribed their changed treatment to the weight of numbers rather than to the American majority's conscience: "There are now nearly as many Irishmen and Irishwomen in this country as in the Old World. There is the largest Irish city in the world in this country ... New York ... there are more Irishmen in the good city of Boston than in any city of Ireland, save Dublin ... " " ... we and our fathers," he went on to claim "have brought to this city that ideal Irish opinion of freedom and of equality of right, of that power which belongs to every man to carve out his fortune in his own way. . ." Such, he said, was the ideal which O'Connell had attempted to realise in Ireland, and which the Irish had succeeded in realising across the Atlantic. But that was not all. "As a not very remote son of Ireland, I look forward" he asserted, "to the time when Ireland shall govern New England, and New England govern the United States". The speech elicited great applause, but when that shrewd Irish-American politician, Patrick Collins, rose, he deprecated Butler's provocative language.[15]

Butler, in his speech, acknowledged that the United States had yet to master her anti-Catholicism. The American refusal of public funds for denominational schools was an enduring grievance. Catholic churches, schools and newspapers, in that order, were the media of expatriate Irish nationalism. The eccelsiastical proprietors and lay editors of the *Boston Pilot*, the Cincinnati *Catholic Telegraph* or the Sydney *Freeman's Journal* produced papers that lived up to their titles. The first and third bore the names of famous Dublin nationalist organs. Michael Davitt was mistaken in supposing that O'Connell "created a national public opinion ... without a press".[16] On the contrary, when, early in his career, O'Connell hailed "the free Press of Ireland", he had fully appreciated its possibilities.[17] The preoccupation of the Irish with themselves, natural though it was, equally naturally intensified the suspicion and dislike that faced them wherever they settled. An intelligent defence of their attitude came from Kevin Izod O'Doherty at the Brisbane celebrations of the O'Connell centenary. The former Young Irelander referred to "those sons and daughters of Australia, who consider that their National sentiment is ... slighted by demonstrations of this kind, believing that they sow ... dissension in our young community". There was far too little in Australia's short history, he argued, to nourish the collective mind of her inhabitants: "whence can we better draw the inspiration to infuse a spirit into ... uninformed clay than from the grand traditions of an older clime? If

15. *O'Connell Centenary Record*, pp 545-7.
16. Davitt, op. cit., p. 35.
17. John O'Connell, op. cit., i, pp 430-2.

we wish to rear our children with ideas beyond those of mere 'bush' experience, we are fain to fall back upon the historic names and events of our motherland". O'Doherty's conclusion, however, showed plainly enough what it was that British Australians found objectionable in the festivities. If O'Connell had not effected "the glorious resurrection" of a parliament in Dublin, its establishment could not be indefinitely delayed because "outside the Green Isle, in England, Scotland, America, Australia . . . the Irish Nation still exists, one and indestructible".[18]

O'Connell's concern with official patronage exposed him to charges of being a placehunter, if not for himself, for his party, including a numerous family. It was his contention that Irish Catholics should start to receive a bigger share of appointments under the Crown. The increase of Catholic office-holders simply began to meet the legitimate claims of a deprived people, and it was not incompatible with the continued pursuit of repeal.[19] While O'Connell's view was perfectly defensible, the reactions of the Irish in Australia and Canada to the accessibility of power and place indicated what might happen if they fared as well in the United Kingdom. Kevin Izod O'Doherty, the revolutionary of 1848, spoke of "the great Anglo-Celtic empire" that had evolved for the race whom O'Connell found "in a condition little better than . . . abject slavery".[20] Over the third quarter of the century the Irish had advanced a very long way politically in the Australian colonies. The careers of two colonial premiers in Victoria—Sir John O'Shanassy, a strong O'Connellite, and Sir Charles Gavan Duffy, once a Young Irelander, illustrate the progress.[21] In Canada Archbishop T. L. Connolly of Halifax, Nova Scotia, a patriotic Irishman, deployed two main arguments when he led Irish Catholics to the support of confederation in the 1860s. Like other proponents of the policy, he feared the unfederated colonies would be irresistibly sucked into the United States. He was afraid, firstly, of the undenominational public education of America. Secondly, he contrasted the status of Catholics in British North America with their inferiority in the United States, where they had "No share in the Executive, no seat in the Senate, and . . . very few members in the House of Representatives." On British territory, especially in the Atlantic colonies of New Brunswick, Nova Scotia, Newfoundland and Prince Edward Island there had been "no period since the days of emancipation, at which Catholics have not possessed that influence in the country to which their numbers and position fairly entitled them . . . The great government of the United States has nothing more tempting to offer".[22] The whole experience of the Irish for many generations, in their own country and later as emigrants, had given them a

---

18. *O'Connell Centenary Record*, pp 598-600.
19. This seems a fair comment on the passage on O'Connell and 'the spoils system' in Angus Macintyre, *The Liberator: Daniel O'Connell and the Irish Party, 1830-1847* (London, 1965), pp 160-2.
20. *O'Connell Centenary Record*, p. 598.
21. For O'Shanassy, see the *Dictionary of Australian Biography*, 2 vols. (Sydney, 1949), ii, pp 208-9; for Duffy, the more recent *Australian Dictionary of Biography*, 4 vols. to date (Melbourne, 1966-   ), iv, pp 109-13.
22. W. L. Morton *The Critical Years: the Union of British North America, 1857-1873* (Toronto, 1964), p. 191.

keen appetite for power. The archbishop overstated his case, yet the ability to satisfy that appetite, to a considerable extent, under the extensive autonomy granted to white settlers by Britain from the mid-century largely reconciled the Irish Catholics of Australia and Canada to the empire.

It was a question of relative strength. Where the Irish constituted a higher proportion of the population than they did in America and Britain, although the Irish minorities there far outnumbered those in Australia and Canada, they were drawn to a more militant nationalism than that associated with O'Connell. Fenianism offered the Irish of America and Britain a sense of dignity and purpose otherwise difficult to attain. But the Fenians, it should be emphasised, admitted their debt to O'Connell. At New York they held their own meeting to honour his centenary. It was addressed by Father Edward McGlynn, subsequently celebrated as a social reformer with radical ideas. Lustily as they cheered for O'Connell, the audience cheered louder still the mention of Fenian names. They accepted, nevertheless, Father McGlynn's verdict: "if the legislative or an absolute independence of Ireland is ever to be achieved, whether by moral suasion or by force, what man or number of men can claim to have done as much as O'Connell to make either possible?"[23] The Fenian-dominated Home Rule Confederation of Great Britain asked to participate in the elaborate commemoration mounted in Dublin that year. They also joined the counter-demonstration by Fenians and Fenian sympathisers against the constitutional nationalists who had charge of the proceedings. The Liverpool South End branch of the Confederation marched through Dublin beneath an imposing banner that depicted O'Connell removing the shackles from Erin's wrists and taking her by the hand.[24] The pictorial homage was deeply symbolic. The Fenians of the Confederation had had second thoughts about the practicality of revolutionary nationalism. A successful immigrant businessman from County Wexford, John Barry, travelled all over Britain in the early '70s persuading his Fenian comrades to organise Home Rule associations and go in for constitutional activity.[25] At the Manchester congress of these associations in January 1873, out of which the Confederation emerged after further meetings, the Glasgow Fenian John Ferguson made the keynote speech, holding up the example of the Liberator: "It was true O'Connell lay dead and buried, but the cause for which he struggled was marching on..."[26] Those present would have remembered, and some had been enrolled in, the British branches of O'Connell's Repeal Association.

At the centre of O'Connell's nationalism lay an area of ambiguity. "Yes ... I *have* an ulterior objective", he announced publicly in 1813 when Catholic Emancipation was the declared aim, "THE REPEAL OF THE

23. *O'Connell Centenary Record*, p. 531.
24. *Ibid.,* pp 26-7, 174-7.
25. Joseph Keating, 'History of the Tyneside Irish Brigade' in F. Lavery (ed.), *Irish Heroes in the Great War* (London, 1917), p. 51. Despite its title, this essay is a valuable source for expatriate nationalism in the North-East of England.
26. *Manchester Guardian,* 9 January 1873.

UNION and THE RESTORATION TO OLD IRELAND OF HER
INDEPENDENCE".[27] Nor was this a momentary aberration. "We would
fain excite a NATIONAL and IRISH PARTY, capable of annihilating any
foreign oppressor whatsoever", the Catholic Committee heard him say three
years earlier.[28] He greeted the news of Napoleon's return from Elba joyfully,
and was 'horribly out of spirits' at the tidings of Waterloo.[29] The threat from
France seemed to afford the best hope of inducing concessions by Britain to
Ireland. "I live to see Ireland free and independent",[30] he told his adored wife
in 1820. And so on; such statements from him, public and private, abound.
What was the nature of the independence for which he yearned? On the
occasion of the O'Connell centenary in Melbourne Sir John O'Shanassy
touched significantly on this question in a different form: "Parenthetically , I
may be allowed to ask, on whom has the mantle of O'Connell fallen in these
modern days?"[31] O'Connell belonged to a class pulled in two directions by its
loyalties and its interests. The surviving Catholic gentry of Ireland were
natural leaders of the national movement in the existing social climate, and
possessed ever stronger incentives to adhere to the Union. O'Connell informed
a Catholic rally in 1812 that whereas he had once had forty kinsmen serving
as officers in the Army of Bourbon France, following the partial abolition of
the Penal Laws he now had sixteen relatives commissioned with the British
Army in the Peninsular campaign.[32] The statistics assembled by Professor H.
J. Hanham in his essay on "Religion and Nationality in the Victorian Army"[33]
show that O'Connell hardly exaggerated when he termed his country "the right
arm of the empire—the nursery for sailors and soldiers".[34] The comparatively
few Catholic officers met with very little discrimination. The rank-and-file were
less fortunate. O'Connell pressed government to see to proper spiritual care for
them. It needed Cullen's exploitation of a recruiting crisis in the wars of the
1850s to obtain a real concession from the authorities who suspected Catholic
priests of being carriers of nationalism as well as of superstition.[35]
Notwithstanding, O'Connell took intense pride in the Irish military
contribution to the stability and expansion of the British empire.[36] At times he
wrote and spoke as though he would be content with something less than
independence under a common Crown. "Twenty-nine years after the Union,"
he said to the House of Commons in 1836, "Ireland was not a province, but a
pitiful colony . . . Do justice to Ireland and England had nothing to apprehend
from the further agitation of repeal, nothing to apprehend from Ireland, but

27. John O'Connell, op. cit. i, p. 420.
28. *Ibid.*, p. 86.
29. *O'Connell Correspondence*, ii, nos 540 and 562, O'Connell to his wife, 2 April, 12 July 1815.
30. *Ibid.*, 20 September 1820.
31. *O'Connell Centenary Record*, p. 587.
32. John O'Connell, op. cit., i, pp 262-3.
33. In M.R.D. Foot (ed.), *War and Society* (London, 1973).
34. O'Neill Daunt, op. cit., i, p. 304.
35. Dublin Diocesan Archives (hereafter cited as D.D.A.), Cullen to William Monsell, M.P., 14 July 1857.
36. E.g., *O'Connell Correspondence*, vi, no. 2665, O'Connell to Richard More O'Ferrall, M.P., 29
    November 1839.

everything to hope. Henceforth separation was at an end".[37]

He surprised even his brother James by such tactics, but was prepared with a simple explanation of his behaviour. The spells of co-operation with the Whigs which characterised his policy for some years were intended to disarm criticism and secure tangible gains. "I am, it is true, *playing a part,*" he told James, "moderating my tone and manner in order to get as much as I can quietly and to leave no pretext for renewing the Coercion Bill", that is, the drastic legislation of 1833, modified the next year and afterwards allowed to expire, "but, after all, it will be found that our only resource is in . . . Repeal".[38] O'Connell's opposition to coercion measures is particularly interesting. He might deny in the Commons that there was any connection between political and agrarian unrest.[39] He did not believe his denial. He genuinely deplored agrarian outrage, and shared the horror which the worst acts of peasant warfare inspired. Besides, this endemic violence was counter-productive in terms of British opinion, when its upsurges coincided with the periodic belief in Britain that Irish grievances were receiving all the attention they merited. "It is in the agitation of the English mind and of the English people that Irish safety consists", he once remarked.[40] On the other hand, he was in no doubt that widespread agrarian unrest in Ireland represented the eruption of fierce national sentiment. A setting of economic recession for well organised political and religious demands, resulting in waves of agrarian outrage, supplied O'Connell's campaigns with an indispensable thrust. He warned W. C. Plunket, the liberal Tory attorney-general for Ireland in 1822, "We are sincerely attached to constitutional connection with England. When I say we I mean the Catholic clergy and Catholic gentry, including the upper class of farmers, but the people, the physical force, is ready to turn out. Let them have but an occasion or give them officers and they will soon find an occasion".[41]

The question posed above requires more consideration. What exactly was the 'constitutional connection' which, according to O'Connell, his own class, the Catholic gentry and the substantial peasantry wished to perpetuate? The letter to Cullen of May 1842 set down that long list of objectives to be won by repeal. Taken together, they assumed a virtually complete freedom of action, in internal affairs, for the restored Irish parliament which was to be popularly elected, unlike its predecessor. The nature of the changes that O'Connell envisaged under the Dublin parliament is apparent from his flat statement to Cullen that 'Protestantism would not survive Repeal ten years'. This extinction, he added, would take place without persecution. It must be supposed that he thought most Protestants would emigrate, as poorer members of the community living in the Southern provinces had been doing for many years, finding their diminished status before emergent Catholic nationalism intolerable. Yet O'Connell said no more in his letter than that in

37. *Hansard,* 3rd series, xxxi, 94-5 (4 February 1836).
38. *O'Connell Correspondence,* v, no. 2076, O'Connell to James O'Connell, 7 June 1834.
39. *Hansard,* 3rd series, xxv, 358 (22 July 1834).
40. *O'Connell Correspondence,* v, no. 1972, O'Connell to P.V. FitzPatrick, 27 April 1833.
41. *Ibid.,* ii, no. 949, O'Connell to Plunket, 4 April 1822.

justice, as distinct from positive law, the Irish had never lost 'their right to domestic legislation'. It does seem that O'Connell, for all his bitter resentment of the British in so many ways, really wanted to keep a self-governing Ireland within the empire. A species of 'external association' with Britain suited his country and the international position of the Catholic Church, about which he cared a great deal. Moreover, there were the Irish abroad to be taken into account. O'Connell's youthful enthusiasm for the United States dwindled when he learnt what negro slaves and Irish Catholic immigrants had to suffer. His friend, Bishop John England of Charleston, South Carolina, a pioneer of Catholism in America and formerly an active nationalist as a priest in Ireland, sent him unfavourable reports of the great republic.[42] "Do not mistake me as to the state of religion in America',' wrote O'Connell to Bishop Doyle of Kildare in 1830 ". . . there is an ignorant rudeness of self-assertion which would domineer over the Church as it is paramount in the state".[43] Like Bishop England, O'Connell perceived in America "the restless genius of false liberalism", a danger to the Church rivalling that from absolute monarchs on the Continent "who not content with Caesar's portion claim what belongs to God".[44] He did not conceal, after the Philadelphia riots of 1844 and similar disturbances of which the Catholic Irish were victims, his harsh estimate of American hypocrisy, intolerance and cruelty. He was powerless to help the Irish in America. He could and did intervene with the British government on behalf of the Irish in Britain and the empire.[45]

Ideally, O'Connell desired a free Catholic Church in a liberal state, preferably a constitutional monarchy. His radicalism, his approval of manhood suffrage, should be seen in that context. That is why in 1830 the Belgian revolution appeared more important to him than the one in France.[46] The affair with Chartism was very brief and the reaction vehement. The Australian and Canadian colonies after the mid-nineteenth century reforms in colonial government resembled the Belgian model quite closely. Although O'Connell was dead by then, expatriate Irish nationalists of the type of Sir John O'Shanassy were justified in thinking that in those colonies they had got what he wanted. For them O'Connell's lasting significance was primarily religious. The work and the legend of O'Connell—as with Gladstone, who so admired him in retrospect—meant different things to different men. O'Shanassy, carefully holding the balance, like speakers wherever the O'Connell centenary was commemorated, observed: "Some will celebrate it from the most National point of view—some from an intensely religious

42. *Ibid.*, no. 1052, Bishop England to O'Connell, 4 October 1823.
43. *Ibid.*, iv, no. 1669, O'Connell to Bishop Doyle, 21 April 1830.
44. *Ibid.*, vii, no. 2914, O'Connell to Fr. W.A. O'Meara, O.F.M., 9 September 1841.
45. *Ibid.*, v, no. 2347, O'Connell to Bishop Griffiths, Vicar Apostolic of the London District, 16 July 1836; vii, no. 2962, O'Connell to Bishop Fleming of Newfoundland, 2 July 1842. These letters exemplify O'Connell's pressure on ministers and Parliament in aid of the Irish in Britain and her empire.
46. He qualified his advocacy of manhood suffrage, as in the debate of 12 July 1839 on the Chartist National Petition, *Hansard* (3rd ser.), xlix, 260; for his comment on the Belgian revolution, see *O'Connell Correspondence*, iv, no. 1714, O'Connell to R.N. Bennett, 5 October 1830.

one".[47] The Liberator's language and his actions, in death as in life, left his admirers to put the emphasis where they would. For some thirty years after his demise the man who most nearly filled his place was a prince of the Church, Paul Cullen, the recipient of O'Connell's confidential exposition of the meaning of Repeal. By becoming the first Irish cardinal he fulfilled one of O'Connell's hopes. *The Times* editorial when he died in 1878 called him an 'ecclesiastical imperialist'.[48] It was fair comment, but it ignored his larger role. By default, and not of set purpose, he acted as the leader of his people. The heads of the independent Irish party in the 1850s and the Fenians in the '60s vented their anger and frustration on Cullen, blaming him for the failure of popular support which put an end to the first and checked the second. Their reproaches are, perhaps, the best indication of the authority he wielded. *The Times* compared him unfavourably with the 'mild and genial' Archbishop Murray whom he succeeded in Dublin.[49] Cullen's public utterances, let alone his vast correspondence, establish his commitment to Irish nationality.

Cullen revered O'Connell and exhorted the Irish, repeatedly, to follow his example. Far from wishing to take the Church out of Irish politics, Cullen ensured that clerical participation should be made more effective by the observance of a certain standard of unity and discipline.[50] He condemned Young Ireland's behaviour towards O'Connell, which he considered the height of folly and ingratitude, but forgave them when they returned to constitutional paths, except possibly Gavan Duffy, whose notorious vanity was insuperable. Cullen did not work for the dissolution of the independent Irish party which he had helped to bring into being. The party destroyed itself. Thereafter, increasingly, Cullen spoke up for Ireland in the absence until the '70s of an Irish Parliamentary party. "Probably no country under the sun has to suffer so much as Ireland, nor is there any other country in which the rulers are so blind to the wants and afflictions of the people".[51] This extract from his Lenten pastoral of 1863 is typical. His warnings against the temptations of revolutionary nationalism implied no sympathy whatever with Britain. He never felt the insidious attraction of belonging to a great empire, as O'Connell had done, and Butt and Redmond, if not Parnell, did. He saw in the British empire a worldwide scourge and the inveterate foe of Catholicism. He insisted, with O'Connell, that revolution must entail disaster for a people quite unable to resist the might of a nation which possessed the political will to crush a frontal attack upon her rule, in Ireland as in India. Cullen believed in the efficacy of O'Connell's methods of popular agitation and Parliamentary pressure. His confidence was spectacularly rewarded by the Gladstonian Church and Land Acts of 1869–70. The lack of a distinct Irish party and the Fenian reluctance

47. *O'Connell Centenary Record*, p. 586.
48. *The Times*, 25 October 1878.
49. *Ibid.*, the obituary of Cullen.
50. For a fuller discussion of Cullen's activity in Irish domestic politics, as summarized here, see E.D. Steele, 'Cardinal Cullen and Irish nationality' *Irish Historical Studies* (1975).
51. P.F. Moran (ed), *The Pastoral Letters and Other Writings of Cardinal Cullen*, 3 vols. (Dublin, 1882), ii, p. 177.

to shelve revolutionary for non-violent tactics were serious handicaps. To offset these disadvantages, Cullen was able to point to the threat from Fenianism, as O'Connell had pointed to that from smouldering peasant discontent. The Fenian menace had international dimensions which rendered it more formidable than the agrarian peril.

Cullen kept in close touch with the Irish abroad through their bishops. The anti-clericalism of the Fenians alarmed him and some of his episcopal correspondents. But, despite the severity of his official strictures on agrarian and political secret societies, Cullen does not seem to have been so apprehensive of the "frightful propensity to illegal combinations" among the Irish as was O'Connell, the lawyer and man of property.[52] Cullen's correspondence with English and Scottish Bishops who consulted him about this problem in their immigrant flocks displays a flexible response to a situation that invited combination. He distinguished between Fenian and other oath-bound societies. If the latter were avowedly Catholic, they might be tolerated, although he wondered, with some reason, whether they would not do their membership more harm than good in alien surroundings.[53] From the outset of his Irish career, which he commenced as Archbishop of Armagh and Apostolic Delegate, Cullen advertised the conviction that, in the words of his pastoral letter of 24 February 1850, "If we have anything to glory in, it is our Catholicity; if our country has a bright name among the nations of the earth, it is because she is Catholic, and on account of the sufferings she bore rather than forfeit this glorious appellation".[54] That awareness was stimulated by the added prestige which the Irish undeniably derived from their swift rise to power in the Church overseas. It is not irreverent to argue that her prominence in the Church, and domination of the episcopate, in America, Australasia and English-speaking Canada was to Ireland what her trade and navy were to Britain, the source of enormous pride. Cullen did not doubt that the Church needed the Irish almost as much as they needed her. "On the [Irish] Church,' he stated to the Cardinal Prefect of Propaganda in 1855, "... depends the future of religion in England, Scotland, the United States, Australia...."[55] He shared O'Connell's poor opinion of English Catholics, "who ... not lacking in pride and egotism ... are ready to sacrifice Ireland." He accused them, a small but wealthy body, of neglecting poverty-stricken Irish immigrants. He thought no better of Scottish Catholics.[56]

Neither O'Connell nor Cullen rejoiced to see their people leaving Ireland. The volume and effects of post-Famine emigration gravely worried Cullen. He detested the British empire, but also those aspects of American democracy

---

52. *O'Connell Correspondence*, ii, no. 558a, O'Connell to Sir Henry Parnell, 13 June 1815.
53. D.D.A., Cullen to Archbishop Dixon of Armagh, 3 August 1857.
54. Moran, op. cit., i, p. 21.
55. Peadar Mac Suibhne, *Paul Cullen and his Contemporaries with their Letters from 1820-1902*, 4 vols. to date (Naas, Co. Kildare, 1961), ii, p. 199, Cullen to Cardinal Barnabo, 28 July 1855.
56. *Ibid.*, iii, pp 247-8, Cullen to Barnabo, 19 November 1856; D.D.A., Cullen to Dr. Tobias Kirby, rector of the Irish College, Rome, 22 March 1867.

which repelled O'Connell.[57] The fate of souls in environments destructive of true religion oppressed him. Belief in "the vitality of the Celtic race" sustained him.[58] Moreover, his reputation in the Roman Curia gave him considerable influence in the selection of bishops for Ireland and, in varying degree, countries of Irish settlement. He used it to secure the appointment of some good Irishmen.[59] Letters to him from Irish prelates illustrate the compelling reasons for the national preference in making these choices. ". . . the Irish arrive", wrote J. J. Lynch, Bishop and later Archbishop of Toronto, "without leaders, entirely defenceless, and the majority impoverished . . . The wonder is that so many have preserved the faith."[60] Irish bishops were a necessity to provide the immigrants with guidance that came easily to men bred in that ecclesiastical tradition. But Irish bishops and priests had the aid of an outlook instilled into their flocks at home. "In their own minds," noted Oscar Handlin, studying the Boston Irish, "immigrants played a clear role . . . they had been carried across the waters by a Divine Providence to present an irrefutable example of fortitude and faith to their unbelieving neighbours . . . and ultimately to bring the United States into the ranks of Catholic powers."[61] This mentality developed, if it did not originate, under O'Connell, and Cullen reinforced it.

57. D.D.A., Cullen to Archbishop Spalding of Baltimore, 12 November 1864 and to Dr. P.F. Moran, vice-rector of the Irish College, 19 April 1864.
58. *Ibid.*, Cullen to Bishop J.J. Lynch of Toronto, 13 May, and to Archbishop Spalding of Baltimore, 12 November 1864.
59. *Ibid.*, Archbishop Hughes of New York to Cullen, 17 December 1858, saying, 'all parties would be reconciled if your Grace should recommend to the Holy See some suitable Irish priest' for the archbishopric of Halifax, Nova Scotia.
60. D.D.A., Bishop J.J. Lynch of Toronto to Cullen, 9 June 1864.
61. Oscar Handlin, *Boston's Immigrants: A Study in Acculturation,* revised edn. (Cambridge, Mass., 1959), pp 185-6.

62. Every student of O'Connell must acknowledge his debt to Professor O'Connell's admirable edition of his ancestor's correspondence, and to three monographs, Fr. J.A. Reynold's *The Catholic Emancipation Crisis in Ireland, 1823-1829* (New Haven, Conn. 1954), Professor K.B. Nowlan's *The Politics of Repeal: a Study in the Relations between Great Britain and Ireland, 1841-50* (London, 1965), and Dr. Macintyre's book (see note 19 above).

Chapter 8

Daniel O'Connell and the Irish-American Nationalist and Politcal Profiles

Lawrence J. McCaffrey

Although the American Irish vocally and financially endorsed Daniel O'Connell's Catholic Emancipation agitation in the 1820s and his efforts to Repeal the Union in the early 1840s, the 'Liberator' of United Kingdom Catholics and the founding father of modern Irish nationalism has never been very popular among the Irish of the American Diaspora.[1] That and other factors made nineteenth century Irish-American nationalism considerably more than an extension of the liberation movement in Ireland. Circumstances and situations in the United States and the personality of the American Irish made Irish-American nationalism more ideological, passionate and violent than O'Connell's strategy for freeing the Irish people and the Irish nation from British domination.

Irish-American nationalism has been saturated with hate; for many a deeper hatred of England than love for Ireland. Despising England served as a catharsis for Irish-American tensions and frustrations, a way of expressing and explaining Irish failure, a striking out at real and imaginary enemies. Britain had to be punished and humiliated, not only as a step in the direction of Irish independence but as an atonement for her sins against the Irish. British laws, cruelty, religious bigotry, insensitivity and indifference to Irish needs and

---

1. An early conflict between O'Connell and the American Irish involved the slavery question. O'Connell an abolitionist and advocate of full civil rights for emancipated blacks condemned Irish-Americans who countenanced black slavery in the United States and refused to accept donations from American Repeal organizations in Southern communities insisting that he would not stain the Irish freedom movement with the sweat and blood of American Slavery. He advised Irish-Americans to support abolitionism in the United States as an extension of the liberal principles they learned in Ireland and a cause consistent with Christianity and their own Declaration of Independence. Many Irish-Americans told O'Connell to mind his own business and to stay out of domestic United States politics, an early indication that Irish-American nationalism was suited to the interests of the American Irish rather than the cause of Irish independence. The controversy over slavery and the personality of O'Connell prevented Irish-American nationalists from consolidating local Repeal associations into an organized national movement.

problems had resulted in the deaths and exile of millions of Irish people.

To the American Irish, Britain was the source of Irish disgrace and humiliation at home and abroad. In one of his poems, 'Remorse for Intemperate Speech', William Butler Yeats described how the Irish left Ireland with a maimed personality, featuring 'great hatred', carrying from their 'mother's womb a fanatic heart'. And during his American exile, John Mitchel, the most passionate and unforgiving of the Young Irelanders, analysed the motives underlying his nationalism:

> I have found that there was perhaps less love in it than of hate—less of filial affection for my country than of scornful impatience at the thought that I had the misfortune, I and my children, to be born in a country which suffered itself to be oppressed and humiliated by another . . . and hatred being the thing I chiefly cherished and cultivated, the thing which I specially hated was the British system . . . wishing always that I could strike it between wind and water, and shiver its timbers.[2]

While there were those who never reconciled themselves to physical or spiritual exile from Ireland or needed a scapegoat for their lack of success in the United States as the essence of a paranoid Irish nationalism, other Irish-Americans, people who had achieved social and economic mobility, worked for an Irish nation state to earn respectability in the general American community. They believed that the existence of an independent Ireland would be an instrument of their assimilation in the United States. These searchers for status and respectability argued that Ireland wearing the British collar and leash was a symbol of Irish inferiority and degradation, encouraging the concept of Anglo-Americans. But a free Ireland 'numbered among the nations of the earth' would elevate her exiled children in the eyes of other Americans. The Irish may have been the first but certainly not the last minority group in the United States to link their destiny with the sovereignty of the ethnic homeland. Contemporary Jews, Blacks and Slavs insist on the continued existence of Israel, African freedom, and the independence of Poland or other countries in Eastern Europe for the same reason that nineteenth century Irish-Americans became involved in Irish nationalism.[3]

Whether their motives originated in enmity for Britain or the desire for success in America, Irish-American nationalists could not understand how O'Connell's non-violent, constitutional, parliamentary nationalism could produce a free Ireland. It depended on the decency, honesty, fairness and integrity of British politicians who had frequently demonstrated and expressed their hatred and contempt for Ireland and her people. And Irish-American nationalists were convinced that the British parliamentary process would

---

2. William Dillon, *Life of John Mitchel,* 2 vols. (London, 1898), ii, 104-105. Thomas Flanagan in "Rebellion and style: John Mitchel and the Jail Journal", *Irish University Review,* i, 1-29, presents a remarkably penetrating analysis of Mitchel as the fanatic hater of Britain.
3. Irish-American nationalism as an ethnic search for responsibility is a main theme in Thomas N. Brown, "The Origins and Character of Irish-American Nationalism," *The Review of Politics,* xviii (July, 1956), 327–358; and *Irish-American Nationalism* (New York, 1966).

corrupt Irish nationalists who participated in its operation, contaminating the very soul of the Irish freedom movement. They insisted that Ireland could only be liberated through revolutionary violence.

As one response to the pressures, hostility and prejudices of Anglo-American Protestant nativism, Irish nationalism jelled and flourished in the ghettos of urban America as a search for identity, an expression of vengeance and a quest for respectability. Before the Great Famine rapidly expanded the communities of the Diaspora, Irish nationalism was more hope and aspiration than reality. While O'Connell's Catholic and Repeal Associations served to educate the Irish in the skills of public opinion politics, to unite and mobilise them for agitation, and to lay the structural foundations of Irish nationalism, there was much to be done before the Irish people could think of themselves as distinctly Irish and realise the implications of that conceptual indentity.

As an eighteenth century, cosmopolitan Whig patriot, O'Connell did not understand the significance of cultural identity as a dimension of nationalism. While Young Irelanders in the 1840s began to push beyond the nationalist frontiers outlined by O'Connell, and in the process created and articulated an Irish cultural nationalism, most of the Irish population was composed of illiterate peasants unable to comprehend the complete message of the *Nation*. And their priests, fearing that Young Irelanders were the paracletes of Continental secularism, radicalism and anti-clericalism, remained loyal to the memory, message and tactics of O'Connell.

Geography and the nature of the economy also obstructed the advance of Irish nationalism. Although a small country, Ireland is divided by a number of small mountain ranges, and in the early nineteenth century, primitive transportation facilities strengthened regional boundaries. In terms of identity, Ireland had less meaning than townland, parish, county or province. And Irish tenant farmers functioned within a ramshackle social and economic system, existing without adequate legal rights or weapons to protect them from exorbitant rents or arbitrary evictions. Alien Protestant landlords versus native Catholic tenant farmers was only one aspect of class divisions and conflicts. Catholic cottiers were as much exploited by Catholic tenant farmers as they were by agents of the landlord system. Among the rural Irish masses, the priority concern was survival rather than national freedom. Tradition and fear induced dependency on landlords, and land hunger diluted much of the Catholic unity and patriotism that O'Connell had forged.

When the Irish came to the United States they brought their townland, parish, county, regional and clan loyalties with them packed in their psychological baggage, but the common ghetto experience and Anglo-American Protestant hatred and persecution contributed to the creation of an Irish identity. Men from all counties and provinces of Ireland worshipped together in the same Catholic churches, voted as a block in Democratic party machines, and worked side by side on the railroads in the mines and factories. Anglo-American contempt for all things Irish deepened the wounds of an already serious inferiority complex, necessitating a search for pride through ethnicity. In their quest for Irishness, Irish-Americans invented their own 'radical' myths to match those of the persecutor, rejecting what they considered O'Connell's 'West British' patriotism, turning to the poems, essays and doctrines of Young Ireland for the source of their cultural and revolutionary nationalism. Young Ireland refugees from the comic opera 1848 cabbage patch revolution left Ireland as dismal failures; they arrived in America as heroes. The emigration factor in Irish history and the development of an Irish consciousness and identity among the American Irish speeded the progress of Irish nationalism on both sides of the Atlantic.[4]

In the 1850s, 1860s, and 1870s, while the Irish nationalist majority in Ireland returned to the paths of constitutional nationalism in the forms of the Independent Irish Party, the National Association and Home Rule, the American Irish thought, talked and planned revolution. Their efforts culminated in the Fenian Brotherhood, the American wing of the Irish Republican Brotherhood. Although revolutionary republicanism in the United States divided on personality and strategy, it was always more passionate than its Irish manifestation.

Even after Fenianism collapsed in the late 1860s following isolated insurrections in Ireland and futile Canadian invasions in America, revolutionary republicanism continued to represent Irish-American nationalism. In the 1870s, the Clan na Gael replaced the Fenian Brotherhood and attempted to make contact with and radicalise the Irish peasant masses through a campaign against landlordism as a prelude to revolution.[5] Charles Stewart Parnell outwitted and outflanked the Clan, capturing the Land League phase of the New Departure, and eventually enlisting Irish-American dollars and enthusiasm behind the Irish Parliamentary Party and the demand for Home Rule. But he and his successor, John Redmond, always talked a tougher, and more anti-British brand of nationalism in America than they did in Ireland. When the Home Rule movement and Parliamentary Party began to collapse following the third Home Rule bill and Ulster crisis, 1912–1914, Irish-Americans seemed more comfortable encouraging Irish rebellion than they . had been while financing an Irish party in the British Parliament.

Although Daniel O'Connell played a minor, more negative than positive role, in the structure and ideology of Irish-American nationalism, his impact on Irish-American politics was considerable. Because of Catholic Emancipation and Repeal agitations in Ireland, Irish immigrants arrived in the United States with considerable experience in the methods of Anglo-Saxon style politics. And Irish political sophistication continued to grow throughout the nineteenth century as they participated in constitutional nationalist

4. In discussing the regional loyalty, educational, and economic factors frustrating the development of nationalism in early nineteenth century Ireland, and the significance of the American experience in forging an Irish identity, I am indebted to the research and writing of Thomas N. Brown cited in the previous footnote.

5. In *Irish-American Nationalism* (1966), Thomas N. Brown presented his thesis that the new Departure originated in the United States, first inspired by Patrick Ford's attacks in *The Irish World* on American industrial capitalism and Irish landlordism as the twin sources of Irish poverty.

St. Patrick's Day Parade, Union Square, New York, 1874.

movements modelled on O'Connell's use of the British constitutional and parliamentary processes. O'Connell could also be described as the first Irish political Boss. Leaders of the urban American Irish from 'Honest' John Kelly of Tammany in the 1870s to Richard J. Daley of Chicago in the 1970s have shared many of the features of O'Connell's political personality. But O'Connell's influence on Irish-American politics is much more subtle and significant than style, the techniques of agitation or Bossism. He was the agent of the Anglo-Saxon Protestant liberal dimension of the Irish political profile in Ireland and the United States.

Even among the many groups of Americans who did and do not like the Irish because they believe that they are the agents of Catholic ignorance and authoritarianism or think they are crude, arrogant and aggressive, there are those who concede them a kind of political genius. Frequently this admission has been made more in a spirit of fear than of admiration. In January, 1916, Sir Cecil Spring-Rice, United Kingdom Ambassador to the United States, incidentally an Irishman, wrote to his Foreign Secretary, Sir Edward Grey, concerning the difficulty of persuading the United States to support the British in their war against the Central Powers. He attributed many of his problems to the anti-British Irish who had "unequalled power of political organisation" and were the "best politicians in the country".[6] And Anglo-American Protestants gazed in amazement mixed with anguish as the Irish seized control over urban America. In the April, 1894 issue of *The Forum*, John Paul Bocock discussed 'The Irish Conquest of Our Cities', claiming that Irish oligarchies controlled New York, Brooklyn, Jersey City, Hoboken, Boston, Chicago, Buffalo, Albany, Troy, Pittsburgh, St. Paul, St. Louis, Kansas City, Omaha, New Orleans and San Francisco. He asked

> What do the majorities of the citizens of American municipalities think of themselves? How has it come about that the system of government so admirably conceived by the fathers has worked and so poorly in municipal affairs? Philadelphia, Boston and New York were once governed by the Quakers, the Puritans, and the Knickerbockers. Are they better governed now, since from the turbulence of municipal politics the Irish-Americans have plucked both wealth and power? . . .

Some contemporary Irish-American scholars and intellectuals seem as concerned about the dark side of Irish political skill as Bocock was back in the 1890s. In his highly regarded, often quoted and much discussed essay, 'The Irish', in *Beyond the Melting Pot* (1963), a book he coauthored with Nathan Glazer, Daniel Patrick Moynihan, an important advisor in both the Kennedy and Nixon administrations, former United States Ambassador to India and envoy to the United Nations, levelled a devastating attack on the Irish role in urban government, insisting that their political style was short on content, lacking a purpose beyond the acquisition of power:

6. Alan J. Ward, *Ireland and Anglo-American Relations, 1899-1921* (London, 1969), 93-96.

The Irish were uncommonly successful in politics. They ran the city. But the very parochialism and bureaucracy that enabled them to succeed in politics prevented them from doing much with government. In a sense the Irish did not know what to do with power once they got it. They never thought of politics as an instrument of social change.

According to Moynihan, Irish-American political perspectives never really advanced beyond the rural parish, old country value system; their attitudes were static and thus essentially conservative. Although the Irish political genius was directed at the seizure and maintenance of power, unfortunately it lacked the idealism and social conscience that translates power into constructive change. American urban problems connected with rapid industrialisation and population growth demanded reform, but Irish power paralysed the responses of city governments, frustrating social improvement, serving as a negative rather than a positive contribution to urban development.

Before *Beyond the Melting Pot* reached the reading public, Thomas J. Fleming, in *All Good Men* (1961), one of a series of novels he has written about the Irish in a New Jersey City, anticipated the Moynihan thesis, presenting it in the words of Larry Donahue, an ambitious, unstable, bitter young politician critical of the local Irish boss and machine:

> . . . This city is a living testimonial to the ineptitude and rotten morals of the Irish who are running it . . . I'm serious. Thirty years of absolute power. What would a Jew have done with it? Or a New England Yank? We'd be living in a dream city with equal housing and equal opportunity and equal justice for everybody.

More recently, in a revisionist lecture. "The Irish in United States Politics", delivered before the April, 1975 American Committee for Irish Studies meeting at Stonehill College, Easton, Massachusetts, Thomas N. Brown intelligently and provocatively argued that historians, social scientists, creative writers and journalists have exaggerated the existence of a unique Irish political style and approach to the American political process. He insisted that the contents and techniques of Irish-American politics have varied from city to city, generation to generation, responding to local issues, values and challenges. Brown offered evidence to indicate that Irish-American politics in Boston have been more Boston than Irish and suggested that the same would hold true for other cities like New York or Chicago.

If Brown meant that there is more than one Irish-American approach to urban problems and that there are varieties in the Irish political personality—O'Connell, Parnell, Redmond, Curley and Daley—he is obviously correct. There is no stereotype Irish politician and the American Irish did take on the tones and colours of regional value landscapes. And while the Irish did arrive in the United States with considerable experience in the arts and crafts of political organisation and action, rough and tumble urban American politics and local challenges did shape their approach to government.

Although scholars, intellectuals and the literati have exaggerated the uniqueness and overly romanticised Irish-American politics, there is a distinct brand of Irish politics, far more subtle and complicated than style or personality. In fact, the flexibility that Brown emphasised is one of its leading components. But Anglicisation and Romanisation, both tempered in the trials and tribulations of nationalist agitations and movements, rather than pragmatism and adaptability are the essence of Irish politics, the sources of American Irish political values and objectives.

The Irish are both the victims and beneficiaries of two kinds of cultural imperialism, Anglicisation and Romanisation. These two outside influences, added to the fading memories of a defeated Gaelic culture, fashioned the values of the Irish at home and abroad, and the English and Catholic dimensions of the Irish personality have been as apparent in politics as in religion and literature. Political Anglicisation commenced in the long struggle for Irish freedom. Protestant patriotism began to vanish with the Act of Union but it bequeathed to Irish nationalism the values of Whig patriotism, with its emphasis on the defence of natural and individual rights as the purpose of good government. In the early decades of the nineteenth century, Daniel O'Connell, a Whig patriot as well as a disciple of Thomas Paine and Jeremy Bentham, organised the Irish masses for political action, instructing them in the use of the instruments and levers of the British constitutional system. In doing so, he impregnated Irish nationalism with a firm commitment to liberal-democracy, a principle embraced by physical force as well as constitutional nationalists.

O'Connell did more than just borrow the principles and methods of British constitutionalism and pass them on to his Irish followers. He also created tactics of agitation that contributed to the advance of liberty throughout the Western World. In his campaigns to emancipate Catholics and to Repeal the Union, he created the first modern political movement in the United Kingdom, one that was based on constituency organisation and support as well as activity in the British House of Commons. And O'Connell was the first European politician to achieve significant victories for individual freedom in the oppressive Age of Metternich by applying the 'moral force' of disciplined public opinion. As he worked with British Whig and Radical politicians to achieve reform and good government for Ireland, he taught his people that the success of democratic politics depended on compromise, the willingness to accept less than the original demand, the notion that some improvement was better than no progress at all.

Later in the nineteenth century, Charles Stewart Parnell built on the foundations that O'Connell so firmly laid. Although less charismatic than the Kerry Catholic, the Wicklow Protestant also added to the contents of Irish political wisdom and success. His determined obstruction of the House of Commons, energetic leadership of the Land League attack on landlordism, creation of the first disciplined party in the British Parliament and masterful employment of balance of power politics which forced the Liberals to adopt

Home Rule taught the Irish democracy how to manipulate the weaknesses and strengths of parliamentary government to achieve power.

Although they were technologically and culturally retarded when they arrived in the United States, because of their experience as participants in Irish nationalist movements that operated within the context of parliamentary government the Irish entered their urban American ghettos clever in the ways of Anglo-Saxon politics, ready to take on the native Anglo-American Protestant Establishment in a struggle for power. While they employed the political methods of their opponents, and embraced the principles of liberal-democracy, the Irish political perspective was also coloured by their Catholic experience, and this religious-cultural influence made them profoundly different in point of view from Anglo-Saxon and Anglo-American liberal-democrats, a difference undetected by Daniel Patrick Moynihan.

A critic of Moynihan's thesis concerning the static, conservative character of Irish politics is tempted to argue that it lacks accuracy, substance, and most important, historical perspective, because the author assumes that throughout the late nineteenth and early twentieth centuries there were large numbers of Americans who viewed politics as 'an instrument of social change'. Moynihan seemed to have accepted a consensus among historians which is more of an anti-Catholic, ethnic, nativist academic prejudice than a scholarly conclusion. This prejudice insists that American social reform is the achievement of Protestant middle class Progressivism accomplished in the teeth of Catholic ethnic opposition.

Moynihan and the academic establishment have been wrong about two things: Protestant middle class reformism and Catholic social conservatism. Throughout the nineteenth century and even today, the American Protestant public opinion and many of its spokesmen have rejected the concept that government could or should intervene to lessen the burdens of poverty and disease. Supported by a crude Social Darwinism, *laissez faire* was always predominantly a creed of the Anglo-American Protestant majority. In criticising the Irish for not using their political power to confront and then solve urban problems, Moynihan expected them to function beyond the frontiers of the American value system. They did, but he failed to recognise it. While Anglo-Americans were insisting on self-help, Irish politicians, however venal, showed concern for the urban poor. Dispensing buckets of coal, food baskets, public works and other forms of patronage employment was often an inefficient and graft ridden system of social justice, but it was the precursor of welfare state liberalism in the United States.

While the Irish operate outside the general American consensus concerning human nature and the meaning of history, paradoxically their conservative, skeptical, often cynical atttudes toward man and his environment have made them more successful practical reformers than ideological liberals have been. They strive for importance of harmonising change with the traditions and continuity of history. Their Catholic sense of community, expressed in the theological doctrine of the Mystical Body, encourages a collectivist rather than an atomistic approach to society. They have no emotional or intellectual antipathy to the welfare state. In contrast, Anglo-Saxon and Anglo-American Protestant liberalism draws its sustenance from an individualistic religious and economic ideology which emphasises the rights of the person against the 'oppression' of the community. The Protestant conscience and value system find it much more difficult to challenge the nucleus of the urban industrial social question than the Catholic community centered point of view. Collectivist answers irritate and antagonise Protestant psychology.

In the twentieth century, following a major economic depression that shook confidence in *laissez faire* capitalism, a majority of American citizens concluded that social security was an essential foundation for human freedom. When they decided that government had an obligation to guarantee that social security, it was Irish politicians in cities, not Anglo-American Protestants in suburban or rural America, who served as the core of minority group coalitions that made possible the New Deal, Fair Deal, New Frontier and Great Society.

In Ireland and the United States, the Irish have blended the methodology and principles of Anglo-Saxon and Anglo-American Protestant liberal politics, a Catholic sense of community, and their own tolerant, gregarious and compromising personalities into a unique brand of politics. And because they participated in and bridged the gulf between Roman Catholic and Anglo-Saxon Protestant cultures, the Irish were the only European ethnics who could have led the American Catholic community into an accommodation with the dominant Anglo-American Protestant ethos.[8]

7. In "Urban Liberalism and the Age of Reform", *The Mississipi Valley Historical Review,* xlix, 231-241 (September, 1962). J. Joseph Huthmacher challenged the academic consensus concerning the reform impulses and achievements of Protestant Progressivism. He argued that the poverty experience of Catholic ethnics and their welfare oriented machine politics made them the main force challenging *laissez faire* liberalism. Huthmacher suggested that Protestant Progressivism was much more concerned with conformity, making ethnics one-hundred percent American, than social improvement. Progressive nativism attacked parochial schools as divisive, imposed prohibition and other puritan panaceas for social disorders, and distinguished between Anglo-Saxons and lesser breeds. Naturally ethnics responded negatively to the nativist rhetoric of reformism. In discussing the reality rather than academic theories concerning the origins of social reform in twentieth century America, Huthmacher showed how ethnic politicians in state legislatures sponsored and supported bills to improve the working conditions of the proletariat: child labor laws, minimum wage guidelines, and sickness and accident benefits. During the administration of Governor Alfred E. Smith in the 1920s, New York state previewed the New Deal. And during the 1930s, Franklin Delano Roosevelt was able to move the United States away from self-help individualism because he had the loyalty and encouragement of Irish dominated urban political machines. Ethnic Catholic community attitudes in contrast to Anglo-Saxon Protestant individualism and the political, social and economic implications of these opposite attitudes is also a main theme of Michael Novak's *The Rise of the Unmeltable Ethnics* (1971). Although many Catholic bishops, priests and journalists have advocated extremely conservative positions in regard to private property and social change, clerical conservatism seems to be Eastern rather than nationwide, and Catholic laymen in America, like those in Ireland do not necessarily follow the dictates of bishops and priests on political, social or economic questions unless such opinions conform to the interests of the total Catholic community.
8. In an article "Thanks to the Irish", published in the Jesuit weekly *America,* vol. 114, no. 20, 694-98 May 14, 1966, Professor Philip Gleason of the University of Notre Dame refuted Catholic writers and intellectuals who have argued that the Irish control over American Catholicism made the church in the United States authoritarian and conservative. He insisted that it was fortunate that the Irish were the first Catholic ethnics to arrive in large numbers because "they were the best equipped among all the immigrating Catholic groups to assist the Church in effecting a positive adjustment to American life."

While Irish-Americans were adjusting other Catholic ethnics to the American system, and pushing a reluctant United States along the road to the welfare state, Irish politicians were quietly achieving a successful social revolution in the status and condition of their own people. In a little over a hundred years, the American Irish moved from the basements, attics and tar paper, wooden crate shacks of Boston, Philadelphia, New York and New Orleans to the front ranks of American social, political and intellectual society, including a temporary residence in that very famous mansion on Pennsylvania Avenue, Washington D.C.[9]

Continental Catholics came to America from ultra-conservative societies where church and state were united, serving as twin agencies of government control and conformity. In the United States they found the liberal-democratic, separation of church and state constitution strange and hostile. Within the United Kingdom the Irish had successfully learned to organize and operate within the British political system in agitations for civil rights and national sovereignty. Because of their liberal-democratic experience in Ireland, their familiarity with the Anglo-Saxon Protestant value system, and their command of the English language, the Irish could communicate with native Americans. Irish political expertise protected Catholic interests in the United States and in the process "Americanized" Catholic ethnics from all parts of Europe. Gleason reflected on the alternative to Irish power in this way:
"In this connection, it might be salutary to reflect for a moment on how much more radically the Catholic Church would have been cut off from American society . . . how much higher the ghetto walls would have been . . . if the Germans or French or Poles had occupied the overwhelmingly dominant position the Irish have historically enjoyed. And this not simply because of the difficulties of linguistic communication, but even more fundamentally because of the psychic identification of Catholicism with a language and culture that seemed so deeply opposed to that of the larger American society."

9. When John F. Kennedy was a candidate for the office of President of the United States, he frequently had to defend himself and other Catholics from the charge that they were enemies of the principle of separation of church and state. But Irish Catholics in Ireland and America from the time of O'Connell have been leading champions of the separation between church and state. In the United States, the Irish more than any other Catholic group have insisted that Popes or domestic prelates could not curtail the expression of political, social or economic opinions of clerics or laymen. In the 1880s and 1890s, friends of the suspended then excommunicated Rev. Dr. Edward McGlynn of New York, advocate of the Land League and disciple of Henry George, insisted that Leo XIII and Archbishop Corrigan were attempting to deny the right of free speech to an American citizen. In defending Father McGlynn they quoted Daniel O'Connell's instruction to the Irish people: "As much religion as you like from Rome, but no politics!" (Stephen Bell, *Rebel, Priest and Prophet* (New York, 1937) 62 ff.)

111

Bibliography

Lawrence J. McCaffrey, *Daniel O'Connell and the Repeal Year* (Lexington: University of Kentucky Press, 1966) contains a section concerning the relations between O'Connell and Repealers in the United States. Thomas N. Brown's essay, "The Origins and Character of Irish-American Nationalism," *The Review of Politics* xviii (July, 1956) and his book *Irish-American Nationalism.* (New York: Lippincott 1966) provide the best insights into the personality of Irish-American nationalism. Brian Jenkins, *Fenians and Anglo-American Relations During Reconstruction* (Ithaca: Cornell University Press, 1969) and Alan J. Ward, *Ireland and Anglo-American Relations, 1899-1921* (Toronto University Press, 1969) are both excellent examinations of the influence of Irish-American nationalism and political power on relations between the United States and the United Kingdom. The influence of Romanization on Irish Catholicism are major themes in Emmet Larkin's essay "The Devotional Revolution in Ireland, 1850-1875," *The American Historical Review,* 77 (June, 1972) and Desmond Fennell (editor). *The Changing Face of Catholic Ireland* (London: Geoffrey Chapman, 1968). In "Catholicism and Irish Identity", *The Holy Cross Quarterly* vi, 1-4, Lawrence J. McCaffrey analyses the impact of Romanization on Irish American ethnic identity. Thomas N. Brown and Thomas T. McAvoy, *The United States of America [A History of Irish Catholicism,* Vol. vi, general editor, Patrick J. Corish (Dublin: Gill and MacMillan, 1970)] contains perceptive comments on the American colony of the Irish Catholic empire. Edward M. Levine. *The Irish and Irish Politicians* (Notre Dame: Notre Dame University Press, 1966) discusses the Chicago Irish machine as it operates under Mayor Richard J. Daley, the most successful of all Irish political bosses. Some of the best and most probing analyses of the Irish-American political style can be found in fiction including Joseph Dinneen, *Ward Eight* (New York: Harper, 1936); Edwin O'Connor, *The Last Hurrah* (Boston: Little, Brown, 1956); and Thomas I. Fleming, *All Good Men* (New York: Doubleday, 1961). Daniel Moynihan's essay "The Irish" in Nathan Glazier and Daniel P. Moynihan *Beyond the Melting Pot* (Cambridge: MIT Press, 1963) has become a popular interpretation of the Irish political style and influence, accepted by many scholars in American studies as gospel. Moynihan praised the ability of the Irish to achieve power but argued that they did not know what to do with it once in office. He claimed that their peasant Irish Catholic values made them a conservative and negative force in American urban affairs. This position was successfuly demolished by J. Joseph Huthmacher's essay "Urban Liberalism and the Age of Reform", *Mississippi Valley Historical Review,* xlix (September, 1962). Huthmacher offered evidence to show that the Catholic communalism of the Irish politicians made them champions of welfare state liberalism in contrast to Anglo-American Protestant advocacy of *laizzez faire* liberalism justified by Social Darwinism. Michael Novak, *The Rise of the Unmeltable Ethnics* (New York: MacMillan, 1971), defending Slavs and Italians, and Lawrence J. McCaffrey, "The Conservative Image of Irish-America," *Ethnicity,* 2 (autumn, 1975), a brief for the Irish, both attack the assumption that Catholic ethnics are a reactionary force in American life. Many Catholic intellectuals in the United States have argued that the dominant position of the Irish in American Catholicism has retarded the political and intellectual advance of Catholics in the United States, but J. Phillip Gleason in "Thanks to the Irish", *America,* May 14, 1966, offers convincing evidence that only the Irish leadership could have accommodated American Catholics to the principles of liberal democracy.

Chapter 9

The Image of O'Connell in Australia

Patrick O'Farrell

In 1855 Michael D'Arcy, editor ot the Sydney *Freeman's Journal* remarked:
"We had once the pleasure of hearing Daniel O'Connell say,—at a time
when New South Wales seemed hardly worthy of the honor of the
remark,—*that in it Irishmen would first begin to love the British
Constitution*—'they will' he said 'have English Law fairly administered.' "[1]

Although O'Connell's prediction was substantially accurate—the weight of
Irish experience in Australia confirms it—its realisation was neither immediate
nor total. A belligerently Irish minority, for which the *Freeman's Journal* was
the mouthpiece, believed that Irish Catholic rights and equality had to be
wrenched from a resistant Australian society, and D'Arcy's reference to
O'Connell in 1855 was in the context of a protest against anti-Irish prejudice
and discrimination, a contrasting of the reality with O'Connell's ideal. Herein
is encapsulated one of the several contradictions which lay at the core of
O'Connell's image in Australia, and which mark his influence on the Irish
Australian scene. O'Connell was taken to be the apostle of liberty and social
harmony under the British constitution, but the translation to Australia of his
aims—and particularly the attempted adoption of his political
methods—produced conflict and division. The dominance of O'Connell in
Irish politics in the 1830s and 40s, seen as the vigorous pursuit of reform
within the boundaries of loyalty to the English constitution, did much to
demarcate and confirm the thinking of the Irish in Australia at a formative
time in their developnent. Yet this stance, if oriented towards imperial unity,
produced an assertive Irish consciousness which appeared as disloyalty to its
critics and led to tensions and rifts within Australian society—and besides, the
attempt to follow closely the O'Connellite pattern of politics was unsuccessful,
because it was irrelevant in Australian conditions.

At the time of its passage, the Catholic Emancipation Act of 1829 had little
impact on the tiny settlement of New South Wales. The population was about

1. *Freeman's Journal* (Sydney), 7 July 1855.

O'Connell's image did not emerge as significant in Australia until local Irish Catholics gained a public voice in the *Australasian Chronicle*, founded in August 1839 by a group of Catholic laymen. Then he soon became both a symbol and cause of division, not merely of Irish Catholics from British Protestants, but of Catholics among themselves. Attitudes towards O'Connell and his causes had colonial implications, raising locally questions of social orientation and procedure on which Catholics were not agreed. At the same time it came to be seen that O'Connell's Irish activities raised questions generally relevant to local concerns in the 1840s when the political character of the colony was at stake—particularly questions of Catholic status and political power, and of liberal and democratic reform of a conservative and privileged order.

W. A. Duncan, the Scots-Catholic editor of the *Australasian Chronicle*, did not support O'Connell's campaign for repeal of the union with Britain. In April 1841 he made this clear, offending many Irishmen, including his co-proprietors of the *Chronicle*. In reproducing the London *Tablet's* case against repeal, Duncan claimed:

> ... repeal ... would be the greatest calamity that could befall the Catholics of the British colonies ... [it would] deprive the colonial Catholics of the influence of the Irish members of the imperial parliament ..." "[This] would entirely leave these Irishmen [in Australia] to the tender mercies of an English Tory parliament ... If there were no Irishmen in the British parliament, as a matter of course the English parsons would have a cabinet to their liking, and then our next 'New South Wales Bill' might 'establish by law' a certain Church corporation here, and endow it anew with one seventh of the territory.[7]

So convinced was Duncan of the threat repeal posed to Catholic interests—that of a return to Anglican dominance—that he campaigned to prevent a local repeal organisation being formed. He failed: a branch of O'Connell's Repeal Association was set up in Sydney towards the end of 1842. It was never large nor strong, nor were the amounts of money it transmitted to Ireland substantial. Indeed it seems likely that it was Duncan's public opposition to repeal, and subsequent efforts to thwart any expression of local support, that most encouraged what he wished to avoid. This paradox is implicit in the immediate response to his anti-repeal editorial. A correspondent ('Hibernicus') took Duncan to task for raising the issue: "it is not wise to agitate the question of repeal in this colony". Yet 'Hibernicus' felt obliged to contradict Duncan's conclusion: "As an Irishman I protest against my country being exposed to the deliberate injustice and blood-stained misrule of England. ..."[8] Duncan's rejection of repeal offered sufficient provocation to some local Irishmen to overcome their inclination to avoid public commitment to such a contentious cause. Duncan was probably correct in his opinion that

---

7. *Australasian Chronicle* 29 April, 4 May 1841. The *Australasian Chronicle* later changed its name to the *Morning Chronicle,* and later still to the *Sydney Chronicle.*
8. *A.C.,* 4 May 1841.

there were thousands of advocates of repeal in the colony, but it is also probable that this advocacy was private and merely sentimental until subjected to Duncan's challenge.

In fact, Duncan himself, on St Patrick's Day 1840, had assessed Irish nationalism in the colony as non-existent: "where shall we look on this 17th day of March for a proof that Irishmen have not forgot their country, save in the tavern and taproom?"[9] A St Patrick's Society was not formed until 1841, and its main purpose was to collect funds to build a church. At its first St Patrick's dinner the themes were loyalty, religiosity and respectability. The chairman, Father Francis Murphy, set the tone in proposing the first toast, to the Queen: "As Irishmen we owe her a special debt of gratitude, which we can never repay, for the kindness and justice with which she has treated a long-suffering and persecuted people (cheers)."[10] The Sydney *Herald* gave great offence by its comment that this dinner was not attended by gentlemen, but by some "respectable citizen-tradesmen". As to Daniel O'Connell, his was the last of a long list of toasts,—to the friend of the people, the advocate of the people's power.

Here, probably, was the reason why O'Connell had received scant attention. The leaders of the Irish Catholic group in the colony could not avoid some nationalist commitment, but they wished it to be muted, and they were certainly not advocates of the people's power. Though separated from the conservative forces in the colony by a social gulf, their economic and political thinking was similar—opposed to the forces of reforming democracy. Besides, these self-made prosperous men were products of pre-emancipation Ireland, and habituated to discretion. The aggressive, heady atmosphere of O'Connell's Ireland of the 1830s took considerable time to appear in Australia, for its surfacing entailed the displacement of old leaders by new, and its dispersion depended on the emergence of new immigrant forces not numerous until mid-century. In the 1840s Irish Catholic conservatism in the colony was sufficiently strong to dampen expressions of enthusiasm for O'Connell the democrat.

O'Connell the repealer was another matter. If O'Connell the democrat threatened their interests, O'Connell the repealer appealed to their identity and pride. Duncan's attack on repeal implied denigration of O'Connell, which was intolerable. Ultimately this, with other sources of conflict, lost Duncan the editorship of the *Chronicle*, and a great boost was given to the cult of O'Connell, who became the epitome of all virtues: "Ireland had never had such a friend since the days of her great apostle . . . she had never produced such a man before,"[11] Father Coffey told the 1842 St Patrick's Day dinner.

Early in 1843, Father John McEncroe moved into the editorship of the *Chronicle*. Stridently Irish, McEncroe lauded O'Connell in particular, as

9. *A.C.*, 17 March 1840.
10. *A.C.*, 18 March 1841.
11. *A.C.*, 19 March 1842.

exemplifying the close connections between religion and nationalism, and also between nationalism and the temperance crusade of Father Mathew: McEncroe was a vigorous advocate of total abstinence. At first he took the view that he should eschew comment on repeal, but, significantly, his reasoning was not that the issue was divisive, but that he could see "no practical utility in agitating at this great distance from the scene of action."[12] However, the trial and imprisonment of O'Connell in 1844 created a new situation which affronted the sensitivities of local Irishmen. By this time, the Loyal Australian Repeal Association was promoting repeal as a panacea to all Ireland's ills, and—revealing the strongly constitutional limitations on its radicalism—praising O'Connell's handling of the Clontarf situation as having "saved his country from being ensanguined with the blood of its loyal and peaceable inhabitants."[13] From an Australian Irish viewpoint O'Connell was the ideal Irish leader, a constitutional nationalist whose claims might find sympathetic echoes in Australia generally. This, and extreme colonial Irish touchiness to questions of status and loyalty led to great indignation when the news reached Sydney in June 1844 of the exclusion of Catholic jurors from the trials of O'Connell and his associates. Forty-six leading Irish Catholics requested the Mayor to convene a meeting to protest against the injustice and insult offered to the Roman Catholics of the Empire: it was the affront to principles of equal citizenship, not the fact of O'Connell's arrest, that stirred them. At the meeting, the first resolution was not one of indignation, but of affirmation by the Catholics of Sydney of loyalty to the throne. The issues of infringement of political rights, raised by the exclusion of Catholic jurors, were used to argue that protest ought not to be exclusively Catholic, but there is no doubt that the first concern of the organisers of the meeting—prosperous Irishmen, aspiring to respectibility—was to insist on Catholic Loyalty. And this certainly was being questioned. Some elements in the colonial press were describing O'Connell as a conspirator, and repeal as treasonable. Not all of this hostility was imported from Tory England. By 1843, repeal had a local implication in that the settlers of the Port Phillip (now Melbourne) district were seeking separation from New South Wales, a move resisted in Sydney. The Port Phillip campaign had something of an O'Connellite complexion, and generally O'Connell as the model for radical separatist democrats was highly distasteful to the New South Wales establishment. Its members were convinced that repeal would destroy the empire, and in consequence, their own position—a threat clearly enunciated by the new editor of the *Chronicle,* McEncroe's assertively Irish nephew Michael D'Arcy. He saw repeal as an instrument for social transformation, which "will emancipate, not only England but Australia, nay eventually perhaps the human race, from the remains of feudal and oligarchical oppression."[14] The New South Wales oligarchy did not relish such a prospect.

12. *A.C.,* 9 March 1843.
13. *Morning Chronicle,* 3 April 1844.

Nor did some Irish Catholics, and the fortunes of O'Connell in Ireland were soon to precipitate a split in the ranks of the local Irish. Upon news being received, in October 1844, of O'Connell's imprisonment, some Irish Catholics again requested the Mayor of Sydney to call a protest meeting. He refused. McEncroe then took the initiative, and a meeting to express sympathy was held. His action seems to have been taken in the wake of the collapse of lay efforts. Some Irish, apparently out of dissatisfaction with their usual leaders, refused to sign the petition to the Mayor, and when he refused to act on it, the petitioners themselves decided not to proceed with a meeting.

Factionalism and faint-heartedness were clearly revealed when news arrived of O'Connell's release. McEncroe advocated a celebratory public meeting, but urged that it be circumspect and inoffensive—devoid of "any spontaneous ebullition of Irish feeling"—lest it be "productive of unpleasant results." Archbishop Polding, preaching in St. Mary's Cathedral in thanksgiving for O'Connell's release praised his religiosity and pacific achievement, and attributed his release to the power of prayer. That being so "it would be in some sort profane to make it a subject of worldly rejoicing." The most prominent of the local Irish agreed with Polding's conclusion—that there should be no demonstration—but for less elevated reasons: for them the fierce sectarian conflict endemic since the late 1830s was the main deterrent. However, their leaders did not necessarily reflect what many Irishmen wanted. An Irishman in West Maitland lamented that no immediate celebration was held there, simply because there was no one to organise it. Eventually a kind of spontaneous demonstration formed around a large bonfire. Those assembled gave nine cheers for O'Connell and repeal, but not before they had acknowledged their British colonial priorities with cheers—if only three—for the Queen.

And in Sydney a meeting was held, revealing a split between respectable conservative Irish elements and the Irish working class. This split had first appeared on St Patrick's Day in 1843, when there were two simultaneous dinners, one attended by those at the top of the Irish Australian social pyramid, the other by those less well placed, At that time the division did not attract public comment, but in January 1845 Dr D. J. Tierney openly disassociated himself from the O'Connell meeting. He declared that "the most dignified as well as most staunch and unchanging friends of Ireland and O'Connell, as well as the most dignified by station" regarded such a meeting as inexpedient, and he would not lend himslf "to a manoeuvre and an evident design to split and thus weaken the friends of Ireland. . ."[15]

An estimated 3,000, mostly labouring men, attended the meeting. Speakers stressed the themes usual in apologias for O'Connell—his avoidance of bloodshed, his mustering of moral power—but they were very conscious of the

14. *M.C.*, 15 January 1845.
15. *Ibid.*

social composition and local preoccupations of their audience. Mr Curtayne assured the meeting that "though he was not able to distinguish among them the élite or the 'dignified in station' . . . he was able to distinguish what was of more consequence, the men whose brawny arms by their industry upheld the state (cheers). Such men were always leagued on the side of justice; it was by such men that the reforms in the political institutions in their country had been effected."[16] Other speakers characterised O'Connell as "the man . . . to whom the poor looked for protection." Others emphasised Australian applications: O'Connell was "the friend of every community which was struggling for its rights and liberties and therefore a friend of this community." There was even a dash of anti-clericalism, in which church interests were blamed for Irish divisions. The only unpopular speaker was one who tried to excuse British policy in Ireland, a usual feature in earlier gatherings.

This meeting was a fleeting revelation of the temper of the Irish-Australian proletariat, concerned with local issues and its own grievances, critical of its established leaders, lay and clerical. Those leaders were anxious to avoid such manifestations in the future, and thereafter it was the image of O'Connell the champion of Catholicism, not O'Connell the poor man's friend, that was dominant in the Australian Irish scene. Besides, by this time attention was shifting away from O'Connell towards famine relief, an area where the clergy could provide church structures to organise collections, a development which helped to confirm their central position in the direction of Irish Australian affairs.

When news of O'Connell's death reached Australia in September 1847, it was the clergy who took the initiative in arranging tributes: all took the form of solemn high requiem masses, plus meetings organised and chaired by leading clergy. In the *Chronicle* a correspondent lamented that he had been expecting influential Sydney Catholics to promote a public meeting to express sympathy, but this had not happened: "O'Connell . . . wrung from the hands of your tyrants those political rights that were so unjustly withheld from you,"[17] he admonished his ungrateful fellow countrymen. How many of them understood? The catafalque used in the requiem mass in Sydney gave rise to curious speculation. Some believed that a French corvette then in port had brought O'Connell's body to enable his colonial admirers to 'wake' him. A woman who believed the catafalque contained O'Connell's remains went about enquiring where he was to be buried, so she might attend.

Predictably, being clerically organised, the Melbourne and Sydney meetings had a strong religious orientation.That in Sydney amounted to a temperance gathering. Laymen, notably the future premier, John O'Shanassy, were more prominent in the Melbourne tributes. There it was resolved that the crape of mourning be worn for three months, no small token of homage in a community where, as one of the speakers remarked, many regarded O'Connell as a

16. *M.C.*, 22 January 1845.
17. *Sydney Chronicle*, 7 October 1847.

turbulent demagogue. A verse tribute of the time promised:

"And even in lands he never hath beheld,
Thy scattered children to his name shall rear
Monuments high as Egypt's Pyramids . . . ."[18]

Efforts to fund a memorial do not appear to have been made until 1863, when they met a poor response. Wealthy Catholics would not participate, and subscriptions were neither numerous nor large.

However, O'Connell's influence in Australia was far more pervasive and important than the explicit acknowledgement of his name might suggest. In the Australian colonies from the 1840s to the 1860s the most aggressive Irish Catholics modelled their politics on O'Connell's—without success, and to the great encouragement of sectarian conflict. O'Connell himself appears to have appreciated the essential differences between the colonial situation and the Irish—the absence of an entrenched ascendancy, an established church, and of a historical national question: he seems to have regarded the system of British government, without these hindrances, as naturally productive of civil and religious freedom. But in the first colonial elections of 1843, the most vocal and assertive Irish Catholics encountered situations of sectarian resistance and of division in the Catholic vote which led them to adopt an O'Connellite stance. The Sydney *Freeman's Journal,* founded by Archdeacon McEncroe in 1850, insisted that the O'Connell model of disciplined Irish Catholic unity, allied with the forces of religion, pursuing a policy of aggressive confrontation of any opposition, was the only appropriate political exemplar for Irish Catholics in Australia. O'Connell's approach had been devised for Irish conditions and had achieved success there. It amounted to blending belligerent appeals to religion and nationalism so as to create a mass popular voting unity for the purpose of remedying the grievances of a Catholic majority. Its every basis was at variance with the realities of Australia. The Catholics were a minority (about a quarter) not a majority, most of them had no serious practical grievances, and such as they did have were not specifically Catholic; the political concerns of the colony bore little relationship to those of Ireland; substantial freedom and equality existed, opportunities abounded, and local issues dominated politics; Catholics of Australian birth did not react to Irish stimuli, and well-to-do Irish Catholics acted in conformity with their economic interests.

Political realities continually contradicted the O'Connellite ideologies. From the 1843 elections onwards, colonial Catholics refused to conform to the imported Irish model. Their voting could not be directed by either clergy or nationalists: they reacted to local issues and personalities, prompted by the ordinary range of political considerations. The Catholic vote was never united, always split. Yet the self-appointed spokesmen of Irish Catholics, through the *Freeman's Journal,* continued to insist that this must cease, that the proper

18. *S.C.,* 30 September 1847.

way for Catholics to act was in unison, apart from the rest of the community and against it, so that the serfdom of Ireland would not be duplicated in New South Wales. Such diatribes confirmed, among non-Catholics, a repellent image of Catholicism as selfish, obsessive, and perversely at odds with the rest of society. Irish Catholics in Australia in the 1860s still gave the appearance of acting out a role of reaction to persecution appropriate to the Ireland of O'Connell, and some were in fact still doing just that, so influential had been the example of his political style.

The adoption of an O'Connellite stance was, however, not entirely self-generated. It was encouraged by sectarian hostility and colonial attacks on O'Connell and his policies. Many English and Scots Australians regarded O'Connell as the symbol and expression of political priestcraft and mob power. The most outspoken enemy of Irish Catholicism in the 1840s was the Presbyterian minister John Dunmore Lang. Lang, consistent with his democratic principles, favoured repeal, but he interpreted the O'Connellite movement as confirming the proposition that "Roman Catholics . . . are always a compact and distinct political party whenever they come into contact with Protestants."[19] This characteristic was of great menace to Australia, given his parallel proposition that Protestants would always be divided politically and thus open to Catholic political dominance. In 1847 Lang made clear that he regarded O'Connell as operating a Roman Catholic dictatorship in Ireland, and that he believed that this was threatened in Australia. In the sectarian circumstances of that time, nothing was more likely to encourage assertive Irish Catholics to embrace O'Connellism than Lang's fear of it.

Important though O'Connell's influence was on the formation of the character of Irish Catholic politics in Australia, those politics soon took on their own local momentum. However, the legacy of O'Connell had a particular bearing on one development in Victorian politics. In 1858, Charles Gavan Duffy became a member of John O'Shanassy's ministry in Victoria's first parliament. The two Irishmen soon fell out, not least because O'Shanassy, a devout O'Connellite, distrusted Duffy the Young Irelander: O'Shanassy believed until his dying day the O'Connellite story that Duffy had been an informer in 1848, and the conflict between the two men had a deleterious effect on the Irish Catholic political interest in Victoria.

Preparations for the celebration in Australia of the O'Connell centenary in 1875 had the same air of caution and initial reluctance that had marked those earlier meetings when O'Connell was alive. The centenary came at an unpropitious time, facing Irish Catholics with that nice choice between being shamed into celebrations or being shamed out of them. In March 1868 an Irishman had attempted the assassination of Prince Alfred, Duke of Edinburgh, in Sydney, unleashing a fierce anti-Irish sectarian reaction. The Catholic Church and the various Australian states were in conflict over the

19. John Dunmore Lang. *The Question of Questions or, Is this Colony to be transformed into a Province of the Popedom* (Sydney 1841), p. 16. See also John Dunmore Lang. *Popery in Australia . . . and How to Check it Effectually,* (Edinburgh 1847), p. 24.

issue of denominational education. In Victoria, the brief premiership of Charles Gavan Duffy in 1871 had heightened sectarian feelings. So adverse was the colonial atmosphere that in Brisbane the initial meeting to arrange an O'Connell Centenary celebration passed an amendment not to proceed: "That it is inexpedient in this dependency, the nation cherishing the memory of many of its illustrious sons, to single out for honour by a public demonstration, one whose fame principally rests on services rendered in particular to the Church in Ireland."[20] The terms of this amendment are revealing. They show that O'Connell's image had been transformed, under clerical patronage, into something narrowly Catholic and Irish, and that an Australian element among Catholics was unwilling to have O'Connell foisted on them as a hero. A Brisbane celebration was in fact held, at which the main speakers were the 1848 transportee, Kevin Izod O'Doherty, and Bishop James Quinn, but O'Doherty took pains to conciliate those opposed to the celebration on other than sectarian grounds; that is, "those sons and daughters of Australia who consider that their National sentiment is, as it were, slighted by demonstrations of this kind, believing that they sow the seeds of dissension in our young community. They are jealous of their Australian dignity, which they consider compromised by celebration of men and events which have no direct connection with their native land."[21] However, Bishop Quinn's enthusiasm was such that he "took back his respected ancestral name" adding thereafter an 'O' to his surname. For O'Quinn, O'Connell's principles were sanctified, for he had possessed the confidence of the Irish hierarchy.

Both in Sydney and Melbourne, strenuous efforts were made by the organisers to avoid alienating the general community or dividing Catholics. In Sydney, the English Benedictine Coadjutor Archbishop, Roger Vaughan, was invited to give the celebratory oration, although the organisers might have chosen any one of the several Irish bishops appointed to New South Wales dioceses since 1865. Their choice of the English Vaughan reflected their wish, just as strong in other Australian colonies, to put forward O'Connell not merely as an Irish nationalist, but as a benefactor of mankind—which is precisely what Vaughan did. His treatment of O'Connell's gifts—those of fusing loyalty with liberty—and of England's relationship with Ireland—the inclination to grant freedom and fair play flawed and frustrated by occasional tyrants and bigots—struck just the balance sought by most Irish Australians. And Vaughan emphasised O'Connell's non-Irish concerns—electoral and parliamentary reform, free trade, the emancipation of Jews, anti-slavery, the rights of man generally. O'Shanassy in Melbourne, Sir George Kingston in Adelaide, and speakers in Perth, placed similar stress on O'Connell's services to human freedom.

The celebrations were not a success. Most of the speakers at the celebrations throughout Australia had either known O'Connell personally, or had, at least, attended his meetings in their youth. The audiences were

20. *F.J.*, 31 July 1875.
21. *O'Connell Centenary Record 1875* (Dublin, 1878), p. 598.

something of the same complexion. When J. G. O'Connor rose to speak at the Sydney commemoration, he remarked that "he was sorry to see so few persons around him who could claim Australia as the land of their birth." W. H. Cooper, the Australian who rose to respond to O'Connor, made a passionate plea for Australian nationalism which implicitly rejected such celebrations as divisive:

> There was too much faction in this country. There was no pure national sentiment. There was no general instinct of patriotism giving vigour to the national heart . . . the capture of Limerick was made a red letter day, but the date of Cook's landing had slipped out of the calendar . . . we had no O'Connell here to oppose his divine eloquence and dauntless heart against the wiles of schismatics among us, and therefore it the more behoved every man who wished this country to rise to the status of a great nation to aid in the destruction of these factions. . . .[22]

The reaction of Catholics to the celebrations was not markedly different from that of the general community—a few in cautious praise, some in condemnation, most apathetic. In Sydney the proceeds from the celebrations were to be devoted to a scholarship at St John's College of the University of Sydney. £1,500 was required; only £440 was raised. In Melbourne, O'Connell was to have a statue, costing £3,000. That project also fell short of target, though the statue was eventually erected in 1891, not, as was hoped, in some commanding public place, but in the grounds of St Patrick's Catholic Cathedral: the situation symbolised the firm location of O'Connell's image within the official Catholic fold. The celebrations also revealed the great distance in understanding and divergence in temper that separated the Irish in Australia from their homeland. The Irish in Victoria had deputed Charles Gavan Duffy to represent them at the Dublin celebrations, but an audience hostile to Duffy because of his conflicts with O'Connell refused to allow him to be heard. This was painful and bewildering to the colonial Irish. During his Australian career, Duffy had become 'the O'Connell of the South': the divisions, distinctions, and enmities of internal Irish politics had become, to most Irish in the antipodes, both incomprehensible and repellent. In Australia, sentiment, inclination—and ignorance—tended to render all Ireland's heroes equal, though somehow the stature of O'Connell was to remain the measure for them all.

22. *F.J.*, 14 August 1875.

Select Bibliography

The basic sources are the newspapers, the *Australian Chronicle* 1839–47, and *Freeman's Journal* 1850 on. On the period, and relevant themes, see James Waldersee *Catholic Society in New South Wales 1788-1860* Sydney 1974; T. L. Suttor *Hierarchy and Democracy in Australia 1788-1870* Melbourne 1965; and P. O'Farrell *The Catholic Church in Australia. A Short History 1788-1967* Melbourne 1968. For Roger Therry see R. Therry Esq. *Reminiscences of Thirty Years' Residence in New South Wales and Victoria* London 1863; for Plunkett, see John N. Molony *An Architect of Freedom. John Hubert Plunkett in New South Wales 1832-1869* Canberra 1973; for Governor Bourke see Hazel King *Richard Bourke* Melbourne 1971; for W. A. Duncan's editorship of the *Chronicle* see J. O'Brien "W. A. Duncan, the 'Irish Question', and the N.S.W. Elections of 1843" *Journal of the Australian Catholic Historical Society* Vol. 4 Part 1, 1972; for O'Shanassy and Gavan Duffy, see Geoffrey Serle *The Golden Age. A History of the Colony of Victoria 1851-1861* Melbourne 1963.

Chapter 10

O'Connell and Rome

R. Dudley Edwards

The Kingdom of Great Britain before the Union with Ireland

Daniel O'Connell was born a subject of George III whose style proclamed him King of Great Britain, France and Ireland. The English rulers of the House of Hanover ruled a Protestant state in which Scotland by the Act of Union of 1707 had been linked under one Parliament in the Kingdom of Great Britain with a Protestant constitution, applying also to their Kingdom of Ireland. The nominal claim to France was an inheritance going back to Edward III which was not rationalised until after the legislative union of 1800 established the United Kingdom of Great Britain and Ireland. This union of Scotland, England and Ireland represented the Hanoverian Protestant rulers by contrast with the Catholic Stuarts who had been displaced at the end of the seventeenth century and who had maintained their three kingdoms separately, being advised by separate parliaments. In matters of religion, the revolution of 1689 had inaugurated a variation in the Protestant constitution between Scotland and England. In England the Established Church was Anglican and episcopalian. In Scotland it was presbyterian. Under the Act of Union of 1800, the Established Church in Ireland continued to be the Protestant episcopalian Church linked to the Church of England. In Ireland the majority, however, continued to be Roman Catholic, excluded from full citizenship, the privileges of which were confined to members of the Established Church. The unprivileged, of course, included the Presbyterians who constituted the overwhelming element among the non-episcopalian Protestants, usually described as dissenters, or non-conformists who predominated in the north of Ireland. The Irish Catholics, like those of England and Scotland, had maintained association with the Holy See in Rome which until 1776 had recognised the exiled Stuart Kings James II and James III. It was largely under Stuart aegis that Irish Catholics had maintained political significance in exile in the employment of European sovereigns, before all was changed by the French Revolution. Their employment at home was obstructed by the obligation to take oaths denying the papal jurisdiction and the claims of the exiled Catholic sovereigns. While the papacy after 1766 became reconciled to recognising the Protestant rulers of the British Isles, the limits diplomatically to this policy were set by British statutes which denied the temporal as well as the spiritual powers of the papacy and would have made it high treason to attempt to alter this state of affairs.

Archbishop Troy and the Union

John Thomas Troy, a member of the Dominican Order, with considerable experience of the Church's central organisation at Rome, had been Bishop of Ossory before becoming Archbishop of Dublin in the 1780s. Troy, a Dubliner, had no pretentions to the social *mores* of the upper class among whom the Catholics constituted a small minority. In a metropolitan centre, he was concerned with the problems of a Church which was emerging, with the passage in the 1770s and early 1780s of acts giving immunity from the penal laws against Roman Catholics, into a position of connivance with the State. These relief acts made it necessary for individual Catholics, clerical or lay, to subscribe to a new oath of allegiance to George III and the Protestant succession. From the standpoint of the Dublin archbishop, the situation was a delicate one as the papacy regarded with distaste the formulae of allegiance sanctioned by the Hanoverian government. A tradition of petitioning the King since George II's time had existed among leading Catholic gentry anxious to testify to their loyalty. With this some of the bishops had been associated, externally, until the necessity of securing immunity from the penal laws became urgent. There was also the question of clerical influence on the somewhat democratically-minded Catholic Committee which maintained personal links with the parliamentary reform movement in Ireland. Troy became of greater importance with the Dublin administration after the reform movement became involved with the United Irishmen and with French intrigue leading to the rebellion of 1798. It was largely due to Troy that it was possible to maintain evidence of non-complicity in the rebellion by the leading Catholic Church authorities in Ireland. Thereafter, when the government decided on the legislative union largely to organise against the much feared Napoleonic France, Troy and the trustees of Maynooth were concerned to secure Catholic emancipation as part of the union plan. While this had miscarried, other aspects such as the pensioning of the clergy and the concession of a papal veto remained part of the policy favoured by Dublin Castle. The refusal however of the government to persist in implementing the arrangement is understandable, since the weak-minded George III became obsessed with the belief that it would be a violation of his coronation oath to admit to a Protestant legislature Roman Catholics whose doctrines, to him, were traitorous. The government had to give up the plan for Catholic emancipation.

In a world in which the American and French Revolutions had sparked off the greatest challenge to the beliefs of the Christian kingdoms of the *ancien régime*, it was essential to establish alliances with every political force likely to put restrictions on the atheistic principles emanating from France. It was for this that the Irish Catholic hierarchy had joined with the government in the establishment by a statute of the Irish parliament of the Royal College of St Patrick at Maynooth in 1795. It was for this that Archbishop Troy and other bishops had consented to a plan of endowing the Catholic Church by the State in return for which the concession by the papacy of a veto over episcopal appointments was an elementary precaution to exclude potential revolutionaries from the government of the Church in Ireland. Protestant susceptibilities, from the King down, made it impossible to carry through such a policy for a generation after the Union. There is little doubt however that the veto would have been conceded as part of a political deal for Catholic emancipation within the first years after 1800. Almost inevitably, the failure to implement emancipation with the Union created a new situation in which other Irish Catholic interests emerged. In these Daniel O'Connell was prominent. These new interests were to change the relations of the Holy See, the English and Irish Catholics, lay and clerical, in the immediately succeeding years.

Failure to Emancipate: The Veto

In the ethos of the eighteenth century the rise of the middle classes presented a challenge to the British representative system. Even before the outbreak of the American War of Independence, the monopoly of political power by a few landed families combined with commercial interests and the middle class challenge expressed itself in the Yorkshire movement in the 1760s, though this was ultimately unsuccessful in its immediate objects. Before parliamentary reform became contaminated by French revolutionary ideals, some Irish Catholics had developed an interest in it though these were only a section of the emerging Irish. After the Union, Catholic elements favourable to government recollected that any concessions had been due to ministerial favour but the failure to secure emancipation weakened this view which gave way increasingly before a more vocal lay party not necessarily committed to the Crown as opposed to parliamentary forces. Thus the question of emancipation came to be a factor in the formation of administrations after 1800. The question of the veto was linked to this as a means for evolving a security for the Protestant Constitution on what was regarded as a necessary compromise to satisfy Protestant anxieties over old fears of papal interference. It was to be on the veto that the policy advocated by Troy and other Irish bishops was altered substantially so that it was possible for O'Connell to describe himself as a Catholic but not a papist, until Rome was prepared to alter its attitude regarding matters of moment to the Irish Catholics. This change came about largely through the influence of O'Connell.

The English Catholics, The Stuarts and The Revolution

Among the various differing elements in the small Catholic community in England, the problem of allegiance had been a divisive one throughout the eighteenth century. Loyalty to the Holy See became less embarrassing after the abandonment of the Stuarts by the Catholic powers in 1766. The influence of France as well as of Anglican ideas maintained an almost gallican attitude to Catholic concepts of Church freedom. As in France many favoured a national approach to ecclesiastical questions which led to some degree of variance with those who favoured a greater degree of centralisation in Church affairs. The experiences of state discrimination against Roman Catholicism maintained an uneasy peace among these elements until there emerged the more tolerant atmosphere of the Enlightenment in which lay Catholic views found themselves opposed by what came to be known as the ultramontane standpoint of the upholders of a more absolute papal authority. With the outbreak of the French Revolution English and Irish refugee elements favouring the *ancien régime* reinforced the cisalpine group, as the English who favoured some state control over Catholic activities came to be called. The strength of this element was far greater than might appear in the controversial differences which were publicised as the papacy itself became allied with the opponents of the French Revolution. The position of the papacy might appear to be complicated as it continued to accord privileges, if not royal recognition, to the last of the Stuarts, Charles III and Henry IX, the latter being a Cardinal of the Church, also claiming to be Duke of York. From the death of the latter however in 1809, the papacy became more prepared to recognise its indebtedness to the British Hanoverian rulers whose diplomatic representatives established links with Catholic Austria and materially protected papal claims to the restoration of its temporal states after Waterloo. The papacy thus, while unfavourable to English gallicanism, was not without reason to favour a political understanding with England which could have led to the concession of the veto, if Protestant susceptibilities could stomach this.

Irish Catholic Traditions Divided

Since the sixteenth century the exiles in Europe had looked back in rancour at the planter class who displaced them at home and who, since Cromwell, had been overwhelmingly associated with Protestantism. They regarded the assertions of independence of English parliamentary authority in the days of Molyneux, of Swift, of Flood and of Grattan, with indifference amounting to contempt. The O'Connells at home in correspondence with their relatives in the army and in the Church on the continent shared these feelings, as did a substantial element among the higher clergy and the gentry. The Catholic Committee in Dublin which since the last days of George II had been sponsoring relief petitions to the Crown was largely dominated by this attitude by contrast to a more democratically-minded mercantile element in the towns who favoured an approach to parliament rather than to the King. On this question the division was very marked, O'Connell finding himself on the side of the democrats, despite the degree of pressure upon him against this by his uncle Maurice, known as Hunting Cap, his adopted father. It was to be O'Connell's main function to bring the Irish Catholic body together in a parliamentary activity which had the most decisive effect on the future relations of the Irish nation with the Holy See, which brought about emancipation and created future political problems not always correctly attributed to O'Connell.

O'Connell Unifies Irish Catholics on Parliamentary Plans

After the Union, the condition of the King's health made him increasingly liable to mental illness. The role of George, Prince of Wales, as Regent for his father in these circumstances made it difficult to maintain exclusively a policy of petitioning the sovereign. O'Connell was not the first to favour an association with the Whigs in parliament who were agreeable to sponsoring petitions against the King's Tory Government's continued resistance to Catholic emancipation. He was, however, more successful than John Keogh and earlier personalities of the Catholic Committee in imposing the viewpoint of the more democratic laity on the bishops and the gentry which ultimately culminated in their acceptance of the policy of parliamentary petitioning. The issue, however, was at first complicated by the revival of the question of a royal veto on papal appointments within the United Kingdom. Protestant parliamentarians almost inevitably came to be influenced by English ideas that papal influence on the Catholics could be subordinated to state control as a guarantee for those who feared any Roman threat to Protestant liberties.

O'Connell Defeats English and Roman Vetoists

When Napoleon made the Pope a prisoner, a decision favouring the veto seemed likely to emerge from Rome, where Monsignor Quarantotti acting for the Pope gave qualified approval to the idea of the veto as part of a proposed plan for Catholic emancipation. O'Connell's attitude was that the veto would convert the secular clergy into government lackeys in the eyes of the people, who would distrust them as they had distrusted the Crown nominees in the sixteenth century. The result, said O'Connell, would inevitably be that from the continent hordes of friars would come into Ireland and gain the confidence of the people as they had done in the worst crisis of the penal laws when hardly a bishop remained in the country. O'Connell's view weakened the favour for the veto of ecclesiastics like Troy who ultimately gave way to the increasing feeling among the younger clergy that government patronage might prove a disaster. The vetoists however had a potential strength in their opposite numbers among the English Catholics and in the fact that Roman influences appeared to be increasingly dominated by favour for the English government. In England, of course, there was not that political objection to the veto which affected the more nationally-minded Irish Catholics. O'Connell successfully organised a resistance to the veto until an anti-veto element became vocal among the English clergy. Even a papal expression of favour towards the veto after the end of the Napoleonic regime had only the result of leading O'Connell to express himself as distinguishing between papal rights in matters of theology and political questions such as the veto which, O'Connell argued, should be settled by the people and not by the Pope. O'Connell's action in this matter virtually terminated the phase in which the English Catholics regarded themselves as competent to speak for the Church in Ireland as well as in Britain. Thus began the acceptance at Rome of a situation in which Church affairs in Ireland came to be regarded as primarily the concern of the Irish clergy and people though Rome, of course, would continue its diplomatic expertise in considering such matters in a British context.

O'Connell's National Movement wins Emancipation

With the establishment of the Catholic Association in 1823 O'Connell developed a technique which brought an extra-parliamentary dimension into the struggle for emancipation. In the course of these years, O'Connell realised that the clergy were potentially a most powerful group in organising a nation-wide movement. Only gradually was it possible for him to secure mutual confidence between what was essentially a popular parliamentary movement and the clergy who necessarily regarded all political matters from a more narrow standpoint. The victory over the vetoists was not achieved without accentuating the common issues for clergy and people, often exposed to local Protestant resentment if not rancour. Not all the clergy were prepared to go with O'Connell in building up a political machine against the Protestant ascendancy. After 1815, the problem of poverty was increasingly a matter of concern in Ireland, which to a large extent was only on the perimeter of the industrial revolution that had brought wealth to so many English manufacturing towns, particularly in the north. It can even be argued that O'Connell did not understand the economic issues which so much concerned J. K. L., James Warren Doyle, Bishop of Kildare and Leighlin, who felt that such issues took priority over everything else while O'Connell was increasingly putting his trust in forging the political weapon through which he was to intimidate successive English governments for over two decades. Percipiently, O'Connell realised that J. K. L.'s support was of outstanding value as an intellectual influence among the bishops. In his efforts to organise the Association as an effective political weapon, O'Connell increasingly stressed the potential mundane advantages for the clergy which emancipation, he argued, could bring about. J. K. L. had been content to give a low priority to the temporal needs of the clergy. O'Connell gave them a higher priority. Perhaps he felt he could only thus secure them in the fight with the landlords who dominated politics and took their views from the Protestant government virtually indifferent to emancipation. The defeat of the existing vested interests in the Irish counties was brought about when the clergy backed O'Connell's candidates for elections. Notably so was this apparent when O'Connell presented himself as candidate, successfully, at the Clare election in 1828; thereafter any English government had to face the fact that a new political

Dan and his Regulars.

machine existed in Ireland capable of dominating most of the county elections. It was this machine which made Catholic emancipation urgently in need of a solution in 1829. It was the priests who were O'Connell's main allies in this achievement and it revived among British and Irish Protestants that fear of Rome which had been such an obsession from Henry VIII to William of Orange. As in the past, mutual hatreds of Anglicans and Presbyterians were laid aside to build up in Ireland, under the influence of Henry Cooke, a Protestant resistance to O'Connellism presented to gullible supporters as the latest manifestation of the dreaded Roman influence. O'Connell, however, often a wishful thinker, totally underestimated this opposition which he saw himself defeating as he defeated the opponents of emancipation in 1829. He still regarded his national movement as essential for the implementation of emancipation, though he did not necessarily realise that this would involve him more and more in establishing close links, not merely with the clergy, but with the Holy See. At the moment of time when he turned to repeal of the Union to place the national movement on a non-denominational basis, he would seem to have thought that in the Church too there could be political devolution which would accord self-government in Church matters of a domestic nature to the Irish bishops. Circumstances were to come about in which however O'Connell would have to bring in Rome to secure his control over the Irish clergy, tempted by an English government offer of patronage if they would abandon O'Connell. Had he not been successful, O'Connell might have been followed by a much more anglicised political group, but it is important to remember that such speculations diminished substantially in value in the aftermath of the Great Famine.

English Post Emancipation intrigues at Rome

The Irish hierarchy's public expression of gratitude for emancipation to the greatest living Irishman, the Duke of Wellington, was not lost on O'Connell. To the ordinary Irish Catholic he was now the Liberator, but the hierarchy did not appear to see him in the role of political saviour any longer. They would revert to the eighteenth century policy of putting their trust in the King's government. So perhaps O'Connellism would have come to an end.

The insular mentality which dominated so many unimaginative British politicians did not comprehend more experienced and sophisticated statesmen with foreign experiences and contacts such as Wellington who, like Castlereagh in the past, had not been afraid of advancing English interests through Roman goodwill. Castlereagh's intervention to save the Papal States for the Pope made possible an indirect British influence on papal appointments to Irish bishoprics. Probably the first name on the hierarchical expression of gratitude to Wellington, that of Primate Patrick Curtis, owed its position at Armagh to a frendship which had originated with Wellington during the Peninsular War when Curtis was Rector at Salamanca. In the years after 1829 it became increasingly evident that even if the veto had been abandoned publicly, the papacy was privately prepared to promote government nominees. This inevitably provided O'Connell with a growing clerical following when, in pursuance of his avowed policy of implementing emancipation, he denounced these government intrigues which accompanied the maintenance in office in Ireland of Protestant administrators, determined to make emancipation for most purposes a dead letter. Thus the repeal movement was initiated in Ireland on a national basis still dominated by a self-orientated clericity and laity.

O'Connell's 'Weapon' and Cooke: Repeal

The attitude of O'Connell towards the clergy, from the first successes at the county elections of the Members of Parliament supported by the Catholic Association, could lead to the conclusion that the Liberator, who was above all a political manipulator, regarded them as the decisive weapon in destroying the landlord monopoly of the county constituencies. To others they would appear to dominate the Liberator, the sinister force once again involved in a determined conflict to destroy Protestantism. Henry Cooke's career was in large part consecrated to this idea.

While Anglicanism in England varies considerably between the extremes to be found in its High Church and its Low Church followers, the experience usually met in its Irish sister Church, the Church of Ireland, has rarely demonstrated any of the catholicity of the High Church. Low Church, which had since the days of William of Orange become more positively embodied in the structure of the Protestant establishment, was particularly strong in Ireland, where it helped to maintain the confrontation between the 'saints' and the 'popish idolators'. In the eighteenth century, the intellectual element among the Presbyterians which subsequently emerged, after 1828, as the non-subscribing Presbyterian Church, had on the whole been detached from the Low Church abhorrence of popery. This may in part have been due to the naive rational belief that Catholicism and the Pope would not survive the Enlightenment. After the legislative Union, the Presbyterians, eschewing their intellectuals, had placed their confidence in loyal, reliable and rigid ministers, who accepted an increased royal endowment, the *regium donum*. This prepared the way for a future understanding among all Irish Protestants increasingly aware of the growing popish menace. The middle-class Presbyterians achieved their political ambition for emancipation in the year before the Catholics and having thereafter far fewer resentments towards the episcopalian clergy, found themselves readily drawn towards one another in the evangelical revival which had flowered not merely in Ireland in the decade after Waterloo. This emotional movement was to be found particularly among the younger clergy and notably among the divinity students of Trinity College, Dublin. The success of some of these in starting soon after emancipation the *Dublin University Magazine* is an illustration of this and of the extent of their obsession with popery in Ireland. In the political sphere, the success of Cooke in 1828 in reimposing on Presbyterians the obligation to subscribe to the Westminster Confession of Faith was a prelude to a close alliance of all Protestants, episcopalians and presbyterians in particular, in the holding of evangelical functions. North and South, Protestant landlords and tenantry, parsons and ministers combined in fervent meetings to bring about the new reformation which too often ended in no more than the denunciation of popery and the organisation of resistance to plans for equality among all denominations to implement the recently enacted statutes. Thus pious beliefs that emancipation would automatically operate were quickly frustrated and thus too O'Connell's intentions to include Protestants extensively in a repeal movement were frustrated, and O'Connell felt himself driven back to his old weapon in maintaining a national movement attempting to restrict foreign influences.

Throughout the later part of O'Connell's career, he exploited a great capacity to proceed simultaneously on two political lines which often converged into one. Thus, at the end of George III's reign on the defeat of emancipation, he directed his forces in the cause of parliamentary reform. Similarly, on the failure of his repeal gesture to the Protestants, the national movement took up the cause of parliamentary reform which it brought to a successful conclusion in 1832. Thus O'Connell turned away from the policy of the Irish hierarchy in putting their trust in the Wellington administration and in doing so brought back into his own hands the control of the laity in the Irish Catholic movement. Inevitably, of course, he found himself pressurised by the hierarchy, particularly after 1830 when the new French Revolution appeared to be remarkably anti-clerical. O'Connell's movement was described as liberal and, increasingly, because of liberalism's anti-Catholic connotations, O'Connellism was more and more obliged to express itself so as to secure clerical approval.

O'Connell's Constitutionalism Qualified by Catholicism

Repeal could be represented as a revolutionary policy, concerned to overturn the government by setting up an independent Irish state, not unlike the revolutionary efforts in the Europe of the 1830s. Certainly, English conservative politicians were highly suspicious and so it was not easy to organise a constitutional repeal body. Even the Irish bishops had theological doubts about the morality of any movement going beyond 'justice for Ireland'. Thus O'Connell found himself increasingly accepting justice for Ireland as his policy. Thus reform rather than repeal came to be the cause he emphasised. As, however, the parliamentary machine depended on the allies that had helped to destroy the landlords, the clergy continued to dominate O'Connell's expressions of opinion. O'Connell's constitutionalism, therefore, continued to be qualified by Catholic political demands. There were times when the movement appeared to lead the Liberator and at no time as positively as

The Irish Agitator tossed by the Papal Bull.

Great Gun — 15 Feb. 1845

during the anti-tithe phase when O'Connell himself was at great pains to keep within the law and said little publicly favouring protestors against the iniquitous tithes. While Presbyterians, like Catholics, resented the tithes the main outbreaks in what came to be called the tithe war were in the more predominantly Catholic parts of the country. The final compromise which terminated tithe collection by substituting a rent charge virtually marked the last common grievance of Catholics and Dissenters against the episcopalian clergy. But the continued identification of the Catholic clergy with O'Connell's political movement accentuated Presbyterian suspicions and reduced perceptibly the participation of Protestants in repeal. If justice for Ireland could only be secured in the views of many Catholics through repeal, it was an achievement which O'Connell's political machine secured at the expense of the loss of confidence from the Protestants, but for a minute handful.

O'Connell's Repeal Attitude towards Rome

The consequences of English diplomatic intrigues at Rome, which necessarily had to be pursued indirectly through ambassadors accredited elsewhere and through the informal representations by English Catholic noblemen usually working in concert with the English Catholic Colleges at Rome, resulted in a papal admonition to the clergy in Ireland to stay out of politics. In the second half of the 1830s, O'Connell had become very close to John MacHale, Archbishop of Tuam whose Connacht province included some of the poorest parts of Ireland, most exposed to Protestant evangelical missionary activities. MacHale, like O'Connell, believed in the efficacy of denunciation to which he resorted frequently, calling in question successive administrations' failures to deal with social problems as well as their incapacity to restrain the over-enthusiastic conversion schemes for starving peasantry organised by evangelical societies. As O'Connell prepared to revert to the repeal programme on the failure of Melbourne's government to live up to his ideas of 'justice for Ireland', MacHale's participation in O'Connell's activities was directly responsible for the intimation from Rome to the Irish hierarchy to stay out of politics. While the Irish ecclesiastical reaction was an unqualified acceptance of the direction and an assurance that episcopal interventions in public matters were confined to occasions of critical religious importance in the face of continued Protestant aggression, O'Connell came to conclude that it was as essential to secure self-government for Ireland in Church as in nation, devoting attention to the weaknesses in the Catholic position of those among the hierarchy least disposed to co-operate with him and most exposed to the insidious advances of Protestant administrators. Concurrently, the Liberator expressed himself publicly and privately in terms of unqualified obedience to the Holy See from which he, indirectly, requested some of the highest personal honours available to outstanding Catholic statesmen. The resultant concessions to O'Connell made leading papal advisers conclude that however

O'Connell Monument in the Irish College, Rome.

liberal his affirmations, O'Connell could be relied upon to be strictly orthodox, a matter in which the aging Irish statesman, increasingly concerned with personal spiritual matters, could not himself be in doubt. Nevertheless, where O'Connell's own movement was concerned, as in the past, he unhesitatingly expressed his views on any actions, even from Rome, which appeared to call in question his bona fides. On at least one occasion, O'Connell embarrassed the Irish hierarchy by calling in question the canonical justification of a papal rescript so that it was necessary to remind him of his oft-repeated assurances to the leading bishops that he would never act without having previously consulted them. Fortunately for him with the fall of Melbourne and the return to power of Peel, there was sufficient evidence of triumphant Toryism and Protestantism to win over decisively a majority of the hierarchy to O'Connell's movement. A new situation arose when O'Connell decided upon a more direct approach in Rome to build up an effective party there to secure his ideas of self-government in domestic matters for the Irish hierarchy.

The Approach to Cullen

Soon after Sir Robert Peel again became Prime Minister, O'Connell made a direct approach to the Rector of the Irish College at Rome, Paul Cullen, one of the most gifted Irish ecclesiastics on the continent, destined to dominate the Irish Church for the generation after O'Connell. He must have found the Liberator's proposals for the virtual endowment of the Church through repeal singularly stimulating.

In the period after the restoration of the Papal States, the Irish College at Rome had included several outstanding ecclesiastics who had devoted themselves to the study and teaching of modern Irish history from the standpoint of 'faith and fatherland'. Probably Paul Cullen and his kinsman Patrick Francis Moran were the most outstanding of these exponents of Irish Catholic nationalism, as the publications which emerged under their auspices throughout the rest of the century were to testify. When O'Connell proposed to Cullen a comprehensive scheme to maintain the highest principles of Catholicism in Ireland in close association with the Holy See, he was merely establishing contact with a Roman ecclesiastic whose inclinations and pursuits were already clearly involving him in just such activities. It is not possible to be sure of the identity of O'Connell's Church adviser in this matter but it may be assumed that if it was not Archbishop MacHale, it was someone whose views were probably closer to the western Archbishop than to any other Irish metropolitan. In the course of the 1830s, the Catholic hierarchy experienced numerous instances when non-denominational education was interpreted more favourably to Protestants, particularly to Presbyterians, than to Catholics. Archbishop MacHale had been one of the first to quarrel with the national education Board from which he severed all connection, thereby shackling himself with the responsibility for providing education for the poor throughout

Connacht. MacHale, sensitive about criticisms at Rome over his alleged preference for his study to the ardous fieldwork of counteracting Protestant missions, was not slow to point out to the Holy See that those of his brethren of the hierarchy co-operating with the Government rather than with O'Connell were compounding the felony of disloyalty to the Church's purest principles on mixed religious education. At first Rome delayed, apparently preferring to avoid being involved in a difficult international situation in which the Chancellor of the Austrian Empire, Metternich, seemed to favour the English as opposed to the Irish viewpoint. Nor does Cullen appear to have taken any prominent part in building an O'Connell lobby until the ground for this appeared to have been stabilised by Peel's policy of endowing Catholicism in Ireland divorced from O'Connell. Perhaps Cullen himself was one of the sources on which Rome increasingly relied when it came to accept O'Connell as one of the most outstanding Catholics in Europe. Rome was not prepared to put all its eggs in the English government's basket.

Reaction Against Peel

Coinciding with the replacement of the Whig government by the Tories, O'Connell's personal significance seems to have fallen as never before when he was defeated at the General Election which confirmed Peel in office. Not for the first time the Irish leader recovered his position spectacularly and built himself up to the most critical pinnacle in the political scene since emancipation through his all-out campaign for repeal. Within a few months of his parliamentary defeat, thanks to the Municipal Corporations Act, O'Connell was elected Lord Mayor of Dublin, an office he enjoyed, discharging its duties with studied fairness. From this position, O'Connell developed the repeal programme which quickly became to Peel's government a major embarrassment. The Prime Minister had certainly travelled far from the days when as Irish Chief Secretary he identified closely with the Orange ascendancy. From the time he gave way on emancipation in 1829 he gradually moved to a more equitable position vis-à-vis the conflicting Irish interests so that in fact he quickly earned the resentment of the ultra-conservatives who were in a few years' time to have the satisfaction of bringing down his government. On one matter there was agreement between these old allies, in their common hatred of O'Connell. With rare exceptions, this mutual antipathy was reciprocated. In these circumstances, it would have been difficult for Peel not to suspect O'Connell of seeking the destruction of the government. The repeal movement then was primarily concerned to destroy the Tories but there was also the danger that it was a camouflaged revolutionary activity to divorce Ireland from Great Britain.

At an early stage Peel had decided to woo the Catholics away from O'Connell but first he determined to deflate the great Irishman whose monster meetings organised at first from the west, and with MacHale, seemed likely to bring Irish administration to a halt. Once the government became convinced that the O'Connellites were meditating treason, it was decided to arrest the leader and his prominent supporters and put them on trial for their suspected nefarious purposes. With O'Connell out of the way, in jail, Peel embarked upon the policy of winning the Catholics by substantially enlarging Maynooth's endowment, by establishing an impartial Charitable Bequests measure favourable to Catholics and by setting up provincial colleges at university level on a non-denominational basis. Before the programme was fully revealed, O'Connell had been released when on a legal appeal the judgement of the lower court was reversed in his favour. O'Connell's first reactions were not unfavourable to the Prime Minister's programme, partly perhaps because of the aura of universal adulation which greeted him on his release, treated in the diocese of Dublin as an occasion for an ecclesiastical *Te Deum*. With the Irish Church, as never before, united in admiration of him, O'Connell's first reaction to Peel's Catholic programme seems to have been one of unqualified approval. Within a few weeks however, the Irish leader had changed his attitude and took the lead in denouncing Peel for attempting a new enslavement of the clergy to destroy the independent Irish nation.

The exact steps by which this change took place might prove impossible to establish but in a short time O'Connell's reversion to opposition seemed justified by the views of leading English and Roman statesmen. The return of the Whigs to power in the summer of 1846 might not have appeared predictable to many contemporaries two years earlier. Once the agricultural crisis precipitated by the Irish famine was known, the stability of the government might well have been called in question by many. Remote from Westminster, the Roman representative of many bishops, Paul Cullen, regarded events following the revelation of Peel's new Catholic policy with considerable suspicion. The endowment of Maynooth had been met with general Catholic approval. Immediately after its passage however, Cullen noted in correspondence with his Vice-Rector at the Irish College, Tobias Kirby, that it had resulted in signs of a 'Castle Catholic' group within the Church in Ireland. On the question of charitable bequests, differences of opinion among the bishops had been followed by indications by some, of their readiness to serve on government boards to secure the best advantages for Catholic charities. Finally the Colleges Bill, condemned as non-denominational by the majority of bishops, created for Cullen the anxiety lest episcopal participation would bring about public connivance unless Rome could be convinced of the necessity to uphold their condemnation. It was in this situation that O'Connell and MacHale became increasingly condemnatory of Peel's Catholic policy. It was probably through Cullen that O'Connell's policy was endorsed despite an *ad hoc* mission to Rome undertaken by Lord Minto to secure approval for the English Catholic plan. Thus O'Connell to destroy Peel appealed to Rome despite his earlier favour for devolution. But when Peel fell, in attempting to cope with the Irish famine, he but anticipated the fate of O'Connell whose movement inevitably became subordinate in the attempts to cope with that catastrophe. Thus O'Connell survived long enough to see his repeal policy relegated to an insignificant position both in Church and state.

O'Connellism Destroyed by the Famine

Within twelve months of his release, O'Connell became aware of the first failure of the potato crop and of its dire possibilities for the Irish people. This event seems to have coincided with a sudden loss of power by the statesman whose aged appearance struck everybody in marked contrast to his previous vitality and energy. With the onset of the Famine, O'Connell quickly concluded that only by the allocation of millions of pounds of public money could the consequences of the destruction of the people's food be restricted. O'Connell's views had little support from the government's experts and almost inevitably he became involved in the intrigue which drove Peel's Tories out of office only to be replaced by Russell's Whig administration as little prepared to listen to O'Connell as Peel. It was in this situation that the aged Irish leader abandoned his movement, becoming convinced that his own death was not far off so that despite optimistic doctors he settled his affairs. A visit to Rome seemed to some of the pious enthusiastic clergy who had greeted as miraculous O'Connell's release from jail a possible way of recuperating so O'Connell left Westminster on his last triumphal tour, being everywhere accorded the honours due to an eminent person until he reached Genoa where he died after the Cardinal Archbishop, aged 88, brought him the viaticum. His end was to Dr. Miley, his champion since the exalting days of the Dublin *Te Deum*, a great disappointment. Miley had set his heart on O'Connell reaching Rome and a public reception by His Holiness the Pope. In the end, he reported, O'Connell was a prey to nocturnal horrors about the next world but he would not submit to being moved from Genoa. Ironically, the man who had accentuated the Catholicism of his nationalism and the Romanism of his religion was not prepared to make the last journey there himself. O'Connell's Ireland was destroyed by the Famine after which, economic and social issues would never again be accorded a subordinate place in the programme of Irish politicians. Perhaps J. K. L. should have been listened to twenty years earlier when he urged the problems of poverty before the interests of the politicians and the churchmen.

For any study on O'Connell and Rome there is an absence of source material due to the fact that since the 16th century it was illegal to bring into the dominions of the King of England any instrument emanating from the Pope or Bishop of Rome. In consequence diplomatic relations did not exist between Great Britain and the Holy See in the lifetime of Daniel O'Connell (1775-1847). On reflection, it will be realised that the struggle for Catholic Emancipation necessitated extreme caution as regards any public association between the Pope and British subjects. Whenever Rome made a pronouncement regarding the affairs of England, Scotland and Ireland or about the three kingdoms as a whole, such statements were made indirectly in communications to leading ecclesiastics. Thus no communications exist directly between the Pope and O'Connell. There are, however, some indirect communications conveyed through properly accredited church officials.

The public attitude of the government of successive Hanoverian sovereigns from George III to Victoria on O'Connell and Rome can be ascertained. Royal policy may be inferred from parliamentary statutes and from royal speeches at the opening or closing of parliament. Beyond this, statements made on public occasions must be construed in their contexts. Equally so statements made on less formal occasions and in correspondence official or unofficial must be assessed historically.

A new rich source of information on O'Connell has been provided by the labours of his descendant Professor Maurice R. O'Connell whose edition of his correspondence is planned to extend to eight volumes. The author is much indebted to Professor O'Connell for putting at his disposal the completed editorial work. Professor O'Connell is not, of course, responsible for the conclusions offered here which may in some instances differ materially from those of the editor of the correspondence. It will be appreciated that views expressed here are presented after attempting to relate to their historical context the Liberator's statements often made to individuals in circumstances in which the comprehension of the recipients had to be taken into account. Thus, it appears to this author, that O'Connell's views in correspondence varied according to circumstances and often conflicted with opinions in which he acquiesced possibly for the rest of his life. The author is conscious of the fact that the whole issue deserves a major study.

The O'Connell archives including the family documentation in the second half of the eighteenth century were acquired by University College, Dublin and have been appraised in a number of finding aids in the Archives Department. These include:

P12/1 Margaret McCarthy (1973/4), 'Undated and Incomplete Items'.
P12/2 Julitta Clancy (1974-5), '1776-1812'.
P12/3 Susan McGann (1974-5), 'Correspondence, 1813-29'.
P12/4 Grainne McCabe (1974-5), '1830-47'.
P12/5 Miriam Lambe (1975-6), 'Family and Legal Documents'.
P12/6 Geraldine Tallon (1975-6), 'Accounts'.

This supersedes the Chronological Index previously completed in the U.C.D. library. For reference to other O'Connell sources including the National Library of Ireland see M. R. O'Connell, *The Correspondence of Daniel O'Connell*.

The following recent works may be consulted:

Aydelotte, (W.O.). 'The House of Commons in the 1840s', in *History*, (1954). 249-62.
Broderick, (J.F.). S.J. *The Holy See and the Irish Repeal Movement, 1829-47* (Rome 1951).
MacDonagh, (O.). 'The Politicization of the Irish Catholic Bishops, 1800-1850', in *Historical Journal*, xviii, 37-53.
Macintyre, (A.D.), *The Liberator, Daniel O'Connell and the Irish Party, 1830-47* (London 1965).
Machin, (G.I.T.), *The Catholic Question in English Politics, 1820-30* (Oxford 1964).
Nowlan, (K.B.), *The Politics of Repeal* (London 1965).
O'Donoghue (P.) *The Catholic Church and Ireland in an Age of Revolution and Rebellion, 1782-1803.* (Unpublished Ph.D. Thesis. N.U.I.).
Reynolds, (J.A.), *The Catholic Emancipation Crisis in Ireland, 1823-29* (New Haven 1954).
Whyte, (J.H.), *The Independent Irish Party, 1850-9* (Oxford 1958).
Whyte, (J.H.). 'The influence of the Catholic Clergy on elections in nineteenth century Ireland,' in *English Historical Review*, lxxv, 239-59.

Chapter 11

The Place of Daniel O'Connell in the Liberal Catholic Movement of the Nineteenth Century

Victor Conzemius

The title of this article may meet with objections. Criticism may stem as well from a denominational viewpoint as from a general historical view. Some may resent that O'Connell is here brought into connection with a stream of ideas of unorthodox, dubious Catholicism, to say the least. In view of the traditional lack of understanding of liberalism in Catholic circles, and that not only on the Continent,—the antiliberal prejudice in the nineteenth century and beyond in the Catholic Church was stronger than the anti-socialist—and of the numerous misconceptions about the signification of 'Liberal Catholicism', such a reaction can be understood. More serious would be the objection of the historian to whom it may seem that thus to entitle the article is to attach an inadequate label to a personage who had only a vague, rather symbolic relationship with the Liberal Catholic movement on the Continent which is linked with the names of Lamennais, Montalembert and Lacordaire. In this essay, brief and imperfect though it be, it is hoped to show that both Catholics and historians may accept in good conscience that O'Connell rightly deserves a place in the Liberal Catholic movement in the nineteenth century.

The article is in three parts. Beginning with an outline of the Liberal Catholic movement it goes on to show why O'Connell's stand on central issues of Church-State relationship reflects an authentic Liberal Catholic attitude. The final section indicates some lines of further research.

It is not easy to define Liberal Catholicism. The term itself smacks of the same imprecision and vagueness as the term 'Liberalism'. Experts on liberalism agree that it is much easier to define it in the context of what it is opposed to than to describe it in positive terms. Just as 'Liberalism' is best described by its opposition to socialism, or the Restoration, or conservatism, the meaning of 'Liberal Catholicism' is perhaps best expressed by its opposition to other attitudes of Roman Catholicism in this period, above all 'ultramontanism'. The label itself is nearly as old as that of liberalism. 'Liberal' was originally coined to designate a faction in the Spanish Cortes after 1812 which sought a constitution. The term 'Liberal Catholics' was first employed towards the end of the Restoration period (1818–29) by the journalists of the liberal *Le Globe* in order to describe their colleagues of the Catholic *Correspondant* who sympathised with liberal ideas. Louis de Carne, founder of the (first) *Correspondant*, declares in his memoirs that his journal stood for Catholicism in religious and liberty in political matters. Here we have an essential point for the understanding of Liberal Catholicism: it is first and foremost a view of Catholics on the relationship between Church and society in the new context created by the French Revolution. More precisely, it is the effort of a group of Catholics to come to terms with new political realities and a new political creed: personal freedoms instead of arbitrary force, political liberties arising not from privilege but from legal rights, the entitlement of peoples to political self-determination, liberty of press and religion, possibly separation of Church and State. Within the orthodox Catholic framework Liberal Catholics abandoned the pre-1789 teaching of the Church on her relationship with the State and society reached out for the possibilities the new situation offered them. Liberal Catholicism therefore is at a far distance from 'Liberal Protestantism', which means the application of liberal principles e.g. the principle of unfettered freedom in theology. Even if one accepts a definition of Liberal Catholics given in 1870 rather casually by Lord Acton ('Liberal Catholics are those who fight not only for the liberty of the Church, but for liberty within the Church'), liberal Catholicism in theology stands mainly for opposition to specific Curial and episcopal encroachments on the liberty of expression of a theologian. In no sense, even in its opposition to Papal infallibility, does it put itself against the teaching authority of the Church as such. Someone who abhorred religious liberalism as much as Newman may therefore rightly be called a Liberal Catholic if in the Roman Catholic context he brought to fruition liberal attitudes which were opposed to the main stream of the ultramontanism of his time and yet had nothing to do with liberalism in theology.

Here another misconception must be removed. Hitherto it has been generally accepted that the Liberal Catholic movement started with Lamennais and made its real impact through his school. Recent research, however, has shown that prior to Lamennais there had been an intellectual movement of Liberal Catholicism as well as more pragmatic activities tending to liberal solutions of problems arising in Catholic political life. The main representative of the intellectual current was the self-styled Baron d'Eckstein (1790–1861), a Danish convert and journalist living mostly in France, who between 1826 and 1829 published sixteen volumes of the periodical *Le Catholique*. Independently of Lamennais and prior to him Eckstein adopted in his writings the principles of liberty and equality and developed a new vision of Christianity based on these principles.

Of a more pragmatic brand is the pre-Mennaisian Liberal Catholicism which appeared in Belgium about 1825. Its spokesmen were to be found among the clergy as well as the laity. These men thought that in the Belgian context an alliance with the liberals could hardly be more disastrous than the rule of the Dutch. Because of their plea for an alliance with the liberals their political doctrine has been called 'unionism'. Together with the Belgian disciples of Lamennais, who at first were not very numerous but increased rapidly around 1829–30, the unionists ensured by their alliance with the liberals the success of the Belgian revolution. Accepting the Belgian constitution, they based their activities as Catholics on constitutional rights and not on privilege. As in Belgium, liberty became the slogan of Catholics in neighbouring countries in their struggle for the liberation of the Church from State bureaucracy. This honeymoon between Catholics and liberals in Belgium did not last for ever; after some years a doctrinaire attitude of liberals, the insistence on an implementing of abstract liberal principles regardless of popular feelings, as well as a tendency among Catholics to preserve by their impact and influence on society positions previously held as of privilege, turned the alliance into stern mutual opposition.

The principal country where Liberal Catholicism became an influential stream of thought was France. The names of Lamennais, Lacordaire and Montalembert were linked with this intellectual enterprise, which if only for a very short period was on the way to become a popular movement. The condemnation of *L'Avenir* in 1832 by the bull *Mirari vos* brought to a halt any further developments in that direction. It should not be forgotten that even in the heyday of 1830 the hard core of Liberal Catholics was a very small one and did not penetrate as deeply into Catholic circles as the subsequent tribute paid to this venture of Catholic journalism may suggest. What Liberal Catholic disciples of Lamennais remained did not constitute a compact school. Rather was it a group of individuals, loyal to the initial impetus, but isolated and compelled to mould liberal ideas into Catholic interests if they wanted to exercise political influence. Sociologically speaking Liberal Catholic circles were continuing the tradition of the 'salons' of the eighteenth and early nineteenth centuries. They consisted mainly of members of the aristocracy and haute bourgeoisie and a few intellectual members of the clergy; general sympathy was not with them but with their ultramontane opponents. When in subsequent years Liberal Catholic ideas came to the fore and gained credit, as for example in the revolution year of 1848, this enthusiasm did not last very long and was crushed by the ensuing reaction in Government and Church circles. The final appearance of Liberal Catholicism at the period of the First Vatican Council was a very brief one, for the infallibility current ran precisely against what Liberal Catholicism stood for. About then too the last and most influential pioneers of the movement were dying.

One of the main reasons for its failure to make a real breakthrough was the lack of an original thinker in its ranks. Much of its programme relied on intuition and vision and rather less perhaps on political thinking and philosophical reflection. Lamennais, it has been remarked, was a prophet who soon became an infidel; most of his followers were men of action, gifted journalists and parliamentarians, but hardly original thinkers.

Less well-known than French Liberal Catholicism is that of Italy. *L'Avenir* of 1831 made no impact on Catholic culture in that country. The roots of Liberal Catholicism lay deep in the national and religious traditions of the country. For this reason we find in Italy a special type of Liberal Catholicism independent of the French model. In the sphere of political action is grouped together all the forces which stood for conciliation between Rome and the national idea as epitomised by the Kingdom of Piedmont. This movement has been called 'cattolicesimo conciliatore' (F. Traniello). On the religious level Liberal Catholicism in Italy had a strong touch of reformism, and pleaded for structural changes in Church organisation. The famous 'Cinque Piaghe' of Rosmini (1848) are its finest and best known expression. Little known and less investigated were the Liberal Catholics at the Roman Curia under Pius IX. On the whole this school of thought had a more profound and continuous, if uncharted, influence on Catholic culture in Italy than has hitherto generally been accepted to have been the case.

The country where Liberal Catholicism had the least chance to develop was Germany. Almost from the beginning we encounter an ever widening gap between Liberals and Catholics. A few Catholics such as Carl V. Rotteck could still manage to reconcile Catholicism with liberal attitudes in politics; in the following generation a liberal Catholic generally was someone who held his Catholic creed very cheap and was patently embarrassed by it. From the beginning political liberalism had a bad reputation in German ecclesiastical circles. Travelling in 1833 through Germany Montalembert collected many compliments for *L'Avenir*, but found that the separation of Church and State and alliance with the liberals were apparently unacceptable to German Catholics. Both Görres the former Jacobin, and Döllinger, the later rebel, concurred in reviling the liberals. Antiliberalism became one of the chief features of the struggle waged by Mgr Ketteler, the leading figure of the German episcopate. With the possible exception of the Reichensperger brothers in Rhenania there were hardly any German Catholics who could claim to be liberal Catholics. There was of course on the more religious level a demand for reform, represented in the 1840s by J. B. Hirscher in the field of practical theology and in the 1860s by I. V. Döllinger in the area of systematic and historial theology. However, it would be misleading to designate these as champions of Liberal Catholicism. Opposition to existing Church structures, for example Roman centralism, is not sufficient in itself to warrant the label of Liberal Catholicism. A construction of this *tour d'horizon* would bring to light in other countries smaller branches and different brands of Liberal Catholicism: in the Netherlands a still more pragmatic one than in Belgium; in Switzerland the outstanding figure of the conservative statesman Anton Phillip V. Segesser; in Poland a cluster of Polish patriots; in Bohemia and Austria reformist groups round the philosophers and theologians Bernard Bolzano and Anton Günther. But the most exciting and refreshing example was the Liberal

Catholics of England. The vitality of the liberal idea in English political life is the likely explanation of why within a minority context such an ideology could flourish and produce several distinguished representatives. Richard Simpson was a recent convert; Lord Acton came from old Catholic stock; and Newman, a Tory in politics, has rightly been called the most open theologian since Origen (Loisy). Even in the shaping of Acton's outlook continental influences were of lesser importance than his English inheritance, that is, a nonconformist community brought up in a longstanding tradition of separation between Church and State and a certain leaning towards Whiggism in politics. What on the Continent, with its centuries old tradition of alliance between Church and State, was beyond the understanding of many Catholics was the natural principle on which the organisation and development of the Catholic community in England was based. Disestablishment had not to be fought for; it was an accepted fact for the Catholics in the British Isles.

Here lay perhaps the basic advantage which enabled Daniel O'Connell to develop an authentic liberal Catholic policy in Ireland without having to present a clear-cut programme in this field. Just as he accepted the framework of the English constitution for his political action, so did he rely on the principle of separation as the basic principle regulating the relationship between Church and State. The Irish experience of a 'poor Church'—not a programmatical declaration of theologians (as we heard at the time of Vatican II), but a hard reality in a context of persecution and discrimination—showed that reliance not on Establishment but on the living forces of society was the Church's best chance for the future. The Irish experience furthermore had shown that the Catholic Church there in the eighteenth century, despite all the shortcomings of its situation, had suffered less from direct intervention in Church affairs than any continental Church living under government protection.

The best known incident which helped to establish O'Connell's fame as a liberal Catholic was his attitude in the Veto affair of 1814, when the Curia was prepared to grant to the British Government a veto on the nomination of bishops, while the State would pay the clergy salaries. O'Connell's speech of 25 January 1815 against the Curial rescript—soon withdrawn by Pope Pius VII—where he refused to take his politics from Rome, was more the expression of independence of mind and national self-consciousness than a statement of Liberal Catholicism.

"I am sincerely a Catholic but I am not a Papist. I deny the doctrine that the Pope has any temporal authority, directly or indirectly, in Ireland; we have all denied that authority on oath and would die to resist it. He cannot, therefore, be any party to the act of parliament we solicit, nor shall any act of parliament regulate our faith or conscience. In spiritual matters too, the authority of the Pope is limited; he cannot, though his conclave of Cardinals were to join him, vary our religion either in doctrine or in essential discipline, in any respect. Even in non-essential discipline the Pope cannot vary it without the assent of the Irish Catholic bishops."[1]

1. John O'Connell, *The life and speeches of Daniel O'Connell, M.P., edited by his son* (Dublin, 1846), ii, 178.

It has rightly been observed (Maurice O'Connell) that attention has been too
exclusively focused on this incident. O'Connell's attitude in 1815 is to be seen
in a larger and more genuine perspective of Liberal Catholicism, where the
anti-Roman and nationalist elements, so prominent in the Veto affair, were
minor factors. Indeed one can find in his speeches and letters a number of
statements where he endorses the principle of religious liberty. Right from the
beginning of his political career in 1807 he claims religious tolerance for British
subjects only on the grounds of a general principle. In a speech in Dublin in
1813 he stated it thus:

> There can be no freedom without perfect liberty of conscience: . . . The emancipation I
> look for is one which would establish the rights of conscience upon a general principle . . .
> which would serve and liberate the Catholic in Ireland but would be equally useful to the
> Protestant in Spain . . . which would destroy the Inquisition and the Protestant Orange
> Lodges together and have no sacrilegious intruder between man and his Creator.[2]

Again and again he professed the same principles. In 1818 speaking at a public
meeting at Tralee; in 1830 when supporting the emancipation of the English
Jews; in 1831 when commenting on political developments in Italy and in 1837
when discussing the situation in Spain; in 1842 in the course of a public
discussion with Lord Shrewsbury. He knew well that the official teaching of
the Roman Pontiffs, clinging to the abstract idea that error has no right to
survive and spread itself and must, therefore, be crushed, was contrary to his
own views. It may well be that his independent stand in these matters damaged
his reputation in Rome. In 1836 he saw himself unfit to become a censor of the
recently founded *Dublin Review* for the reason that he could not support the
official Catholic views on the relations between Church and State.

In 1863 Montalembert, speaking at a celebrated meeting at Malines
(Belgium), spelled out the same principles in words which sound like a belated
echo of O'Connell's profession of religious liberty. This was a fitting tribute by
someone who, when travelling as a young man in Ireland in 1830, had been
favourably impressed by O'Connell's campaign for the Irish people and had
hailed him in 1847 in Paris as a preceptor of Catholic nations.

Another aspect of the Liberator's commitment to the Irish cause which
merits consideration is that he did not seek the religious emancipation of his
community in the first place but looked to larger political liberties resulting in
greater religious freedom. Yet while refusing to have his politics dictated by
Rome or vested Church interests he skilfully used the parish organisation of
the Catholic Church in his country as an instrument for the financing of his
campaign (Penny-action). Thus he made the existing Church structures in
Ireland serve the national cause. Some have criticised him for this as bringing
the clergy into politics. But in an age when 'political theology' or even
'theology of revolution' or 'theology of liberation' have become fashionable in
theological circles, O'Connell's solution appears as an extremely lively and
successful example of how Church structures can be made to serve political

2. *Ibid.*, ii, 264.

emancipation. The difference is that to-day there is much theoretical discussion about a theology of liberation but little action, little real influence of theology on political structures. In O'Connell's time there was much less discussion, but perhaps more successful political action, thoroughly liberal because it left the Chutch unhampered in its own realm, no servant of the State or of a political party but an advocate of the liberty of society. There is perhaps no other country in Europe where Church organisations have so directly contributed to serve the cause of liberty and political emancipation than Ireland. It is only the Belgian revolution, the result of a 'monstrous alliance' between Catholics and liberals, as the Papal Nuncio in The Hague put it, which comes closest to the Irish.

A more detailed study of O'Connell's religious ideas and his relations with the Catholic clergy would give a better picture still of his particular type of Liberal Catholicism. We can only point to the interest such a study would present. Here independently of this O'Connell's influence on the Catholic movements on the Continent deserves separate investigation. His fame had reached gigantic proportions already in his lifetime. The scope of such a study would not be to assemble tributes from obituaries, periodicals and *obiter dicta* and so add to the O'Connell myth, but to gain some idea of the extent to which he was used as a symbol by nationalistic Catholic propaganda. Such a study would not be confined to an investigation of Liberal Catholic sources but would extend to ultramontane as well. Each understood him in a different way and shaped his image according to its own interest. If one instinctively feels that the 'ultramontanes' were very far from the real O'Connell, whose views on religious toleration and the separation of Church and State would have profoundly embarrassed them, it must also be realised that on the Continent even Liberal Catholics did not grasp the entire implications of his views. A majority of Liberal Catholics would not have gone as far as O'Connell in these fundamental matters. The Liberal Catholicism of O'Connell thus appears beyond any doubt not only to be such; in fact of the various types of Liberal Catholicism it seems to have been the most radical in the ideological and the most successful in the political field. His stimulating influence on democratic movements in the Catholic world and beyond makes him more than a distant father-figure of modern Catholic culture; perhaps at no other time save in the early middle ages have the Irish had a stronger impact on Continental culture than—thanks to O'Connell—in the first half of the nineteenth century.

The article is based on earlier notes of the author and had to be written without access to a specific library on the topic. For a recent discussion of Liberal Catholicism see M. Prelot: *Le liberalisme catholique* (Paris 1969); V. Conzemius: 'Les foyers internationaux du catholicisme liberal hors de France au XIXe siècle: Esquisse d'une geographie historique', in *Les Catholiques liberaux au XIXe siècle. Actes du colloque international d'histoire religieuse de Grenoble des 30 sept.—3 octobre 1971* ed. by J. Gadille (Grenoble, 1974), pp 15-51; Id. 'Liberaler Katholizismus in England'. in *Studien der Thyssen-Stiftung zum XIX. Jahrhundert* (Göttingen, 1976).
On this particular topic the article of Maurice R. O'Connell, 'Daniel O'Connell and Religious Freedom'. in *Thought*, Vol. 50, no. 197 (June 1975) sheds new light. A study of the Irish question in German journalism before 1848 has been made by K. Holl, *Die irische Frage in der Ära O'Connells und ihre Bedeutung in der polit*, Publizistik des deutschen Vormärz (Main, 1958).

Chapter 12

The Influence of O'Connell's Example on French Liberal Catholicism

Henri Rollet

(translation by M. H. Kelly, Department of French, UCD)

I

In a recent work of considerable historical value on Liberal Catholicism in France,[1] the name of O'Connell is mentioned only once, in passing, in a statement by Falloux, who will be mentioned later. This near-silence might suggest that, unlike the Belgian liberal Catholics, who occupy an entire section of the bibliography, the Liberator's influence was non-existent. Such a suggestion would be false. O'Connell's real influence was considerable, but it was above all the influence of his example.

O'Connell could have become the leader or the spiritual mentor of liberal Catholics throughout Europe. He did not seek this position, so committed was he to the liberation of his country. But he was nevertheless their model.

At every stage of their campaign in France, the liberal Catholics were clearly applying the principles that inspired him, referring to the key points of his programme, and imitating his basic attitudes. Any personal contacts he may have had are of negligible significance compared with the crucial importance of his example. Liberal Catholicism in France had its own specific problems, very different from the Irish ones, and had to find its own solutions.

II

Montalembert's Fascination with Ireland

Charles de Montalembert was born into an ancient and illustrious family in London in 1810. His father, who became a diplomat under the Restoration,

1. *Le Liberalisme Catholique* (Paris, 1969) edited by Marcel Prelot and F. Gallouedec Gennys, published by Armand Colin.

was living in exile, and his mother was English. His grand-father Forbes exerted a decisive influence on his early youth and provided him with an English culture unusual for a young man of his generation.

During 1828–1829 he lived for a long period in Stockholm, where his father was a French diplomatic representative. There he spent much of his time in libraries. He read Grattan's speeches, which affected him deeply, bound him for ever to Ireland, and inspired him to write a history of Irish resistance from the fall of the Stuarts to the Act of Union. Montalembert was aware of the battle being fought by O'Connell at that time for Catholic emancipation. He felt that writing his book would contribute to that cause by arousing French sympathies in its favour. The friends in whom he confided his plans did not encourage him. Cousin in particular wrote: "The Irish people are outside the European movement. They are unworthy of freedom because they have been slaves . . . Peoples always deserve their fate".

In Stockholm, Montalembert began to write his work. But the more he progressed, the wider the subject became. Then he learned that Catholic emancipation, to which he had wished to contribute, had been enacted. Shortly afterwards a *History of Ireland* was published by the poet Moore. He abandoned his project in despair, saying with Grattan: "My heart was in my cause".

But his love for Ireland had not diminished and as soon as events permitted, he paid a visit there, arriving on 4 September 1830. Liberal above all else, he came to see a country where, as in Poland which had been erased from the map, as in Belgium which was annexed and in open revolt, and as in divided Italy, a people suffered and struggled under the leadership of an exceptional man: Daniel O'Connell. It would not appear that the internal organisation of the Irish Church, its relationship with the state, the behaviour of the clergy and the initiative of the laity caught his attention to begin with. Far from it. The young man of twenty had come to discover the land of Saint Patrick and to commune with its people in order to serve them.

Six weeks later, Montalembert returned from Ireland, confirmed in his views, but also enlightened about matters of which he had known nothing. He had loved the country, he had received the hospitality of its people, he had heard their lament, made the more moving by the infinite dignity of its expression, he had comprehended their hope and the immense trust they placed in O'Connell. His meeting with the latter had been disappointing because the Liberator, surrounded by visitors and petitioners, saw the young man as just one more admirer. But this momentary disappointment did not affect Montalembert's activity.

On the other hand, the young Frenchman had discovered a Church unlike either the three hundred Swedish Catholics or the august Church of France. A poor Church with no concordat, whose bishops, revered by their people, lived a very simple life, whose priests had saved their country, forming the backbone of its moral resistance, and remained closely united to their flock, a Church whose clergy and faithful could join together behind a layman to claim its rights. Such was the revelation that Montalembert took back from Ireland, it was to constitute almost a plan of action for liberal Catholics.

It must be pointed out that the contrast with France seemed all the more striking to the young man since the Church of France, much weakened by twenty-five years of persecution, by the collapse of the clergy and by the disappearance of seminaries and institutions, had joyfully welcomed the return of the King, and had taken the greatest advantage of the régime's constant though at times burdensome support. The French Church had witnessed the growth of priestly and religious vocations, had reestablished its teaching, and vastly increased the scope of its institutions. The union of crown and altar, dazzlingly reaffirmed at the consecration of Charles X, was emphasised by the King, a sincere convert though slow-witted and clumsy, who proclaimed it with ostentation.

When Montalembert returned to Paris on 4 November 1830, the anti-religious reaction which followed the July days of 1830 was at its height. The Church was attacked, denounced and linked with the overthrown monarchy. The bishops, nostalgic for the departed Bourbon king, were silent. The great liberal voices announced the disappearance of the bishops and the death of God. The common people of the towns, the emergent working-class, completely disoriented by the transition from a rural to an industrial life, turned away from the monarchist clergy and prepared to fight it.

III

O'Connell's influence on 'L'Avenir'

When Montalembert arrived in Paris, he found that a new paper was rousing enthusiasm in Catholic circles. It was L'Avenir, which had been appearing since 16 October, with the motto 'God and freedom'. Founded by the abbé de Lamennais, this newspaper succeeded during the year of its existence in giving form to the liberal Catholic movement, in defining its doctrine, in expressing its ideas, and in leaving a deep and lasting impression on French Catholicism.

On 5 November, Montalembert went to see Lamennais, who offered him a regular column which the young man accepted enthusiastically. On the 12th, he met Lacordaire, a young priest and highly talented preacher. A close friendship developed between them which lasted until the priest's death. De Coux, who took charge of social and economic matters, joined them shortly afterwards. This team was the basis of the paper, and Montalembert was responsible for foreign affairs.

We must distinguish here between the underlying thought and the daily news. Through Montalembert O'Connell exerted an important influence on both. Naturally it was first and foremost to be felt in the paper's foreign policy, or to enter more into the spirit of L'Avenir, in the attitude of liberal Catholics towards other nations. Profoundly European, L'Avenir supported without hesitation the liberation of oppressed peoples, whose demands it felt keenly. At

Investiture of Daniel O'Connell with the Holy Order of the Guild of St. Joseph and Mary, Virginia Street Chapel, Ratcliffe Highway.

the time of the Belgian war and the Polish revolt, Ireland could have been relegated to secondary importance. But this did not happen. On the contrary, Montalembert continuously recalled Ireland's right to freedom and the battle undertaken by O'Connell to have it recognised. In the process, the assertion of rights became separated from the events which demonstrated it, and the doctrinal nature of the assertion was emphasised. It was no longer because of a particular statement by O'Connell that *L'Avenir* spoke of him, but because he put himself permanently at the disposal of oppressed peoples. This is an important point. Montalembert had, of course, had direct contact with Ireland and not with Poland, and this made it easier for him to see O'Connell's importance as going beyond any specific event. It must be said, however, that there was complete agreement on the matter between the editors of *L'Avenir,* and that Lacordaire and Lamennais shared an equally great admiration for O'Connell.

The position of the Church, as Montalembert had seen it in Ireland, inspired the basic point in the doctrine of *L'Avenir:* the freedom of the Church. Since the Church had suffered so much from its former alliance with the fallen royalty, they felt that the time was ripe to refuse alliances with anyone, to evangelise without the support of the state, without concordats, without subsidies, but with all the benefits of freedom.

This doctrine caused a scandal, and won over only a fraction of the younger clergy and a few avant-garde laymen. It meant breaking off the political alliance of the bishops, of many priests and of the Catholic nobility with the Bourbons' 'legitimist' party. This seemed unthinkable to Christians who had benefited so much from the support of the Bourbon Monarchy. Montalembert respected this loyalty, he shared it himself, but he refused to translate it into a political commitment. And above all, the clergy set great store by the concordat, material security, and the prestige it conferred on them. More remote from the faithful than were the Irish clergy, they relied more on prestige. In short, the French Church, which had suffered so much under the Revolution and the Empire, was not disposed to risk the adventure proposed by *L'Avenir.*

Nevertheless, this attitude did not stop the idea of the Church changing in the minds of Catholics. They saw it as more autonomous, relying less on the support of the government and taking more responsibility for its own destiny. The effects of this development, unnoticed at the time, became visible fifteen years later.

Montalembert, however, supported his claim by showing his readers the life of the clergy in Ireland. His articles were frequent, suggestive and effective. In January 1831, *L'Avenir* described a mass in a country chapel and concluded: "The foreigner who saw these things had also knelt with these poor Christians and when he stood up again his heart was full of pride and happiness, thinking that he too belonged to this religion which never dies and which, at a time when disbelief hastens to dig its grave, can be found again in the deserts of Ireland and America, as free and poor as when it was born".

On the separation of Church and State, Lamennais wrote: "How will the Church live without endowments? God can answer me that, but what I do not know is how she will live without freedom .... As for tomorrow, we only know one thing: Providence will be up before the sun. Do you not have the example of Ireland and America? Zeal will create immense resources. The people never love the priest so much as when he is as poor as themselves. Nothing is so much respected as legitimate independence purchased by voluntary privations".

Throughout his articles, Montalembert showed how the faithful contributed to the upkeep of the priest and the Church, how simply the pastors lived in their 'episcopal thatched cottages', and how the association of laity and clergy round O'Connell had produced extraordinary results.

His articles aroused enormous interest. Alfred de Vigny, at the time one of the Young leaders of Romanticism, though an unbeliever, wrote to him: "I envy the Ireland of today for the freedom and poverty of its clergy, for the election of its bishops and their 'episcopal thatched cottages', a combination of words quite unknown to us ...."[2] On 13 June, Montalembert reported a famine which was devastating the country, and his moving article brought in contributions amounting to 80,000 francs in three months.[3]

IV

The General Agency for Religious Freedom

The founders of *L'Avenir* saw their paper as an instrument to be used in support of a demand, that of freedom, the kind of freedom which was never given and had to be fought for, as O'Connell had done. In the first issue, Lacordaire wrote: "People are free when they wish to be free, when they can unite and die rather than give up the smallest part of that which alone bestows value on human life".[4]

And Lamennais told French Catholics: "There are twenty-five million of you .... You possess recognised rights; if they are taken from you, you have only yourselves to blame. They will only be safe from attack when you have seriously decided to defend them .... You must complain less and learn determination; what are you lacking but that spirit of unity which gives heart to the weakest and which breeds strong and lasting action?"[5]

The three friends laid the foundations of this spirit of unity on 16 December 1830 in the room of the Rector of Juilly College, *abbé* de Salinis. The intention was to form a vast league of all militant Catholics covering the whole of France. At the head of this vast association a General Agency was set up in Paris, consisting of a seven-man central council together with affiliated

2. In a letter of January 1831.
3. 400,000 Francs today (£40,000).
4. *L'Avenir*, 16 October 1830.
5. *L'Avenir*, 26 November 1830.

contributors donating a yearly 10 francs each. Associations of militant Catholics were to be formed in each diocese: "Each of them will undoubtedly have its own life, its own finance, its own mode of organisation and activity according to each area's needs; but by establishing relationships with the General Agency, a more universal and regular action will result therefrom which will relate all resources to all needs".

What did these militant Catholics want? The Agency's programme specified three points.

Its aims were:

1. "The rectification of any act against the liberty of the ecclesiastical ministry by civil actions in the Chambers of Justice and before all courts from the Council of State to the Justice of the Peace".

2. "Support for every primary, secondary and higher education institution against all arbitrary acts constituting an infringement on the freedom of education, without which there is neither Charter[6] nor Religion".

3. "The preservation of the right, common to all Frenchmen, to come together to pray, study or to attain any other legitimate end for the benefit of religion, of the poor and of civilisation".

Lemennais presided over the Council of the Agency; Lacordaire, De Coux and Montalembert were its most active members. From the outset the last-mentioned indicated the origin of this undertaking, unprecedented in the history of French Catholicism: '. . . If discouragement were ever to take hold of us, if ever our tired hearts were to doubt God and his eternal solicitude, let us dwell on the miracles of the Catholic Association which began with only seven members and after fifteen years of battle brought about the religious independence of Ireland and laid the foundations of its national independence'.[7] The ancestry was clearly, even pointedly affirmed.

Immediately, liberal Catholics set to work. History has recorded some of their activities. Lacordaire, a former barrister, asked for his reinstatement to the Bar and was refused; legal action was taken against a general who had Capuchin friars thrown into prison for vagrancy; some of the Trappist monks of La Meilleraye were saved by the General Agency from expulsion; it also enabled other victims of arbitrary measures to resettle in Ireland and England.

V

The freedom of Primary Education

The basic freedom denied to French Christians in 1831 was the right to teach. Napoleon had given the monopoly of teaching to the Imperial University and the Restoration did not alter the situation. Undoubtedly it turned a blind eye to the Christian Education of girls because the State was not interested in it, and

6. The French constitution after 1814.
7. *L'Avenir*, 18 January 1831.

allowed the development of schools and colleges run by the religious. But it was no more than toleration. Outside the law, no religious teaching establishment could feel its future to be secure.

It was precisely the closure of one of these establishments, the Manécanterie in Lyon, by the Minister for Public Instruction which prompted Montalembert, Lacordaire and de Coux to open a little school in Paris, in the rue des Beaux Arts, on 9 May 1831, to bring the problem to public attention. The following day, the police Superintendant arrived to confirm the offence and the following day he closed the school and brought the three men responsible before the magistrate. The court of summary jurisdiction, having heard a moving statement from Lacordaire, declared the case outside its competence to judge; the case was sent for a full hearing. On the eve of the trial, the sudden death of his father made Montalembert a peer, answerable only to the House of Peers. Montalembert demanded to benefit from his juridicial privilege. He appeared on 19 September with his two friends. When asked his identity his prompt reply was: "Charles de Montalembert, school-teacher and peer of France".

The trial offered a choice platform to the young militant whose speech found a deep response throughout the whole country. Montalembert's eloquence revealed itself in all its mastery, and greatly assisted the cause of liberal Catholics, who won the support of public opinion in the affair. But in the High Court, the law prevailed and a fine of 100 francs, the minimum penalty for the offence, was imposed on the three accused.

The public opinion campaign was not long bearing fruit. By an Act dated 28 June 1833, Guizot, a protestant, recognised the freedom of Primary Education subject to certain guarantees. This unquestionably gave security and impetus to the existing establishments, as well as to the many new ones which were set up.

The time had now come for liberal Catholics to move on to the battle for freedom in Secondary Education.

VI

Early attempts to gain freedom of Secondary Education

Following the suspension, in November 1831, of *L'Avenir,* which by that time had lost most of its subscribers as a result of its increasingly sharp attacks on the episcopate and the conservative wing of the clergy, and following the condemnation of Lamennais by Gregory XVI, liberal Catholics began to look like officers who had lost their troops and whose leaders were wounded. This explains their cautious attitude between 1833 and 1837. In fact, they were relying on the good will of Guizot, who favoured a just solution.

But the liberal and only superficially Catholic bourgeoisie which had allowed the religious to teach the people, refused to entrust them with a future electorate.[8] Hence, when Guizot proposed legislation of liberal inspiration, the Chamber amended it so completely that it became unacceptable to Catholics; the Minister withdrew it. For the next four years, 1837–1841, the demand was unceasingly put to the House of Peers, with Montalembert seizing every opportunity to raise the question. This led to the new Minister, Villemain, to propose a second bill. He surrounded the freedom to teach with such harsh conditions regarding qualification of teachers and state supervision that they seemed a veritable provocation to Catholics. Three times Montalembert took the floor to declare his unyielding opposition. The episcopate condemned the bill and Villemain withdrew it.

Hence, it was clear that only a fierce assault on public opinion could hope to bring irresistible pressure to bear on the government. But Montalembert felt he was alone in undertaking this struggle. One day the Minister, Villemain, said to him in these precise words: "We have a better man than O'Connell; but you do not have Ireland behind you". The left wing in public opinion was hostile to the clergy; the right was deeply divided between the Legitimists, who detested the liberal Catholics, and the Orleanists, who were extremely reluctant to embarrass the government. Moreover, Montalembert knew that the bishops were worried and reluctant, beginning with Archbishop Affre of Paris, and found himself alone within the Church. He repeated to himself the words he had written on 31 May 1834, expressing so movingly the Christian's lament: "I am only an obscure and forgotten child, a layman answerable to the Church and to God for my own salvation alone". These crucial words expressed the recognition that the laity lacked any status whatsoever.

By his interventions in the House of Peers and by his repeated efforts to enlighten the episcopate, Montalembert nonetheless played an important rôle in the demand for freedom to teach. The decisive action, however, was that of the brilliant journalist, the convert Louis Veuillot, who as director of the paper *Univers* exerted a considerable influence on the French clergy. Veuillot was by no means a liberal; he found the very word intolerable. But he declared himself frankly in favour of the freedom of education, and constantly referred to it in his newspaper. This generalised campaign on many fronts persuaded Villemain to propose a new bill, but he laid down strict requirements for qualifications which seemed to make the recruitment of teachers impossible and, fearing the Jesuits, he forbade all congregations to teach. The bill had a stormy reception, Villemain lost his sanity, and the bill was abandoned by his successor.

VII

Committee for the defence of religious freedom

All these vicissitudes showed the inadequacy of a loosely organised campaign.

---

8. Franchise was based on taxable valuation. Voting rights were limited to those with incomes above a certain level.

Each setback confirmed Montalembert's will to mount an action like O'Connell's. In October 1843 he issued a widely discussed pamphlet from Madeira, where his wife was convalescing. It was entitled 'The duties of Catholics on the question of freedom of education'. In it, he referred explicitly to the work of the Liberator. Asking for a large number of volunteers, disciplined action and petitions, the author declared: "With such arms, Catholic Ireland guided by its noble bishops, reconquered its rights, drove back mighty England and is proud to have accomplished what so many statesmen declared for so long to be impossible: political equality of Catholics and Protestants within the vast British Empire".

Recalled to France by the campaign against Villemain's second bill, and determined to get the movement under way, Montalembert arrived in Plymouth on 11 March 1844 and went to London to greet O'Connell and receive his encouragement. A significant action indeed.

The end of 1844 was entirely given over to setting up the 'Organising committee for the defence of religious freedom', and the eighty diocesan committees. The outcome, without precedent in French history, was a vast body of militants and supporters, determined to obtain freedom of education under the leadership of Montalembert. He had, however, suffered two disappointments. First, unlike what had happened in Ireland, the bishops refused to lead the movement. This was because the July Monarchy no longer permitted the enforcement of hostile legislation, and the bishops enjoyed a certain peace which they were not willing to exchange for liberty. Their more or less benevolent abstention made the task all the more difficult. Second, because of its extensive readership, the help of *Univers* was indispensable in influencing public opinion.[9] Veuillot, however, directed his paper in a very personal way, disregarding the precautions desired by the bishops, and paying too little heed to Montalembert's directives. Moreover, in nearly every province, it was necessary to approach the legitimist lesser nobility, the 'Notables', who were not liberal and had suffered from the positions adopted by Montalembert. The greater part of them responded to the Committee's appeal, and it adopted the motto 'God and my right'.

It immediately organised a vast petition which collected nearly three thousand signatures in a year and a half. It defended the Jesuits against the opposition attacks and arranged that their dispersal was such in name only. In the 1846 elections, under limited franchise, one hundred and forty four candidates were elected who had included freedom of education in their programme. The Minister, Salvandy, tabled a new bill which forbade Congregations to teach and placed free schools under the control of the University. The Committee, or Catholic Party as it was sometimes called, led a strong campaign against this fourth bill, and it was withdrawn on the eve of the 1848 Revolution.

Under the Second Republic, a liberal Catholic, Falloux, who became

9. The organ of the liberal Catholics, *Le Correspondant,* had very little appeal among the clergy after 1843.

Minister for Public Instructon, formed an extra-parliamentary committee which drafted a decidedly liberal bill. It was made law on 15 March 1850. It granted freedom of secondary education, and entered history as the 'Falloux Act', which is still in operation. Veuillot had fought against it, considering it insufficient and only accepted it on the orders of Pius IX.

The battle undertaken by liberal Catholics after O'Connell's example had various results. It enabled bills to be defeated which in place of freedom offered only a travesty, and it prepared the way for the Falloux Act. On a political level, the fierce opposition to the government dissociated the Church from the Crown and created widespread support for it in 1848; there was no persecution, instead priests were called on to bless the trees of liberty. It brought about a temporary union of Catholics of every hue: legitimists in the style of Berryer, Orleanists close to Guizot, liberals of different shades, social Catholics who rallied to the 'New Era' in 1848. It was a fragile but long-remembered alliance. The idea of forming a broad Catholic party stayed in peoples' thoughts: Albert de Mun tried to revive it in 1885; it was considered after the Catholic Reconciliation in 1893, and again in 1924 against the persecution of the Cartel of the Left.

VIII

The layman's right to intervene

But the most original contribution of liberal Catholics following in O'Connell's footsteps was to have undertaken, in and for the Church, action by the laity. At the outset, Montalembert wanted to see the bishops leading his Committee. They refused for fear of a confrontation with the government of Louis-Philippe. Archbishop Affre was especially clear on this in spite of the insistence of people like the *abbé* Dupanloup and *père* de Ravignan.

Some bishops tried to justify their refusal on doctrinal grounds. Mgr Blancart de Bailleal, Archbishop of Rouen, declared: 'The laity have no call to get involved in the Church's affairs. They would be better employed praying'. Mgr Mathieu, Archbishop of Besançon, denounced the intervention of the laity violently in an appeal to Rome. the Bishop of Evreux even went so far as to say that by so acting, Montalembert was not behaving like a Catholic.

For the first time in Christian history the problem was posed of the right of the laity to intervene, not in profane matters relating to doctrine, a right which had been denied to Galileo, but in the choice and expression of the Church's attitude to the world. In Ireland O'Connell had not had this problem because the fact that the bishops were merely tolerated by the English government prevented them from leading a movement which they wholeheartedly supported. In Belgium the bishops had guided the Catholic party, and its lay leaders had been their spokesmen.

Montalembert was hurt by these attacks. He received encouragement from the Papal Nuncio, Mgr Fornari. But above all, this doctrinal debate led to an important statement by the Bishop of Langres, Mgr Parisis, which became a milestone in the gradual assertion of the role of the laity within the Church:

'We are told that you do not have a mission: true enough, you have no mission to sit in a Council nor to take a direct part in the doctrinal judgement of the scattered Church . . . but does not Saint Paul tell us that, even among the faithful, each one receives the communications of the Holy Spirit for the common good? Has not every Christian the mission to play a part in fighting the enemies of God according to his means? In Tertullian's beautiful words, is not every citizen a soldier in time of great public dangers? The intervention of the laity is not only useful, today it has become necessary. It is in the deliberations of public assemblies that attacks are made on the Church and steps taken against religious freedom. Who will defend religion there if not the laity? Whenever a layman, by his silence or by his inaction, would be in danger of allowing the progress of evil, it becomes no longer merely his right, it becomes his sacred duty to speak and to act. By remaining silent he would become a prevaricator or even an accomplice, and when the ruin of religion in a great kingdom is at stake, such complicity is terrible even before men, but above all before God.'

All later action by the organised laity finds its source in O'Connell's initiative, taken up by the founders of the Catholic party in Belgium and later by the liberal Catholics in France. Having extracted approval from some bishops and a resigned silence from several more, Montalembert's friends opened a way which was followed by Ozanam and the social Catholics of 1848, Armand de Melun, Albert de Mun and the founders of the Catholic Workers' Circles in 1871, Christian democracy in 1893, the French Young Catholic Association, the *Sillon* movement, the Young Catholic Workers, etc.

IX

Montalembert's tribute

At the beginning of 1847, Montalembert and Veuillot, with about fifteen friends—'officers without troops'—went to see O'Connell, who was staying in Paris on his way to Rome. The Liberator, close to death, received them in an hotel on the rue de Rivoli. Montalembert gave him this greeting:

'We are all your children, or rather, your pupils. You are not just a man for one nation, you are a man for all Christendom . . . Wherever Catholics return to the practice of civil virtues and dedicate themselves to the conquest of their legitimate rights, after God, this is your work. Wherever religion strives to emancipate itself from the yoke that many generations of sophists and legists have forged for it, it is to you, after God, that it owes it'.[10]

10. This interview, reported by Veuillot, appears in R.P. Lecanuet, *Montalembert*, I.

Some recommended works for further reading.

LEFLON, Jean, *La crise revolutionnaire 1789-1846* (Paris, 1949). Published by Bloud & Gay in the series "Histoire de l'église depuis les origines jusqu'a nos jours", directed by A. Fliche and V. Martin. On the revolutionary crisis 1789-1846 in the history of the Church.

GIRARD, Louis, *Le liberalisme en France de 1814 a 1848* (Paris, 1967). Published by the Centre de documentation universitaire, in the "Course de Sorbonne" series. On liberalism in France 1814-1848.

LE GUILLOU, Louis, *L'evolution de la pensée religieuse de Felicité de Lamennais* (Paris, 1965). On the development of Lamennais' religious thought.

GILLET, Marie Martin Stanislas, *Lacordaire* (Paris, 1951).

DANSETTE, Adrien, *Histoire religieuse de la France contemporaine* (Paris, 1965). A religious history of modern France.

DANIEL ROPS, *Histoire de l'Eglise du Christ*, vols X & XI (Paris, 1966-7). A history of the Christian Church.

LATREILIE, Andre, & REMOND, Rene, *Histoire du Catholicisme en France*, vol. 3 (Paris, 1964). A history of French Catholicism.

LECANUET, R.P., *Montalembert*, 3 vols (Paris, 1898).

TRANNOY, Andre, *Le romantisme politique de Montalembert avant 1843* (Paris, 1942). On Montalembert's political romanticism before 1843.

HERBERT, M., & CARNEC, A., *La loi Falloux et la liberte d'Enseignement* (La Rochelle, 1953). On the Falloux Act and freedom of education.

PRELOT, Marcel, & GALLOUEDEC GENNYS, F., (editors), *Le liberalisme Catholique* (Paris, 1969). On Catholic liberalism.

FINLAY, James C., *The liberal who failed* (Washington, D.C.), 1968.

Chapter 13

Fr. Ventura's Funeral Oration for Daniel O'Connell

Francisco Andreu C.R.
(translation by David Nolan, Professor of Italian, UCD)

When the news of Daniel O'Connell's death at Genoa on 15 May, 1847 and of his last wishes reached Rome, and from there spread to the Catholic world, it was clear that the legacy of his heart to Rome was not only the clearest sign of his love for the Church and for its Head, but justice was also being done: the heart of the leader of the Irish Catholics, it was evident, had its rightful place in Rome. The obsequies which were held in the Church of Sant 'Andrea della Valle were an equally clear indication of the admiration which Romans felt for the great Irishman. The committee set up for the funeral honours did not have to look far for one capable of pronouncing a worthy oration on O'Connell. The automatic choice fell upon Fr. Gioacchino Ventura,[1] who was then at the peak of his fame as an orator.

Ventura was born in Palermo on 8 December, 1792. He studied under the Jesuits, and later entered the Theatine Order, of which he became Superior General in 1830. Faithful to the ideological trends of French ultramontanism, he had followed, in all its phases, the progress of Lamennais' thought: from reaction to liberalism; from support for restoration of the monarchy to taking sides with revolutions against absolutism.

Although they were far apart in nationality, education and cultural formation, Ventura and O'Connell were close in spirit and shared an almost complete communion of aims and ideals, especially with regard to the problem of the Church and Liberty—a problem which deeply concerned Christian states that had been shaken by the French Revolution. Ventura grew up in an Italy where stories of the Terror filled him with horror for every type of violence and, like O'Connell, were to make him support later on 'passive

---

1. For the life and works of Ventura, cfr. P. Cultrera, *Della vita e delle opere del P. Gioacchino Ventura.* Palermo 1877; A. Rastoul, *'Le P. Ventura',* in *Les grands hommes de l'Eglise au XIXme siecle,* Paris 1906; F. Andreu, 'P. G. Ventura; Saggio biografico', in *Regnum Dei, Collectanea Theatina,* 17 (1961); Idem, 'Liberta e Religione nell'Elogio funebre del P.G. Ventura per Daniele O'Connell', *Ibid.,* (1947).

resistance and active obedience'. As a young man he had exalted the return of the Holy Alliance and had not regretted the annulment of recent constitutions. But from then on, he had taken a special interest in the religious and political situation of England, the movements of the Anglican Church favourable to the Church of Rome[2] and, above all, he had pointed out the heroic example that Irish Catholics were giving to Europe.[3] As time passed Ventura's thought and action underwent change. This new approach came about as a result of meditation on the religious and social teaching of the Gospel, and of the spectacle of the persistent opposition of the Restoration States to the authority of the Church, which had perhaps trusted and relied too much on their protection. Again his views were conditioned by what he regarded as the legitimate claims of nations who were determined to follow the ways laid open by the Revolution. Ventura gradually inclined towards the new spirit of liberty and equality, in themselves true Christian values, which was abroad in Europe. This spirit united the middle-classes and the proletariat in a common effort designed to prevent a return to the absolutist regime based on privilege and power. He had come by reflection and experience to where O'Connell in fact found himself by birth and education. In 1830 O'Connell and Ventura found themselves battling on the same front. The former was in a more advanced position: he had, due to certain historical circumstances, lived in an environment in which Church and State separation was a reality, and in which the Church's freedom was effective, even under a regime where Irish Catholics were on the political sidelines.[4] Ventura hoped that this situation, in which the Holy See implemented its religious laws without interference from other States, would be approved by all States, especially Christian ones. Such an aspiration was very far from the official Church doctrine.

For this reason, although *L'Avenir* championed every liberty when it appeared in October of 1830, and was welcomed by Ventura, it quickly provoked his criticism and opposition and led to a break with Lamennais. This break was soon set right when in December of the following year the Pilgrims of God and freedom arrived in Rome to seek judgment from the Holy See on their doctrine and activities, and were greeted personally by Ventura.

This friendship with Lamennais led to bitter trials for the Superior General of the Theatines as he lost the esteem of Gregory XVI and left Rome.

Both Ventura and Daniel O'Connell experienced the same kind of suffering during these years: Ventura because of his ideas on religious liberty and on the separation of Church and State; because of his opinions about the political revolt which broke out in the Papal States of Romagna in 1831, a revolt that was for him an omen of the end of what he saw politically as an adulterous connection; again because of his appraisal of the Spanish Civil War between the Liberals, supporters of Isabel, and the Carlist traditionalists; and finally

2. *Enciclopedia ecclesiastica. Opera periodica compilata da G.V.T.* (Gioacchino Ventura Teatino, Naples 1822, iv, p. 345; v p.87 and *passim*.
3. *Joachimi Ventura . . . De Jure Publico Ecclesiastico Commentaria*, (Rome, 1826), i, p. 261.
4. M.R. O'Connell, 'Daniel O'Connell and Religious Freedom' in *Thought*, vol. 50, no. 197 (June 1975).

because of the defamatory accusations and suggestions about the very orthodoxy of the views he advocated. O'Connell likewise suffered as he witnessed the decline of his own relationship and that of his cause with the Vatican, and he was refused by Gregory XVI, or by his representative, the privilege and consolation of the portable altar which he so ardently desired. But both champions of the faith also felt equally deeply a sense of acceptance of the wishes of Gregory XVI and both effected a quick reconciliation with him.[5]

The publication of *Mirari Vos* on 15 August, 1832, which reaffirmed the then official doctrine of the Church on religious liberty, imposed measures of restraint, both on the Irish leader and on the Theatine orator.

Again *Singulari nos* of 24 June, 1834, proscribing *Paroles d'un croyant*, was another step backwards. One had to remain silent and await a time more propitious to new ideas. By 1847 things were very much changed. The reign of Pius IX had given new inspiration to Ventura's words and thinking, just as it inspired hope even in those Italians with little or no religious belief who were anxious for independence.

The themes which had long inspired the words and practice of the great Irish leader, now thronged into Ventura's mind, without as many reservations or pretences: democracy, decentralisation, autonomy, popular control of public expenditure and, above all, freedom of religion. Freedom is, of course, civil liberty which must be advocated by the Church, which had until then been considered by many Italians, especially those interested in political independence, as the enemy or at least opponent of the civil liberties. So, the Theatine thinker—following, once more, the example of the Irish leader—had moved from tradition to the modern spirit.

The Obsequies[6]

The solemn obsequies for Daniel O'Connell took place in the Church of Sant' Andrea della Valle, on 28 and 30 June. All the clergy of Rome shared in the expenses and Pius IX, among his generous contributions, sent rich drapes from the Pontifical Chapel for the funeral rites and declared all the altars of Sant' Andrea della Valle privileged for the days of the ceremonies. The coat of arms and a commemorative inscription which stood out over the main door of the church invited Roman citizens and pilgrims to Rome to pay their last respects to the champion of Religion and Freedom, while another inscription on the inside of the same door listed his main achievements.

Under Maderno's great dome, a majestic catafalque, with inscriptions by the renowned latinist Francesco Mauro on the base, rose to a height of over six metres. Overhead a great medallion in bas-relief showed the image of Daniel O'Connell dying, whom the statue of Religion, which overlooked the funeral

5. M.R. O'Connell, *ibid.* p. 183; F. Andreu, 'P. Gioacchino Ventura', see above, pp 80-81.
6. The following details are derived from the appendix to *Elogio funebre di Danelo O'Connell . . . recitato dal R.mo P. D. Gioacchino Ventura* (Rome, F. Cairo, 1847).

monument, seemed to beckon to his eternal reward. Both were the work of the sculptor Rinaldi. Three other memorable events of O'Connell's life were depicted at the same level on the other three sides: in the first could be seen the leader who pleaded the cause of Irish Catholics in the British Parliament; in the second, O'Connell in his robes as Lord Mayor of Dublin was being received by the clergy on his arrival in the capital, when he was the first Catholic on whom the honour was bestowed after two centuries of oppression; in the third, the leader freed from prison appearing on a triumphal chariot pointing to the Mother of God as restorer of his freedom. All along the nave inscriptions were to be seen on each and every one of the pillars with biblical verses referring to the virtues and actions of O'Connell.

An uninterrupted pilgrimage of the faithful visited the Church from the earliest hours of 28 June to pray for the soul of the dead leader. The pontifical mass was celebrated by Dr. Girolamo dei Marchesi d'Andrea, Archbishop of Mitylene, who had previously been Papal Nuncio in Switzerland and was now Secretary of the Sacred Congregation for the Council. The students of the 'Seminario Romano' assisted at the altar while those from the Irish and Scottish Colleges assisted at the catafalque. The Vicar of Rome, many bishops and prelates, members of the Diplomatic Corps and of the Roman nobility, the general staff and various troops of the Civic Guard graced the occasion of a most splendid and edifying ceremony. The music was played by members of the Philharmonic Academy of Rome, under the direction of Andrea Salesi. At the end, His Eminence Cardinal Baluffi, Archbishop of Imola, blessed the remains.

On the 30th, the obsequies were celebrated by members of the Propaganda Fidei, which O'Connell had promoted actively in Ireland. The Pontifical Requiem Mass was said by Dr. Cometti, Archbishop of Nicomedia and the students of the Irish College served the mass. Round the catafalque were the superior generals of the religious orders with those of the Propaganda Fidei and Germanic colleges. The blessing of the remains was done by his Eminence Cardinal Castracane degli Antelminelli, Bishop of Palestrina and Grand Penitentiary. O'Connell's fourth son and Fr. Miley, his confessor, were also present in a section reserved for them.

Funeral Oration

For an hour and three quarters on the first day and for an hour and a quarter on the second, Fr. Ventura gave an oration in two parts about O'Connell. This was undoubtedly his greatest oratorical success.

1st Part: *Daniel O'Connell caused the triumph of liberty through religion*

In the flame of the fiery eloquence of Ventura, the Irish leader stands out on the glittering horizon of the early nineteenth-century with almost unequalled majesty and power. Daniel O'Connell is "the greatest character of modern times ... before the appearance of Pius IX". A man of Providence for his people, everything in his life seemed providential. As a young student at Douai College in France, O'Connell was present at the enactment of the drama of the Revolution, where every possible mistake seemed to be united to every possible crime. In a monarchy degraded to the point of destroying itself by its own hand, in the apotheosis of Reason as a goddess dripping with blood and slime, in a people "oppressed by cowardly tyrants in the people's name", the young Irishman glimpsed, not the dawning of a new order, but the decline of a soulless world. The Revolution created in him the deepest horror of blood and violence; and it convinced him that "there is nothing more insane nor more ruinous than proclaiming Man's rights while treading underfoot the rights of God".

With rapid and gloomy strokes the orator outlined the state of Ireland when O'Connell climbed on to the Irish political stage. "Irish there were, but no longer an Ireland". The people and the Church had no rights; laws designed to make the Irish into the most humiliated and oppressed of peoples, while Catholics could neither invoke nor expect justice from the Protestant magistracy.

To raise his brothers from subjection, O'Connell relied for effective action on his eloquence and on the integrity of his life. Ventura neither avoided nor justified the religious illusion under which O'Connell laboured in his duel with D'Esterre. He attacked the barbarous practice of duelling, and went on to document brilliantly the faith and religiousness of the Irish champion who, by winning the love of his fellow patriots and the admiration of his adversaries, became "the effective King of Ireland".

Ventura deemed O'Connell's greatest innovation to be the Catholic Association. "Similar to the associations of the primitive Church, it creates a sort of state within a state, without affecting the State". By means of this association he set a mass of eight million people on the way to the pacific conquest of civil and religious independence. Without leading them beyond legal bounds or the limits of duty, he obliged the greatest European power to bow to the law of one man. At this point Ventura, through his mastery of metaphysics, illustrated the great principles of Christian ethics on which the Catholic Association was founded.

One of the principal reasons why Ventura found O'Connell so attractive was because he restrained his people from violence and armed rebellion. Known to the people of Rome as an ardent lover of liberty, Ventura never wished to be considered as an agitator, never as an apologist of revolution or of mutiny.[7] For this reason he preached a distinct separation between "active resistance or sedition" and "passive resistance or legality".

In this Ventura was also in agreement with Shelley, who in his *Address to the People of Ireland* (1811) had decried violence and lauded the power of love and reason.

7. A. Rastoul, *Le P. Ventura* (Paris 1906), p. 60.

"The policy of violent resistance", said Ventura, "in failure or in triumph is always ruinous. Triumphant, violence usually changes people but leaves things as they were. The men on each side are different, but the process of oppression nearly always remains the same. The slave becomes a tyrant and the tyrant a slave: this is the fate of such a process. The sovereignty of all and the servitude of all brings benefits to very few. If eventually the movement produces an improvement, this happens only a long time later, when its creators have paid for it with their lives and when traces of such passions as led to the triumph have been erased."

Catholic doctrine, on the other hand, while condemning rebellion and violence, teaches the use of passive resistance only and active obedience: "passive resistance, whereby the subject refuses to obey an order that goes against his conscience and God's law; but, passively, undergoing without resort to material force such honourable punishments as are brought about by his conviction."

"When it is a case of the profession of the true Faith it is easier to destroy the persecutor by allowing our blood to be shed than by trying to shed his. A martyr in his grave is more terrible to the tyrant than the rebel who confronts him armed on the battlefield".

While laying down passive resistance, Catholic doctrine also suggests active obedience. If it is necessary to resist by suffering, it is also lawful to obey by action designed to free oneself from unjust oppression. "In condemning rebellion, Catholic teaching does not proscribe action; by prohibiting violent resistance, it does not forbid demands made through the channels of legality and justice; by wishing the subject to respect the rights of power, it does not demand capitulation of one's own. In this manner, it reconciles human dignity and the order of society."

It is easy to imagine the effect the orator had on his listeners, in those days of burning passion when, using O'Connell's words as his own, he cried to the Romans: "whoever uses force, is not worthy of freedom; whoever breaks the law, betrays his native land; whoever convinces you to resist, exposes you to perish; whoever preaches insurrection to you, plots treachery against you; fly from him, arrest him, hand him over to the authorities so that he may be brought to justice!" With these basic principles of true freedom, the Irish leader triumphed. At the elections of 1828, O'Connell exclaimed to his Clare voters: "Ireland is liberated". As he foretold, so it happened. When as representative he took his seat in the House of Commons, it was Catholicism which was taking its seat after three centuries of banishment. The battle for civil and religious emancipation in Ireland was long and fierce: many members of the Commons opposed it, the Lords uttered threats, the Anglican church protested, even George IV refused to sign and broke his pen swearing "God damn O'Connell". But all in vain. Surrender became inevitable and the Emancipation Bill which so honours, if rather belatedly, English justice and common sense, was passed "as if it were a peace treaty that had to be signed after a defeat".

The last moments of the Liberator.

And Independence? Death prevented the Leader from seeing his work carried out in full, but "Independence was to come". England and Ireland were to be, to the mind of the great man, not two opposing countries, but two jewels of the one crown, two supports of the one throne . . . for the accomplishment of the sublime ends which providence had destined for them".

The triumph of O'Connell's cause had not only a national value but an historic, universal one. "The history of our century", said Ventura, "was written in the sixteenth century". Heretics in that century lined up against the Church demanding reform. The Church answered by bringing about reforms in the Head and the members. The nineteenth-century revolutionaries cried out for freedom. The Church raised the standard of liberty which, beforehand, had only aroused horror as it was heavy with so much blood. The triumph of O'Connell then showed that true liberty is a daughter to religion and that without religion, freedom degenerates into base bondage. And in a rush of enthusiasm the orator asked: "where do you think that now one may find the audacious provokers of laws of discrimination, the base worshippers of Power, the upholders of the doctrine that would subject the entire Christian world to the power and the whim of a handful of men who call themselves the State and would create universal slavery?" Where are the supporters of absurd centralisation that strangles local autonomy, the regions, the Church itself? There can only be one answer: "They are to be found among the most fanatical demagogues, among the disciples of Jacobinism and of rebellion".

The Catholic Church on the other hand has always been the friend of all true liberties: "As it was the Church that defended the metaphysical freedom of the human mind against the philosophers and heretics who denied it; as it was the Church that created domestic liberty; raising the status of wives and blessing children; as it was the Church that introduced civil liberty, abolishing among nations traffic in slavery and in human lives; so the Church alone can proclaim political liberty specifying the real and true limits of obedience and command, the real and true rights, the real and true duties of the people and their rulers."

In the second part of his oration Ventura was to speak similarly of freedom of conscience: "In an absolute sense this is certainly indifference, atheism, ungodliness, as it is the denial of all revelation, of all positive religion, of all rules of belief and action; in a relative sense, however, in relation to civil power, which has not received from God the mission of preaching and interpreting the Gospel, it is a Catholic principle which the Church has professed, has taught, has defended; this it could not renounce without renouncing its divine mission, without destroying itself; it is a necessary condition of its existence and propagation".

The effect of the first part of his discourse on the Roman audience was enormous and had vast reverberations. While most of those present applauded, some rushed in protest to the Quirinal as if they feared that a new reign of terror was about to break out in Rome as well.

In the event, after the celebrations of St. Peter's feast-day, Ventura continued the second part of his speech on the 30th without interference.

2nd Part: *Daniel O'Connell caused the triumph of religion through liberty*
In the first part of his discourse, Ventura had attacked the prejudices of revolutionaries against the Church; in the second he attacks many Catholics for their suspicions of liberty. Influenced by the events of the end of the 18th century in which "liberty always went hand in hand with blasphemy and sacrilege", people's minds were made to see liberty itself as "necessarily the enemy of religion". Indeed, as the Altar had crumbled beneath the blows of the same axe that had destroyed the Throne "the idea was prevalent that only in unity could they rise again. As a result Throne and Altar aroused the same concern; in the minds, hearts and mouths of right-thinking people they were united". It seemed then that "if the throne could not do without the altar, neither could the altar do without the throne".

This was a prejudice "produced by great ignorance and superficial faith", and was in fact a serious doctrinal error. "It meant making divine religion into a human institution dependent upon human support. But this meant leaving faith, morals, devotion and the Church itself in the hands of the civil power which, as its protector, would not hesitate to usurp the offices of its high priest."

Where "a whole generation of apostolic men" did not seem enough to dissipate such prejudice, one man's zeal sufficed: Daniel O'Connell. He reminded the Catholics of the world in revolt that freedom "is not a gratuitous concession by authority" but "a pacific conquest by the people", and that religious independence was henceforward the only way open to them to achieve the triumph of religion. The struggle of the Leader to demolish these prejudices, in the political and religious fields, had its epic moments. Rome itself seemed at times to distrust a man who "amidst general apprehension", was "alone in trusting completely the Church's wisdom". But the Irish Church, which in its glorious poverty had rejected the bejewelled hand of Anglicanism, saying that "golden chains are still chains", had also asked "not to be helped to live well, but to be allowed to do good", that Church needed liberty above all, as did the people who, following the spirit of Scripture, had looked "first and foremost and at any price" for the kingdom of God and its justice.

All believing nations benefited from this triumph. "O'Connell's apostolate had made a universal dogma of the principle of the independence of Church and State".

In a magnificent flight of imagination, Ventura glimpsed a new era for the Church of Rome dawning over O'Connell's tomb. He saw not only freedom granted to the Church in England, but even Catholicism sitting on the throne that had been occupied by Henry VII. In company with Joseph de Maistre he anticipated a day not too far distant "when mass would be said in St. Paul's in London". He saw Anglicanism, "this scandalous exercise of the royal rights of a Christian sovereign", expire at the feet of the same throne, after "the strong arm of O'Connell had pierced it with the sword of liberty". He did not doubt that Swiss and German Protestantism would follow the footsteps of their English counterpart which "afforded them strength, authority and support", while the British Empire, as was the case with the Roman Empire, was to prepare the way "for the preachers of the Gospel who would everywhere establish the empire of the Cross".

Having recalled that the Church transformed ancient barbaric paganism into "the miracle of the Christian monarchy", carried along by the irresistible enthusiasm of his own eloquence, he confronted governments and rulers with the crux: either respect the independence of the Church or perish. If such governments "ignore the doctrine of religious freedom for their subjects . . . the Church is capable of doing without them, and perhaps adopting democracy. As she did with paganism, the Church will convert democracy to Christianity, blessing it as if baptising a savage matron, and will acknowledge such of its children as are brought to power on the tide of events. On the brow of such a ruler the Church will place the seal of divine benediction and say to him: Reign, and he will reign."

But Ventura dealt only in passing with the acceptance of democracy by the Church and the agreement that would involve. He was to study the subject a year later in his hapless discourse on the Vienna dead.[8] The dominant theme of the panegyric on O'Connell was liberty and religion, a theme that inspired the great man's life and one which gripped Ventura's audience, as it was a problem that was close to the hearts of both the people of Ireland and the people of Rome. Ventura committed all his energy to this problem and O'Connell derived all his fame and glory from its solution. Fr. Ventura's speech was seen as an event in politics. It was firmly believed, a fact confirmed by his biographers, that the inspiration for the oration came from Pius IX himself, who was a personal friend of the orator.

The discourse naturally had its opponents. The daring of certain expressions had alarmed "those obscure political figures who started back in fright at the word liberty as if it were a ghost, while they were plagued by it as if by remorse". At the same time many confused ideas had been clarified by the address itself and turbulent passions resolved. The cry: "Long live liberty" was now to be sometimes answered: "Yes, in the way preached by Ventura". Addressing the Roman people, the orator had said: "No, no you are not the enemies of the Papacy, of ecclesiastics and of order. If you love honourable liberty, you still love the sovereignty of the Head of the church and of religion." On that utterance, a murmur of universal approval was heard which was on the point of bursting into a clamorous ovation when it was stopped by the prompt intervention of the orator.

8. *Discorso funebre pe' Morti di Vienna* (Rome, 1849). It was delivered in Sant'Andrea della Valle, 27 November 1848 and published with a preface and a Note to the Pope's Flight; it was put on the Index by the Holy Office in a decree dated 30 May 1849, which was promulgated on 6 June by Pius IX from Gaeta. In Montpellier, Fr. Ventura accepted the decree 8 September, 1849. P. Cultrera *Della Vita e delle Opere del R.P. Gioacchino Ventura* (Palermo, 1877) pp 97 and 107.

Fr. Ventura hoped reasonably that he had first of all served the cause of religion by his discourse and then the cause of public order. This was recognised by the head of the Ecclesiastical Censure Board, Mons. Graziosi, who, in according the imprimatur, sent a letter to the author in which he gave it as his opinion that the oration was "not only most eloquent but also clearly designed to setting many ideas to rights".[9]

The publication of the funeral oration a few months later was a literary success. Its publication in translation in various languages brought one hundred thousand francs to Ireland alone. In France, more than anywhere else, it aroused the enthusiasm of a large number of clergy who shared the Theatine's ideas. Dr De Sibour, then Bishop of Digne, sent him a prompt pledge of complete support and agreement "as a friend and as a bishop". "Your weighty message," he wrote, "had enkindled in the heart of the Romans flames of the purest patriotism; it has awakened in the Eternal City echoes dormant for centuries. Blessed by the Supreme Pontiff it has gone beyond the limits of church and city and, from the lofty Vatican, it had come to be heard not only in Italy but in the entire world. We have all read there the manifestation of the most exalted thinking that seeks to disperse mysteries and to shine out as brightly as the truth".[10]

In the same period, Fr. Leroy, a Breton priest who claimed he was a Socialist, translated the funeral oration and entitled it: "The Church and liberty",[11] a title that rendered the content of the oration. Fr. Ventura thought then of his old friend, Lamennais, and conceived the hope of leading him back from apostasy to Mother Church. Was not O'Connell's path the one followed by Lamennais, before he went astray? Were not the ideas of the oration those for which the one time apologist had fought and suffered so much? Pius IX himself, who had not forgotten how much the unfortunate Félicité de Lamennais had done in his better days for the cause of Rome, entrusted to the Theatine the task of telling Lamennais that he had the Pope's blessing and that Pius awaited him with open arms. In August, 1847 Ventura wrote to his "most dear friend and brother" a moving letter, hoping "to see him return under the old standard to do battle together, as before, for the greater glory of religion and the greater good of humanity".[12] He sent a copy of his discourse and a portrait of Pius with the letter. Lamennais was not untouched by such a clear proof of affection. He answered on 3 November following, thanking his friend and sending his best wishes to the Holy Father. He also promised to keep the Pope's picture as a souvenir. Ventura's generous heart must have bled, however, when he read that although they remained "forever friends at heart, we have totally ceased to be so in our spiritual convictions".[13] Perhaps, observes Rastoul,[14] some years before when Lamennais had not yet renounced

9. Cultrera, op. cit., p. 49.
10. As quoted in French by Cultrera, op. cit., pp 53-4.
11. Rastoul, *Le P. Ventura* op. cit., p. 69.
12. Quoted by Cultrera, op. cit., p. 64. Ventura's letter and the answer of Lamennais were also published in *Annales de philosophie chretienne*, 4th series, xvi, pp 390-391.
13. This too is in Cultrera, op. cit., p. 65.
14. Rastoul, op. cit., p. 70.

Christ, the noble gesture of the Church's representative would have held him back. But the hour of *rapprochement* and repentance was past. Borne down by the weight of his proud independence, it was as if the spirit of the great apologist of the Church had descended into an abyss where the light of Heaven does not shine.

Two hundred years now separate us from Daniel O'Connell's birth. The ideas of O'Connell and Ventura have gone through many stages from the constitution given by Pius IX to the Papal States, to the encyclical on democracy addressed to the whole world by Pius XII, and to the Vatican II doctrine on religious freedom. It is true that the issue involving the reconciliation of freedom and religion does not excite people's feelings to-day to the same extent as it did in 1847, the Year of O'Connell's death. To-day revolutions have substituted the myth of Labour for the myth of Liberty. The Church has changed with the times and adapted to them, reconciling now, as always, the external principles of faith with the needs and just demands of peoples.

If the issue of religion and freedom is not such a live one to-day, their reconciliation is yet essential to the health of the Church and of civilisation. The Irish leader, therefore, and the Italian orator successfully championed a cause that will always concern the interests of civilised peoples.

Chapter 14

O'Connell and Slavery

Douglas C. Riach

".... Did you ever see a large barrel on two small sticks—with a short, thick neck and a buffalo's head—put it before an audience of five thousand, set it to bowing and the audience to shouting—and that is O'Connell...."[1]

Thus one American abolitionist, Henry C. Wright, on Daniel O'Connell. If the description was hardly flattering, it nevertheless gave some indication of the fascination O'Connell had for those who were leading the movement to free the American slave. The Repeal movement was often depicted as an attempt to liberate the enslaved Irish, yet O'Connell was prominent in the campaigns to abolish Black slavery also, first in the British West Indies, and then in the United States. His commitment to anti-slavery provided an illustration of the internationalism, the concern for the oppressed throughout the world, that was such an integral part of his life and career.

Slavery as an institution had received in the past powerful intellectual, economic and political sanctions. Yet there were also profound contradictions between, for example, the notions of subordination and equality in the Christian tradition, and by the nineteenth century an influential movement had emerged which declared that Black slavery was a sin, and which sought its immediate, unconditional abolition. Anti-slavery as an idea would have appealed not only to the humanitarian but to the utilitarian in O'Connell: slavery was not only less productive than free labour, he maintained, but it was detrimental to the slave and slaveholder alike. Why he engaged himself in anti-slavery to the extent that he did, however, is rather more difficult to explain. Various suggestions were offered: that he was seeking to acquire a reputation for philanthropy: that he was trying to curry favour with such English radicals as Joseph Sturge: that in condemning the existence of American slavery he was seeking to underline his own preference for monarchical institutions. However, these signally failed to account for his conduct on the issue as perhaps did his own insistence that he quite simply represented disinterested philanthropy, and critics of his abolitionism outrageous inhumanity. But the question of motivation remained of some interest, not least because there were many who were convinced that, particularly in his support for American anti-

1. H.C. Wright to L. Poole, Manchester, 3 February 1843. "English, Irish and Scotch Letters Addressed to H.C. Wright, 1843-1847", v.i. Harvard University.

slavery, he was joining with men who were anti-Catholic and part of a British-inspired plot to disrupt the American Union. Moreover, it was argued that in espousing the cause of the Black slave he was damaging the interests of Ireland by splitting the Repeal movement and undermining the support which had been building up for this in the United States.

The Irish Quaker abolitionist Ebenezer Shackleton, comparing the conditions endured by both Irish peasants and Black slaves, concluded:

"In America the slave is called a slave—he is black, and is flogged: in Ireland he is called a labourer—he is white, and is only starved."[2]

Similarly, the great Negro abolitionist Frederick Douglass who was horrified at the poverty he saw in Ireland, and who spoke at a Repeal meeting in Conciliation Hall, frequently quoted O'Connell's statement that the history of Ireland could be traced like the blood of a wounded man through the snow, and Douglass went on to ask that if this were true of Ireland, how much more true was it not of the history of his own people. O'Connell's own interest in anti-slavery can be dated to 1824 when the English abolitionist James Cropper came to Ireland to outline a scheme which he hoped would at one step free the West Indian slave and improve conditions in Ireland. Cropper argued that a revitalised Irish textile industry could pay for the importation of East Indian sugar and that this would both boost the Irish economy and lead to a collapse in the West Indian islands which would secure the abolition of slavery. If the financial disinterestedness of Cropper's plans was questionable, his horror at the plight of Ireland was not. His scheme was backed by O'Connell's Catholic Association, and from that moment onwards O'Connell would stress the similarities between the conditions of the Irish and Negroes, their intertwined destinies, and his conviction that the Irish people should remain in the vanguard of the emancipation movement. O'Connell recognised that in fact the material conditions of the Irish peasants were in many cases worse than those of the slaves, but this, he insisted, was not the sin of slavery: nor was it, he declared, any reason to cease from working in the emancipation movement.

O'Connell soon emerged as a leading figure in the British anti-slavery movement. His growing abolitionist reputation was noted in New England and when the future President of the American Anti-Slavery Society, William Lloyd Garrison, visited England in 1833, O'Connell was one of the people whose support he was most anxious to enlist. British and American abolitionists exulted in the language he employed at anti-slavery meetings in Exeter Hall, as when he claimed that the British people had been "cheated ... bamboozled ... and swindled" into accepting the payment of twenty million pounds of compensation when slavery was abolished in the British colonies in 1833. The abolitionists believed that slavery was an iniquity and would brook no delay in securing its abolition. They felt that an

2. Letter in *Freeman's Journal*, 26 August 1840.

individual's response to Black slavery was either principled and worthy of praise or expedient and worthy of censure. O'Connell recognised this and his declaration that he could be placed in the first category was seconded by such anti-slavery groups as the Glasgow Emancipation Society which specifically addressed him in 1835 as one Parliamentarian who could be relied upon not to compromise or vacillate in his efforts to abolish the system of Negro Apprenticeship that had been inaugurated in 1833, but which O'Connell had denounced as merely a system of slavery in disguise.

O'Connell, of course, displayed his customary adroitness in suggesting that his involvement in the anti-slavery movement—for which he said he was willing to risk assassination—could be effectively contrasted with that of English Tories in general and Robert Peel in particular. He clearly reckoned that Ireland's reputation for unselfish philanthropy would not be tarnished by his claim that in the House of Commons he had refused the aid of twenty members representing the West Indian interest who had suggested that if he stopped attacking slavery they would assist him in Parliamentary matters relating to Ireland. Again, when pointing out that the Synod of Armagh in 1170 had prohibited Irish trade in English slaves, he seldom failed to suggest that England was proving singularly dilatory about returning the compliment.

Though he took some pleasure in scoring points such as these, and though he made much of his abolitionist record at the State Trials in 1844 in order to indicate how far removed his general conduct was from mere expediency, abolition was not for him something which simply provided humanitarian credentials that could be easily won and cheaply paraded.

Thus he was soon made aware that, contrary to his earlier beliefs, the claims of the Irish people (at least as he defined these) and the interests of the Negroes in the West Indies could, and did, come into conflict.

In 1838 the abolitionists were anxious to bring Apprenticeship in the West Indies to an end, but O'Connell and the Irish party were fearful that if they voted for a crucial motion designed to expedite this, they would break the Lichfield House Compact by going against the Whig government. O'Connell himself voted for the motion, but the abolitionist *British Emancipator* considerably embarrassed him by publishing a list of Irish members who had in this instance decided that a vote for Ireland was not compatible with a vote for the West Indian Negro. Similarly, O'Connell found that the demands of anti-slavery could conflict with economic interests which he had long supported. Though a free-trader, he found himself in a considerable quandary in the 1840s when proposals were made to equalise sugar duties and thus make Brazilian and Cuban sugar, which was slave-produced, more competitive with West Indian sugar, which, following the termination of Apprenticeship in 1838, was produced by free labour. Those abolitionists who opposed reducing the duties on Cuban and Brazilian sugar did so on the grounds that such a reduction would stimulate slavery and the slave-trade there: advocates of the scheme argued that it would provide cheaper sugar for the British people. The abolitionists were deeply divided on this emotive and perplexing issue, and at one point O'Connell feared that the British and Foreign Anti-Slavery Society was on the point of breaking up. He himself had to come to terms with the question not only as a member of this body, but as a Member of Parliament and as the leader of the Irish Repeal Movement. Despite his laissez-faire beliefs, O'Connell initially opposed the reductions on anti-slavery grounds, but the difficulties he encountered in reconciling conflicting interests were compounded by the fact that the Repeal press in Ireland was adamant in demanding that the priority was to ensure that people could obtain sugar as cheaply as possible. With some justification, O'Connell could not bring himself to believe that, for all their protestations of concern, either the Whigs or the Tories were at all interested in the South American slaves, especially when one Irish M.P. who had objected as an abolitionist to the reductions, was himself found to own a Brazilian mining company which kept slaves. At a time when his loyalty to successive Whig ministries was coming under attack in Ireland itself, he finally resolved the issue by declaring in the Repeal Association that he had not voted in the crucial debate on the duties: he had had a headache, found a pair and gone home.

Anti-Slavery, therefore, provided O'Connell with searching tests of his philanthropic convictions, his evaluation of priorities and his grasp of practicalities, and this was most clearly demonstrated in his involvement with the American anti-slavery question.

The abolitionists in both Britain and the United States tended to think of themselves as constituting a transatlantic reform community, and since from as early as 1829 he had been delivering speeches exposing the discrepancy between American protestations of love for freedom and the existence of Southern slavery, it was inevitable that O'Connell should attract the attention of the American abolitionists. They saw him as a man who, like themselves, championed an unpopular reform cause, and his manner of doing so never failed to fascinate them: it was O'Connell, as Bostonian Wendell Phillips admitted, who gave the abolitionists their first lessons in the techniques of non-violent mass agitation. They were grateful, too, for the way he was instrumental in persuading British abolitionists to concentrate their efforts on American slavery after 1836. He wanted to "begin the work with the vile and sanguinary slaveholders of Republican America. I want to be *directly* at them. No more side-wind attacks: firing directly at the hull, as the seamen say, is my plan."[3] He was as good as his word, for he went on to focus attention dramatically on American slavery by publicly accusing George Washington of having been a slave-holder, and Andrew Stevenson, then American Ambassador to the Court of St. James, of being a slave-breeder. For this he was challenged to a duel by Stevenson, lionised by the American Anti-Slavery Society, and lambasted in the Southern press.

By 1837, O'Connell was in possession of evidence that his abolitionist condemnations of American slavery were proving of considerable

---

3. Quoted in H. Richard, *Memoirs of Joseph Sturge* (London, 1865), pp 175-6.

embarrassment to the Irish-Americans, while also at this time the American abolitionists were reaching the conclusion that only he had the stature and influence to persuade the Irish-Americans to support the anti-slavery movement. O'Connell's own first public thoughts on this subject had been delivered in Glasgow, where he had declared that if ever he had a free moment he would write an Address telling his countrymen in America to "laugh the Republican slaveowners to scorn and ridicule". Events were to suggest that there was an element of levity in his words that was rather inappropriate, given the explosive impact his anti-slavery strictures would have on Irish-America.

In 1842, O'Connell, with Father Mathew and some 60,000 other Irishmen, signed the Address which urged the Irish-Americans " . . . . By all your memories of Ireland, continue to love liberty—hate slavery—CLING BY THE ABOLITIONISTS—and in America you will do honour to the name of Ireland". It was, of course, given an ecstatic welcome by the abolitionists. At a meeting in Boston's Faneuil Hall, William Lloyd Garrison likened the claims of the slaveholders that the slave was incapable of taking care of himself to England's claim that Ireland was not fit to rule itself: and a resolution was passed, declaring:

> "That this meeting most cordially wishes old Ireland success, in all her righteous efforts to redeem the Emerald Isle from every species of British oppression, and especially in the grand movement of Daniel O'Connell, for the Repeal of the fraudulent act of Union between his country and England."[4]

Notwithstanding all this, however, (nor the claim by one abolitionist present that he had stood watching while Castlereagh "took the bribe for the betrayal of Ireland"), John Hughes, Irish-born Roman Catholic Bishop of New York, condemned the Irish Address as a forgery and added that if it should prove genuine then it should be rejected by every Irish-American as an unwarrantable piece of interference in American domestic affairs.

Hughes' advice won general acceptance in the Irish-American community which feared both status and economic competition with the Negroes, but whose position on the slavery issue, it has been suggested, was "related to the real source of the Catholic Irish antagonism—dislike of the Abolitionists".[5] The latter, it was felt, were hostile to the Catholic religion and to the Irish immigrants, and were advocating Repeal in a specious attempt to curry favour and win support. These were clearly important sources of discord, but there was one further explanation of the Irish-American hostility to the abolition movement. O'Connell consistently maintained that the Irish-Americans would bring credit to Ireland if they supported the anti-slavery campaign. Irish-American newspapers such as the *Boston Pilot*, however, frequently complained that O'Connell was undermining the Irish-Americans' attempts to win acceptance in American society by his insistence on addressing them as a

4. *Tenth Annual Report of the Massachusetts Anti-Slavery Society* (Boston, 1842), pp 9-25.
5. G.M. Potter, *To the Golden Door* (Boston, 1960), p. 374.

"distinct class" on a subject which many feared would ultimately lead to the disruption of the American Union. O'Connell remained oblivious to this objection:

> "Over the broad Atlantic I pour my voice", he declaimed in Dublin, "saying, 'Come out of such a land, you Irishmen, or, if you remain, and dare countenance the system of slavery that is supported there, we will recognise you as Irishmen no longer.' "

Such statements, however much they thrilled the abolitionists, proved ineffective because they failed to appreciate that the slavery issue provided an important test of the Irish-Americans' Americanness, and one in which O'Connell's definitions of Irishness would, if accepted, prove damaging. A measure of the Irish-Americans' thinking on this issue was provided when Wendell Phillips sought to remind his audience not only of O'Connell's abolitionist record but of the Apostolic Letter of Pope Gregory XVI prohibiting slavery and the slave trade: one Irish-American present rose to inform Phillips that the Irish-Americans were ruled neither from Home nor Rome.

For their part, the abolitionists in America believed that the Irish-Americans had been deceived into accepting such attitudes by, in Garrison's words, "a stupendous conspiracy . . . between the leading Irish demagogues, the leading pseudo-democrats and the Southern slaveholders". Garrison went on to accuse the American Democratic journals and the Southern States of having two reasons for supporting O'Connell's movement for Irish Repeal: their wish to enlist the votes of Irish-Americans, and their desire, by sending money to the Loyal National Repeal Association, to "stop O'Connell's mouth on the subject of slavery". O'Connell's Repeal Association was subsequently inundated with exhortations from the abolitionists and complaints from the Irish-Americans, each of which simply fuelled the other. Thus protests from the Albany and Louisiana Repealers against the Irish Address led to rejoinders from the Pennsylvania Anti-Slavery Society. O'Connell's reply to this provoked the Cincinnati Irish Repeal Association to insist that the future of the American Union depended on the continued existence of slavery, and this in turn was answered by O'Connell's famous Cincinnati Address, which was read at the Repeal Association in October 1843. This was O'Connell's most important statement of anti-slavery beliefs. It contained much practical advice as to how the Irish-Americans could without violating their constitutional obligations work to secure for Negroes their civil rights, and lofty sentiments concerning the manner in which slavery itself violated a law higher than the American Constitution. To those Irish-Americans who on grounds of nasal sensibility objected to Negroes, moreover, he retorted that there seemed some evidence for stating that the foul odour of tobacco-spittle was the prevailing smell among native, free Americans.

All this of course had an extremely disruptive effect on the Irish-American Repeal movement, especially in the South. The Baltimore Repeal Association denounced the Irish Address and those in Natchez and Charleston dissolved after his reply to the Pennsylvania abolitionists. In general, the Cincinnati Address had less of an impact because the Second National Repeal Convention had met in New York before it was issued and also since any antagonism it aroused was replaced by the widespread feelings of sympathy felt for O'Connell after his trial and imprisonment: thus the Savannah and Charleston Repealers re-formed soon after hearing of his arrest. O'Connell could hardly ignore such reactions since they were well documented in the Irish Repeal press, but his efforts to declare a moratorium on the slavery issue in 1842, though backed by some Repeal Associations in the border States, failed. He then sought to solve the problem in two ways: first by repudiating the more radical of the abolitionists in America, and secondly by showing that his abolitionism had not after all had an entirely ruinous effect on Ireland's Repeal prospects. In particular, he repudiated the religious views of William Lloyd Garrison, thereby trying to suggest that his concern for the slave had not warped his judgement, and to deflect accusations that he was in alliance with men who were virulently anti-Irish and anti-Catholic.

"Popery is priestcraft confessed. Protestantism is Popery concealed." So declared one abolitionist who professed to abhorr both religions, while Garrison himself declared in Belfast that in a choice between "Popery which goes against the chains of slavery" and "that Protestantism which puts them on", he would opt for the former. Nevertheless, Catholics remained convinced that such incidents as the reluctance of English Quakers to use the word 'emancipation' in reference to the slave because it smacked too much of Roman Catholic Emancipation, provided telling evidence of the anti-Catholic animus of most abolitionists. With notable exceptions, those in America were not active in the growth of nativist hostility to the Catholic Irish, but the poet John Greenleaf Whittier confessed—and even his epithets are revealing—that many in America allowed their "just disapprobation" of Catholicism to "degenerate" into a "most unwarranted prejudice against its conscientious followers". This was precisely what did happen when the American Garrisonians became exasperated by O'Connell and indeed, after a report was reprinted in Garrison's *Liberator* ridiculing the 'idiotic' look that came over O'Connell's face as he crossed himself before dinner, the Irish leader once more condemned the Garrisonians and issued what was in effect the Irish Address in reverse by calling on the American abolitionists to cooperate in the spread of Christian charity with the Catholic Irish in America. The reactions of Catholics to Garrison's visit to Dublin in 1846 and even to the works of Harriet Beecher Stowe after 1853 indicate that strong suspicions existed about the abolitionists' religious prejudice. It would have been a gesture of great magnanimity and no small significance for the future of Irish abolitionism if O'Connell had persisted with his earlier arguments that the only justifiable Catholic response was to engage the more energetically in anti-slavery to ensure that Protestants alone did not obtain credit for displaying abolitionist convictions. As for his own Church in Ireland, however, it was both anxious to avoid any rupture in its transatlantic connections and heavily influenced by men such as Bishop John England of Charleston, South Carolina, who was born in Ireland but whose exposure to the South had convinced him that the entire Catholic tradition condemned not slavery but the slave-trade: only O'Connell and the historian of the United Irishmen, Dr. R. R. Madden, remained convinced that St. Patrick, for example, had exhibited some aversion to both.

Garrison's anti-sabbatarianism and his hostility to a paid clergy were inimical to O'Connell. But the Garrisonians were sure that he had sought to discredit them solely to appease the Irish-Americans. Their association with him—through, for example, their reception and circulation of the Irish Address—had conferred on them a certain status. Now, having abjured political action for themselves, they felt that he had been bought off by Irish American money. Wendell Phillips fulminated:

> "'Tis the beginning of the end .... He would be proslavery this side the pond—'a mere pealer' as we say—He won't shake hands with slaveholders no—but he will shake their gold . . . he is emphatically 'The Great Beggarman' . . . well we can do without him—Anti-Slavery kisses no man's toe."[6]

In contrast to this, Phillips claimed in 1872 that in Conciliation Hall he had witnessed O'Connell rejecting a bill for one thousand pounds that had been sent from slaveholders in New Orleans, on the grounds that it was the "unpaid wages" of the slaves, and both O'Connell and his son John claimed on several occasions that money had been returned when it was accompanied by arguments in favour of slavery. However, the O'Connellite policy had been worked out at an early date. Unless money was actually sent on the condition that O'Connell keep silent about slavery, it was accepted, on the grounds that those who sent it must love Ireland more than they did Black slavery. On other occasions also O'Connell publicly returned money: he refused for example to accept a bill from the Repeal Association in New Orleans when the accompanying letter contained resolutions in which "the duty of allegiance to the British crown was set at nought, and a system of force and violence suggested in its place."[7]

The Dublin Unitarian James Haughton was one abolitionist who urged O'Connell on many occasions to prevent the Repeal cause and indeed the name of Ireland being sullied by slaveholders' gold. It was clear from his dramatic words such as "blood-stained dollars" that Haughton was trying to posit standards against which the morality of the Repeal cause could be measured. In an attempt to demolish such reasoning, the Young Irelander, Father Kenyon, later asked Haughton whether, if he were drowning in the Ganges, he would accept the aid of a proffered walking-stick from a passing

6. W. Phillips to R.D. Webb. Boston, 29 June 1842. MS.A.1.2.v.12, pt. 2, p. 61. (Anti-Slavery Letters to Garrison. Boston Public Library).
7. *Nation*, 1 June 1844. For similar reasons, he later returned money to Repealers in New York and Boston.

Thug. Kenyon concluded:

> "Money is the algebraist's x; it may represent anything; let it stand then for a walking-stick. Be the slaveholders of America Thugs for the nonce . . . . Let the Union be the gulf and Lord John Russell the pair of crocodiles; and there's an end on't."[8]

These two viewpoints, Haughton's and Kenyon's, embodied conflicting views of the nature of the Repeal movement, and, ultimately, of what constituted human freedom. Once more, however, the debate on these issues was important for O'Connell in practical terms, since the Irish-Americans showed little sign of being mollified by his disavowal of Garrison, while within Ireland there was growing opposition to his involvement in American slavery. Subtle differences in approach became evident. Thus the Repeal press from 1840–1842 tended to deplore in terms which suggested some sympathy for the victims the existence of slavery in British India: thereafter the tendency was to point to slavery there as evidence of English iniquity. With some difficulty O'Connell succeeded in curbing the opposition of such newspapers as the Dublin *Pilot* and the *Freeman's Journal,* but the Young Irelanders on the *Nation* proved increasingly unwilling to interfere in any way with the 'institutions' of the American South. This was so largely because slavery was emerging as a factor influencing Anglo-American relations. It is clear from the reaction of the Repeal press, and notably the *Nation,* to such issues as British efforts to secure the right to search American vessels engaged in the slave-trade, and the American annexation of Texas and war with Mexico, that they saw American slavery not as a heinous sin but as potentially providing a *casus belli* between England and America from which Ireland could only benefit. Following a series of angry scenes in the Repeal Association when critics such as Thomas Davis tried to argue that in terms of foreign policy, O'Connell's abolitionism was disastrous, O'Connell declared in 1845 that the English

> "can have us . . . the throne of Victoria can be made perfectly secure—the honour of the British empire maintained—and the American eagle in its highest point of flight, be brought down . . . let them give us the Parliament in College Green, and Oregon shall be theirs and Texas shall be harmless."[9]

Somewhat disingenuously, given its own calculations on this topic, the *Nation* sought to continue the metaphor by spluttering about the sparrows of Downing Street; the Repeal Associations in Portsmouth, Norfolk and New Orleans dissolved; and the implicit offer—later made explicit when O'Connell suggested that he could act as a recruiting sergeant for England if Repeal were granted—also offended the pacifist views of such abolitionists as Haughton who subsequently took O'Connell's Peace Resolutions to be a devious attempt to drum his youthful critics out of the Repeal Association.

8. Letter in *Nation,* 30 January 1847.
9. Report in *Freeman's Journal,* 1 April 1845. For a more detailed analysis of this and related points, see my article in *Irish Historical Studies,* vol. XX, no. 77, pp 3-25.

Haughton in fact became Treasurer of the Irish Confederation, founded by the more militant of the Young Irelanders, only to resign because the attitudes of that body made him very much aware of what the alternatives to O'Connell's abolitionism were. Another Dublin abolitionist had written that the Young Irelanders were willing to see "all the Blacks in Negroland chained and paddled and flogged out of existence". Though Duffy, Davis and Smith O'Brien would have rejected this, Mitchel was already influenced by Carlyle's racism, and all were anxious to avoid alienating the Americans on the slavery issue. O'Connell's denunciations of American slavery, in contrast, were occasionally so severe as to offend even American abolitionists, while the offence he gave to the South, and in particular the manner in which he invoked the dreaded spectre of slave-revolts there, were surely a contributing factor in the development of sectional intransigence in pre-Civil War America.

American slavery was merely one of the topics on which he disagreed with the Young Irelanders, but it was an important source of discord and the debates on the issue which took place regularly within the Repeal Association again illustrate the tendency of American slavery to become a focus for purely domestic quarrels. In this process the plight and cause of the Black slave was often lost sight of, though seldom by O'Connell himself. Even as the catastrophe of famine loomed in Ireland, O'Connell did not renounce his abolitionist beliefs.

And these proved curiously usable. The American abolitionists continued to worry at the example Irish leaders other than O'Connell were setting the Irish-Americans on the slavery issue. When John Mitchel went to the United States, for example, he became a staunch supporter of slavery, and even his old allies John Martin and Father Kenyon were horrified at his proposals that the slave-trade be re-opened and that his Irish friends would do well to answer in the affirmative if they were asked whether they would like an Irish Republic with an "accompaniment of slave plantations". To counteract this type of pernicious influence many pamphlets containing extracts from O'Connell's anti-slavery speeches were issued. The American abolitionists pointed to O'Connell as one great European national leader who, unlike the Hungarian Louis Kossuth, was prepared to risk much for the Black slave, and as one great Irishman who, unlike Father Mathew, was not prepared to abandon the principles of the Irish Address. After the Irish-American riots against the Draft Laws in New York in 1863, further pamphlets of his speeches were issued in an attempt to persuade the Irish-Americans that their obligations to O'Connell included an obligation to serve the cause to which he had dedicated himself. After the Civil War, the abolitionists were even of the opinion that appeals to O'Connell's memory could effect such changes as less corrupt ward politics in the cities. Despite their earlier misgivings, the abolitionists often declared that O'Connell had set a noble example to institutions such as the Free Church of Scotland and the Quaker Relief Committee in the Irish famine, both of which accepted donations from the American South. The abolitionists, in short, were very much aware of O'Connell's usefulness for their cause. More than this, however, many of them intensely admired a man who, after all, had been the single most important champion which the anti-slavery cause had obtained outside the United States. Both Phillips and Frederick Douglass recalled O'Connell's services to American anti-slavery when they later supported Parnell's activities in America.

The Irish-Americans also found in post-emancipation America that it was to their advantage to stress O'Connell's, rather than their own, anti-slavery record. Thus at the O'Connell Centenary Celebrations in Boston the organisers were anxious to receive tributes to his abolitionism from Garrison, Whittier and Phillips. Yet even here, it can be suggested, O'Connell's impact on individuals went beyond mere calculations of his usefulness. John Boyle O'Reilly for one had been involved in the organisation of the Boston Celebrations. After his escape from exile he had become editor of the Boston *Pilot* and though he had initially defended that paper's pre-war position on slavery (and therefore, by implication, its strictures on O'Connell), he became, after Phillips's death, the man who was regarded by many American Blacks as the foremost White champion of their campaign for civil rights. Indeed one contributor to O'Reilly's *Pilot* felt that the techniques of Irish agitation remained of some relevance for the American Negro; mindful of the boycott against Irish landowners, it was suggested that similar procedures be taken against those who discriminated against the Blacks in America.

Robert Tyler, son of the American President and a prominent supporter of Repeal, once said that in his views on slavery, O'Connell did not represent the views of a "hundredth part of the Irish people". This was an attempt to reassure American critics of O'Connell, rather than an example of mathematical accuracy. Yet there can be little doubt that his anti-slavery was objected to by many in Ireland, and that after his death there was little marked sympathy for it either in Irish politics or in Irish historiography. O'Connell had offered very little in the way of sustained analysis of the forces which had combined to create and uphold slavery. Yet there was much in his abolitionism that was of lasting significance. Garrison recognised this. He had already described O'Connell as "incomparably more than a mere geographical Irishman", and it is clear that his statement for the Centenary Celebrations in Boston was meant to be more than merely a tribute to O'Connell's memory: the image of a more unselfish nationalism which Garrison invoked on that occasion was undoubtedly hurled as a challenge to succeeding generations.